Learning Together in the Early Years

Relational pedagogy underpins the core principles of both the cognitive and social/emotional development of young children, as evidenced in the Reggio Emilia preschools and the *Te Whāriki* curriculum in New Zealand. Emphasising the links between people, places and ideas, and the effects of these on education, educators and learners, it is integral to the English *Early Years Foundation Stage*, and forms the basis for early years provision around the world.

This book brings together contributions from international experts on early years education to explore and debate relational pedagogy across different countries and in the context of a broad international field. The three sections of the book cover the following areas:

- culture, environment and adult–child relationships – how children and adults relate to the culture, ethos and environment in which they function;
- adult–child relationships – how education and care environments directly relate to learning and teaching;
- adult–adult relationships for professional development – in training situations and parental partnerships.

The book will be of interest to all those who want to delve deeper into how these interactions affect teaching and learning and to understand how the context can have its own impact on pedagogical outcomes. Researchers in early years education and students on early childhood education courses will find much here to inspire and challenge their thinking.

Theodora Papatheodorou is Professor of Early Childhood and Research and Director of CREATe (Centre for Research into Education And Teaching) at Anglia Ruskin University.

Janet Moyles is one of the UK's most respected names in early years education. She is affiliated to Anglia Ruskin University as Professor of Education and Research.

Learning Together in the Early Years

Exploring relational pedagogy

Edited by
**Theodora Papatheodorou and
Janet Moyles**

Routledge
Taylor & Francis Group

LONDON AND NEW YORK

First published 2009
by Routledge
2 Park Square, Milton Park, Abingdon, Oxon OX14 4RN

Simultaneously published in the USA and Canada
by Routledge
270 Madison Avenue, New York, NY 10016

Routledge is an imprint of the Taylor & Francis Group, an informa business

© 2009 selection and editorial matter, Theodora Papatheodorou and Janet Moyles;
individual chapters, the contributors

Typeset in Times New Roman by
Keystroke, 28 High Street, Tettenhall, Wolverhampton
Printed and bound in Great Britain by
TJ International Ltd, Padstow, Cornwall

British Library Cataloguing in Publication Data
A catalogue record for this book is available from the British Library

Library of Congress Cataloging in Publication Data
Moyles, Janet R.
Learning together in the early years: exploring relational pedagogy / Janet Moyles
and Theodora Papatheodorou.
p. cm.
1. Early childhood education. 2. Child development. 3. Children and adults.
I. Papatheodorou, Theodora, 1953– II. Title.
LB1139.23.M69 2008
372.21—dc22
2008002203

ISBN 10: 0–415–46932–5 (hbk)
ISBN 10: 0–415–46933–3 (pbk)
ISBN 10: 0–203–89416–2 (ebk)

ISBN 13: 978–0–415–46932–6 (hbk)
ISBN 13: 978–0–415–46933–3 (pbk)
ISBN 13: 978–0–203–89416–3 (ebk)

Contents

Illustrations

Tables

Contributors

Caroline Bath worked in early years education for fifteen years in West and South Yorkshire and was involved in promoting inclusive practice for young, disabled children. This engendered her interest in the field of children's rights and participation, and study for a doctorate at Sheffield University which led to teaching in HE and the completion of her doctorate in 2006. She now leads the Early Childhood Studies course at Sheffield Hallam University

Tal Ben-Tov is a pedagogic counsellor and supervisor for student teachers in the Department of Preschool Education at Seminar Hakbutzim College in Tel Aviv. She is a certified kindergarten teacher and holds an MA in Preschool Education and a BA in Education and Israel Studies. Currently, she is a Ph.D. candidate at Anglia Ruskin University. Her research interest is developing toddlers' emotional competences through a programme aimed at their care-givers' professional development.

Sue Bingham is a part-time M.Ed. student at the Faculty of Education, University of Cambridge and a part-time early years adviser for a local LEA. Her research interests have focused on the emotional and social development of young children and how teachers in early years settings can support this.

Liz Brooker is Senior Lecturer in Early Childhood at the Institute of Education, University of London. Her interest in the educational experiences of ethnic minority children, which led to the book, *Starting School: Young Children Learning Cultures* (2002, Open University Press), stemmed from her own experience as an early years' teacher. She continues to study transitions, includ-ing those of babies and toddlers, and her book, *Supporting Transitions in the Early Years* (2008, Open University Press), explores the varied experiences of children from birth to age 5 as they move into school and preschool in the UK and internationally.

Sue Callan is Senior Lecturer in the Centre for Early Childhood within the Institute of Education at the University of Worcester and is responsible for delivery of the Foundation Degree Early Years programme in outreach settings. She has been an adult education tutor for fifteen years, specialising in community-based preschool practice and working with mature students in both personal tutor and mentor roles. Sue is coordinator of the UW FDEY Partnership Mentor Team, supporting mentors from six partner institutions.

Eryl Copp is Course Leader and Manager of Professional Practice in Early Years at Worcester College of Technology. She is a mentor tutor and personal tutor for the Foundation Degree in Early Years. Eryl has taught in primary and nursery schools and has been a nursery school head and external assessor.

Florence Dinneen is Head of the Department of Reflective Pedagogy and Early Childhood Studies at Mary Immaculate College, Limerick, Ireland. She graduated from University College Cork, a constituent college of the National University of Ireland, with a Ph.D. in Philosophy in 2002, after completing a BA degree in Early Childhood Studies in 1999. In 2001 she was awarded a Government of Ireland Research Scholarship in recognition for her doctoral work on the concept of *Educare*. Currently she is leader of a new four-year degree programme in Early Childhood Care and Education at Mary Immaculate College where she is also Consultant Supervisor for the practical placements. Her main research interests are centred on the training of *educarers* and her publications to date reflect this interest.

Johanna Einarsdottir is Professor at Iceland University of Education. She received a Ph.D. in Early Childhood Education from the University of Illinois in 2000. Her professional interests include early childhood education, early childhood teacher education and qualitative methodology. She is currently conducting research on early childhood teachers, children's views on their preschool education, and transition and continuity in early childhood education. She has published her work in the U.S.A. and Europe.

Kate Fowler is Senior Lecturer in the Centre for Early Childhood team within the Institute of Education at the University of Worcester (UW). Kate has taught in nursery, primary and middle schools. She has been a link tutor supporting teacher mentors of Initial Teacher Education students studying PGCE and BA(Hons) Primary QTS at UW as well as a tutor mentor for students on these courses. Time has been spent as course leader for the BA(Hons) Early Childhood at UW and she is currently Continuing Professional Development Coordinator in Early Childhood within the Institute of Education at UW.

Bryndis Gardarsdottir is Assistant Professor at Iceland University of Education. She received a Masters degree in Early Childhood Education from Queen Maud's College of Early Education and The Norwegian University of Science and Technology in Trondheim in 1996. Her professional interests include early childhood education and teachers' professional development. Besides research on parental cooperation, she is conducting research on discourse in relation to the preschool in Icelandic media, and another in relation to assessing preschool children's well-being and learning dispositions.

Jan Georgeson graduated from Oxford University (1980, Experimental Psychology) and did research on reading and visual perception. She took a

PGCE at Bristol Polytechnic in 1984 and taught children with special educational needs in secondary, primary and preschool settings. She completed a doctorate in Educational Disadvantage and Special Educational Needs at Birmingham University (2006). Her research is influenced by sociocultural and activity theory, and she is currently working on research projects investigating Disability and Parent Partnerships.

Kathy Goouch is Senior Lecturer at Canterbury Christ Church University. After a long teaching career in primary schools and kindergartens in London and in Kent, her research interests now are in play, children's early interactions and story-making. Her published work has also included early literacy research, most recently co-editing *Understanding Phonics and the Teaching of Reading: Critical Perspectives* (2006, Oxford University Press). She is currently researching the nature of interactions in baby rooms in nurseries.

Christine Hey is Senior Lecturer on the BA (Hons) Early Childhood Studies at the University of Derby, with a particular interest in early language and communication, and managing the early years' curriculum to promote young children's holistic development. She has many years experience of early years education including private, maintained and peripatetic provision.

Kim Insley is Tutor at the Institute of Education, working and teaching on the Primary PGCE (music, mathematics and professional issues) and the Masters modules for Nurture Group training. She has been a primary classroom teacher, subject coordinator, PGCE course leader, consultant and adviser in primary education. She has researched music education in primary schools, focusing on the practice of the non-specialist class teacher, and now leads the music specialism module within the Primary PGCE. She has written about the curriculum in Nurture Groups and her most recent publication is one on teachers and the law.

Janet Kay is currently Principal Lecturer in Children and Childhood at Sheffield Hallam University. Her previous professional background is in social work with children and families, mainly child protection. She has worked in higher education for seven years and is currently researching for her doctorate. She has published a number of books in the field of early years, covering a range of subjects, including child protection, policy, behaviour and practice issues.

Sylvia Lucas works at the Institute of Education, University of London as a support tutor on the Nurture Group courses, which she originally led. She is a former Nurture Group teacher, setting up one of the first nurture groups in Hackney. She has been a headteacher of four primary schools in east London. She undertakes a range of consultancy in primary practice and school leadership, and is currently adding to her publications with articles and a book on the Nurturing School.

Paulette Luff is Senior Lecturer in Early Childhood Studies at Anglia Ruskin University. She is a doctoral researcher in the Centre for Research in Education

And Teaching (CREATe) and is currently completing research exploring early years' practitioners' uses of child observation. She has worked in the field of early childhood for more than twenty years, as a teacher, foster carer, school–home liaison worker and as a lecturer in further education.

Eva Maagerø is Associate Professor in Norwegian Language at Vestfold University College, Tønsberg, Norway. She teaches linguistics, language development, literacy, text theory, semiotics and multimodality on Bachelor and Masters programmes. Her research interests are language development, literacy, textbook analysis, social semiotics, multimodality and systemic functional linguistics. Together with Birte Simonsen, she has recently completed a project in kindergartens in Lillesand, Norway, where English as a foreign language was introduced to children from ages 3 to 6.

Janet Moyles is Professor Emeritus at Anglia Ruskin University where she currently has a 0.2 role in supporting research activities. Janet was formerly Senior Lecturer at the University of Leicester. She has conducted a number of research projects with various organisations and published widely. Her books include *Early Years Foundations: Meeting the Challenge, Effective Leadership and Management in the Early Years, The Excellence of Play* (2005), *Statements of Entitlement to Play: StEPs* (2002), *Just Playing?* (1989) (all published by Open University Press), *Recreating the Reception Year* (2003, ATL) and *Images of Violence* (2004, Featherstone).

Ruby Oates is Programme Leader for the BA (Hons) Early Childhood Studies at the University of Derby. She originally trained as a teacher and has teaching experience in the maintained, further and higher education sectors. She was a curriculum manager of early years in further education prior to moving into higher education. Her current research interests include the professionalisation of the early years' workforce and the notions and experiences of practitioners in relation to their professional status.

Theodora Papatheodorou is Professor of Early Childhood and Research at Anglia Ruskin University. She is currently Director of Research and of CREATe (Centre for Research into Education And Teaching) at the Faculty of Education. Theodora has conducted research and published in a wide range of topics (including young children's behaviour, the role of learning support assistants, early years' curricula, stories and story-playing, intercultural preschool pedagogy, pedagogical approaches to supporting the mother tongue and student learning) and participated in the evaluation of major programmes (On Track and Violence against Women). She is the author of the book *Behaviour Problems in the Early Years: A Guide for Understanding and Support* (2005, Routledge).

Jane Payler is currently Senior Lecturer in Early Years Education at the University of Winchester. She has researched interprofessional education for professionals in Children's Services and the experiences of young children with special educational needs at Southampton University. Her Ph.D. and M.Phil. research, both funded by the ESRC, were into aspects of learning processes in 4-year-old children, particularly relating to interaction. Jane has previously been a health education officer in inner-city Birmingham; worked as a crèche supervisor for three years; and lectured in colleges of further education over a fourteen-year period in early years, health and social care.

Sally Peters is Senior Lecturer at the University of Waikato, Hamilton, New Zealand. Her Ph.D. study explored the experiences of children, parents and teachers during the children's transition to school. This interest in 'border crossing' has been developed further in a number of projects, including a three-year Teaching Learning Research Initiative exploring 'key competencies' in a number of early childhood and school settings, and a Centre of Innovation project looking at crossing borders between home, early childhood education and school.

Alison Robins is Senior Lecturer in the Centre for Early Childhood Team within the Institute of Education at the University of Worcester. She is coordinator of the Sector-endorsed Foundation Degree in Early Years and was involved in the development and validation of the degree, which currently runs at six partner institutions. She has taught in primary and middle schools, has been a SENCo and deputy head, and has worked as a teaching assistant training officer for Worcestershire Local Authority.

Jill Sachs has extensive experience in early childhood development, and until recently held the position of provincial ECD responsibility manager for the KwaZulu Natal Provincial Department of Education. In this capacity she was responsible for provincial policy development and implementation, including the training and curriculum development of over 4000 reception year teachers. As Education Programmes Manager she is the designer and developer of all the Early Years Education (eYe) training programmes offered by the arts-based accredited South African Caversham Centre. She is much sought after as a presenter, and has a passion for personal development and creativity. She studied at the University of South Africa for a Higher Education Diploma in ECD and a further Diploma in Education Guidance and Counseling.

Andrew Sanders is a former practitioner in and manager of early years settings, and has a special interest in 'what works' and the practical issues of quality services for children and their families. In a broad sense this expands towards the emergence of new initiatives and ideas, topical questions, communicating and shaping policy and practice and key workforce developments. He currently lectures in a range of disciplines on the BA (Hons) Early Childhood Studies at the University of Derby and has an Associate Lecturer role with the Open University.

Birte Simonsen has practised as a primary and secondary schoolteacher for twenty-five years. Since 1993 she has been Lecturer for Student Teachers at Agder

University in the field of education. She is now Dean of the Teacher Education Section. She has participated in different development and research projects connected to ICT and school, and she has also published articles in books and journals on early language teaching and learning.

Jon White is Senior Lecturer at the University of Derby teaching on the BA (Hons) Early Childhood Studies, Education Studies and the Master of Education programmes. He has a background in teaching and working in a wide range of learning environments including the prison service and overseas. With an interest in the relationship between the teacher and student, Jon is developing a framework for learners in higher education to enable more effective participation in early years education.

David Whitebread is Senior Lecturer in Psychology and Education within the Faculty of Education, University of Cambridge, and a former director of the Early Years and Primary PGCE course. His research interests are concerned with learning in young children, including the role of play, thinking skills in young children, and the development of self-regulation and independent learning. His publications include *The Psychology of Teaching and Learning in the Primary School* (2000, Routledge Falmer) and *Teaching and Learning in the Early Years, 2nd edn* (2003, Routledge Falmer).

Val Wood began her career as a nurse and midwife in Northwest England. She moved into teaching in further education and went on to lead a Faculty of Health, Early Years and Social Care in a city college. She led a successful bid for a Centre of Vocational Excellence in Early Years during this period as well as other collaborative community initiatives. She is currently Senior Lecturer on the BA (Hons) Early Childhood Studies programme at the University of Derby.

Ellen Yates is Associate Lecturer on the BA (Hons) Early Childhood Studies programme at the University of Derby. She is an experienced early years' teacher and continues to work as a supply teacher for part of her week. She has taught young children in the United Kingdom and also in the Far East. She is particularly interested in children's creativity and the role of the curriculum in supporting this; she is herself an able ceramicist.

Acknowledgements

The editors would like to thank and acknowledge the support which we have received from a number of colleagues before and during the preparation of this volume, which is the output of a conference on the topic of relational pedagogy. Reflecting the true spirit of relational pedagogy, both the conference and this volume have been born out of an attempt to bridge the arbitrary and false dichotomies and divides between the remit of practitioners, policy implementers, students, academics and researchers. We feel we took this first step thanks to the many colleagues who responded and contributed to this endeavour. It is not possible to name all and everyone individually, but we would like to acknowledge and thank, first of all, Dr Lyn Ang (University of East London), Dr Cathy Ota (University of Brighton), Paulette Luff and Christine Such (both from Anglia Ruskin University), who, as members of the conference organising committee, reviewed and provided feedback for the submitted abstracts for the conference.

We are thankful to conference keynote speakers – Professor Pat Broadhead (Leeds Metropolitan University), Professor Bert van Oers (Free University of Amsterdam), Professor Maria Luisa de Natale (University de Catolica, Milan) and Dr Sally Peters (University of Waikato, New Zealand) – who opened, inspired and stimulated the debate about the meaning and place of relational pedagogy in the twenty-first century. Our thanks also go to all paper presenters, workshop and poster session organisers and, of course, all the conference delegates (early years practitioners, local authority officials, students, academics and researchers) whose diverse voices contributed to the discussion of the concept of relational pedagogy. Such active participation informed and advanced our thinking and understanding of the concept and this is, we hope, reflected in this volume.

We would also like to thank Harriet Hill, Director of the Essex Early Years Education and Childcare Services, and Dr Tony West, from Research and Development Services at Anglia Ruskin University, who wholeheartedly embraced and supported the conference, and who were integral to its becoming such a forum for the discussion of relational pedagogy. We are thankful to Trudi Bishop and Liz Hagon and their team at Essex Early Years Education and Childcare Services, and colleagues and students at our university – too many to name them all individually – whose collective endeavour and effort reflected the true spirit of relational pedagogy.

We would like to thank the authors of the chapters included in the volume; they all took the time to develop and review their chapters and respond promptly to our requests. Last but not least our thanks go to Alison Foyle, the series editor, who has given us the opportunity to publish this volume and open the debate about relational pedagogy.

Theodora Papatheodorou
Janet Moyles

Introduction

Theodora Papatheodorou and Janet Moyles

This book has been inspired by selected papers from a conference on Relational Pedagogy, organised by the Centre for Research into Education and Teaching (CREATe) at Anglia Ruskin University in April 2007. The conference was held in collaboration with the Essex Early Years service and it was attended by a wide range of early years professionals, including early years advisers, trainers, local authority officials, academics, researchers and students, from local, regional and international organisations.

The aim of the conference was to open the dialogue about the meanings of relational pedagogy for the twenty-first century. It intended to offer opportunities for the participants to consider the ways in which practitioners, professionals, academics and researchers work together for and with babies and young children. The conference aimed to do so by returning to the roots of early childhood care and education. It become the forum where participants were encouraged to revisit traditions and were inspired to think innovatively.

The articles included in this book, all of them extensions and adaptations of conference presentations, have been organised under three major strands which are explored further in Chapter 1 and in the introductions to the sections:

1   Culture and environment, and adult–child relationships;
2   Adult–child relationships at micro level;
3   Adult–adult relationships for professional development.

These headings are in some ways rather arbitrary – relational pedagogy is a concept that is all-pervasive and trying to define specific topics to categories of any kind has been a challenge. Nevertheless, we felt it important to delineate some boundaries in order to make greater sense for our readers.

The editors are delighted to be able to present this collection of 17 articles in an endeavour to stimulate awareness, debate and dialogue about relational pedagogy in international early years contexts. This edited collection is presented as follows. In Chapter 1, we offer a definition of the term 'relational pedagogy', discuss the underlying principles of the concept and identify its implications for professional practice. This discussion draws on the work and research of the contributors to this book, as well as on relevant literature on relational pedagogy, early childhood and education in general to provide a rationale for reclaiming and embracing relational pedagogy in our work with and for children.

Following the introduction to Part I, there are five papers dealing in various ways with the culture and environment pervading relational pedagogy and with adult–child relationships. These five chapters deal with curriculum, citizenship, caregivers' voices, nurturing inspiration and the uses of observation in understanding relational pedagogy.

Part II contains six chapters which explore pedagogy at the heart of relationships between adults and young children, which is explored briefly in the introduction. The chapters explore the use of English as a foreign language with young children, self-regulation in potential conflict situations, how babies and toddlers construct relationships with their key workers in nurseries, co-construction and scaffolding to support children's meaning-making, and forging and fostering relationships in play.

In Part III, the five chapters investigate adult–adult relationships for professional development. The areas covered include team-working in early years settings, the impact of relationship training on early years workers, reframing Early Childhood Studies degrees to achieve higher quality training, parental participation and fostering identity, and relationships through mentoring.

As may be seen, the papers from the conference were, of necessity, very eclectic. All the presenters showed a deep commitment to exploring in person and in writing a wide range of issues inherent within the concept of relational pedagogy and enabling others to enhance their understandings. All the chapters are based on the contributors' own research and investigations. The editors have retained the 'voices' of the writers in the true spirit of relational pedagogy! This means that each chapter may be read both as part of the whole but also individually on its own merits. The chapters cover a range of perspectives and have come from as far afield as New Zealand and Europe, making the book truly international. We feel certain that there is much for early childhood practitioners across the world to learn and appreciate from this varied and inspirational collection.

1 Exploring relational pedagogy

Theodora Papatheodorou

Despite the increased volume of literature addressing the concept of relational pedagogy, the place of the concept in professional writing is rather limited. Reasons for such an omission may range from difficulties in understanding the concept of pedagogy; conflicting and polarised discourses and policies about education (e.g. child-centred versus teacher-centred education, outcomes/competencies-based versus processes education); global imperatives and demands for a view of education as a private economic good; and perhaps little confidence in, and trust of, professional wisdom and experience of early years practitioners.

In this chapter, I will attempt to define the term *relational pedagogy*, discuss the underlying principles of the concept and identify its implications for professional practice. The discussion will draw on the work and research of the contributors to this book, as well as relevant literature on relational pedagogy and early childhood and education in general to provide a rationale for the argument that we – early years professionals in any capacity – need to reclaim and embrace relational pedagogy in our work with and for children.

Introduction

The difficulty in embracing the concept of relational pedagogy may be due to the fact that pedagogy itself is a difficult concept to understand and comprehend. Pedagogy is a widely used term in education in Europe and that was my own personal experience, as I was initially educated and worked in the Greek educational system. Pedagogy had a central place in my education as a nursery teacher. On the Continent, the term is used to refer to modules, whole programmes of study and even departments in education faculties. In general terms, pedagogy is understood as the art and science of educating the child and the adult alike. In English educational literature, the term *pedagogy* appeared mainly during the 1990s and it has been considered as being synonymous with teaching, defined as the act and performance of curricula delivery (Alexander 2000; Lewis and Norwich 2005).

Pedagogy, however, is broader and wider in meaning and purpose. For example, in *The Study of Pedagogical Effectiveness* (SPEEL), Moyles *et al*. 2002: 5), state that:

> Pedagogy ... connects the relatively self-contained act of teaching and being an early years educator, with personal, cultural and community values (including care), curriculum structures and external influences. Pedagogy in the early years operates from a shared frame of reference (a mutual learning encounter) between the practitioner, the young children and his/her family.

According to Brooker (2007: 14):

> learning is now seen to be very much the outcome of relationships: between children and their friends and classmates, between children and the adults who care for them in every setting, and between the professional educators and the families and communities who have provided children's earliest experiences.

We would add not only cultural and ethnic communities, since relational pedagogy also encompasses the building of true communities of learners (McCaleb 1995) especially in the early years. It is the learners who are crucial, content being important only because, through it, relationships can be revealed. It is these very relationships that make relational pedagogy difficult to define because they are never static, continually changing and evolving. It is a co-creative process, 'organic' in the sense that relational pedagogy is responsive to the needs, passions and interests of learners (Gold 2005).

Etymologically, pedagogy comes from the Greek word 'παιδαγωγική' which has two components: 'παιδί' meaning child and 'άγω' literally meaning lead but, in the word pedagogy, 'άγω' has the meaning of guide. Metaphorically speaking, the interpretation of 'άγω' as 'guide' suggests that two (or more) people walk side-by-side and hand-in-hand along a route or path that has been walked before by one member of the group, and that member has now taken the role of guide and facilitator in the new journey.

In these terms, in the case of educating young children, pedagogy means that the adult and the child embark on a journey together. The adult remains the knowledgeable one but that knowledge is facilitative: the adult is the facilitator rather than the one who sets a clearly predetermined path or route. This notion of pedagogy is best reflected in concepts such as the 'zone of proximal development' (ZPD), 'scaffolding' and 'mediation', all of which form central ideas about learning in the early years (Bruner and Haste 1987; Vygotsky 2002). It has also been encapsulated in Tal Ben-Tov's term 'guide', which she uses to refer to tutors of early childhood practitioners attending the *Learning to Live Together* programme (Chapter 4).

The ontological foundations of relational pedagogy

Pedagogy – by focusing on the individual as a human being, be it the young child, the teacher, the parents/carers and their being together and their interconnected experience – takes an ontological dimension (Levine, in Meek 1996). It implies a relation, an obligation and the infinite attention which we owe to each other. It invests a dialectical relationship between learner and teacher and acknowledges the particular cultural, social and structural context where such relationships can develop (Levine, in Meek 1996). Understanding pedagogy in these terms means that 'relationality' is its core element.

Contributors to this book place interactions and communication at the heart of relational pedagogy which is viewed as a reflective and negotiative process that requires reciprocity, initiation and the sustaining of joint involvement episodes (Dinneen, Chapter 14). All contributors emphasise the importance of intuition, wisdom and trust (see especially Insley and Lucas, Chapter 13; Fowler and Robins, Chapter 17). Relational pedagogy is viewed as the 'in-between' space occupied by all those involved in the learning process (Oates *et al.*, Chapter 15). In this space conflict may arise, if feelings and others' views are not considered, but these conflicts are also negotiated through a dialogical process. Bingham and Whitebread (Chapter 8) suggest that relational pedagogy is for individual and group self-regulation and, as Bergum (2003) has claimed, it is where we are found and feel at home. It is about sensory and emotional experiences for young children and intimate relationships.

Those who visit the renowned Reggio Emilia preschools in Italy are privileged to witness this kind of pedagogy. Despite the fact that the creative approach adopted in Reggio Emilia preschools captures the eye and imagination of the visitor, looking more carefully and listening to the early years practitioners there, it becomes apparent that their pedagogy focuses on children's self-awareness and well-being acquired through, and because of, the relationships they develop with others (see Cameo 1).

Cameo 1

The teacher is working with a group of four children (two girls and two boys), all sitting around a table. On the table, there is a small basket with little wallets (approx. 9 × 5cm) made from card, glue, colouring pencils, coloured buttons of different sizes and texture, glitter glue, scissors and small folded papers. One of the girls is cutting the folded paper in half and placing the pieces into the basket with the wallets. A boy and a girl are decorating the little wallets with the colouring pens and/or by sticking on colourful buttons. When they finish each wallet, they place it back into the basket and take another one to decorate. The fourth child (a boy) is decorating one of the papers which the first girl has already cut into halves. The preschool

continued

teacher is sitting next to them. The boy addresses the teacher and the teacher replies with a question. The boy responds. The teacher takes a piece of paper and writes a three-word sentence. The boy copies it on to the small piece of paper which he has decorated. He then takes one of the wallets from the basket and inserts the piece of paper. The preschool teacher keeps the wallet in front of her.

The boy moves on to another table and joins four other children. Another girl comes to join the nursery teacher and the other children. The girl takes a small piece of paper from the basket and starts to decorate it. The teacher addresses the girl who, in turn, replies. The teacher takes a piece of paper and writes down a four-word sentence. The girl copies the sentence, then takes the wallet which the other child has just left. The teacher requests the wallet back, saying something. The girl seems disappointed. The teacher takes the basket with the wallets and places it in front of the girl for her to choose one. The girl does so and puts her piece of paper into the wallet. The teacher keeps this wallet in front of her.

In this cameo, it seems that two things are happening; that is, the decoration of the wallets is a collective task, but the messages are individual and written individually by each child (with adult support). Asked about this activity, the preschool teacher explained that the following day it was Ciara's birthday. Every child wanted to send Ciara a very special message. So she asked each child individually what they wanted this special message to be. Then she wrote it down and the child copied it on to the message slip. The preschool teacher explained further that because not all the children are equally skilful in decorating the wallets, they do this job collectively. This is to avoid children's disappointment if they compared their decorated wallets with those of others. So, the decoration of all wallets was left to children who were confident and willing to do so. The teacher emphasised that the important thing was the special message the children would send to Ciara, not its packaging (the wallet).

In this kind of pedagogy, the individual is valued and supported through collective endeavour and effort. The subtle messages for Ciara and other children is that what matters is:

1   how they relate to others and how others feel and think about them, not what they receive – 'being' matters more than 'having';
2   the individual's contribution to collective tasks and efforts, not the type of contribution.

Both of these messages are also reflected in the curriculum experiences of young children in countries such as China, where 'being' (especially as a community member) is a vital component and the good of the individual comes second to the supportive collective ideals (Moyles and Liu Hua 1998).

Children's (and other learners') self-awareness, self-worth and self-esteem derive from how others relate to them and the acknowledgement of their contribution to group and collective efforts and work (see also Papatheodorou 2007a). Awareness of others and self-awareness *because* of others has a prominent place in the philosophy and praxis of Reggio Emilia. This is not necessarily explicitly discussed with and articulated to children. Instead, as Brownlee (2004) would argue, the children are respected as being knowing and capable agents and they are given the experiences and support they need to identify the relationships of what they do and why, so as to find valid personal meaning which is also validated by those who share the same cultural and social space.

This central premise of the Reggio Emilia pedagogy is also echoed in the South African concept '*Ubuntu*', which means 'I am because of others' and highlights the uniqueness of each individual and the transformational power and influence each can make in the lives of others (see Sachs, Chapter 5). It is also embraced in the Maori word '*ako*' which means both 'to learn' and 'to teach' and reflects the reciprocal and bidirectional processes embraced in the inspirational *Te Whāriki* curriculum, implemented in the early years settings in New Zealand (see Peters, Chapter 2). These concepts entail, as Farren (2006) states, a *pedagogy of the unique* and a *web of betweenness* highlighting the contribution which each individual can make in the learning process and the relational dynamics of various contributions that recognise the humanity in the other.

The cognitive dimensions of relational pedagogy

By its definition and connotations, relational pedagogy immediately brings to mind social relationships. Drawing upon the principles of constructivism and socio-cultural theories (Bruner and Haste 1987; Vygotsky 2002) and the work of Baxter and Magolda, King and Kitchener and her own research, Brownlee (2004) has defined relational pedagogy in terms of three parameters:

1   showing respect to the student as a knower;
2   providing learning experiences that relate to students' own experience;
3   articulating and facilitating a constructivist approach to learning by emphasising meaning-making rather than knowledge accumulation.

This means that the learner (whatever the age) does not come into a learning environment as an empty vessel to be filled. The learner has experiences and knowledge that become the lenses through which new knowledge, information and experience are filtered and understood to identify relationships between them and construct new ideas that have personal meaning and inform their actions. Again, this was witnessed in one of the Reggio Emilia preschools, where the atelierista was observed working with two children (see Cameo 2).

Cameo 2

The atelierista is working with two children who have lumps of clay in front of them. Through the guidance of the atelierista – in the form of suggestions, modelling and perfecting of skills required – the lumps of clay are gradually transformed and refined to take on a new form and life. Both the atelierista and the two children are deeply involved, absorbed and working intensely on their sculptures. They seem to be completely cut off from the happenings around them.

  The children are not left to their own devices but are facilitated to use different tools, to handle the clay in different ways, incorporate new and different materials, to make judgements about the ones that blend and fit well with clay and refine skills required to use the materials. Most importantly, the two children are not given the same guidance and instructions. Instead the guidance is informed by what each child is trying to do and the ways each handles the clay. The children themselves, through constructive facilitation, gradually come to form ideas on how to work with and manipulate clay and to produce refined and meaningful representations, distinctly different from each other. In this instance, didactics take the form of indirect and, when necessary, direct facilitation of children to explore possible alternative avenues and pathways that their work may take and offer specific skills to apply or test such alternatives.

The above observation exemplifies the pedagogy of listening, understood as 'being fully attentive to the children . . . seeking to follow and enter into the active learning that is taking place (Edwards *et al*. 1998: 181). If children use a hundred languages to express themselves (Forman and Fyfe 1998), we – the adults – also need a hundred languages for listening and responding. Non-verbal communication (such as little utterances, facial expressions, body language and gestures, nodding, approval glances, smiles, eye conduct, discreet help) form an integrated, coordinated system of communication that is valued as equally as verbal communication. Through such communicative mediation children learn ways of being, doing, saying things and understanding their culture (see Maagerø and Simonsen, Chapter 7; Georgeson, Chapter 10; Payler, Chapter 11).

  This observation also demonstrates that 'relationships and learning coincide' (Malaguzzi 1998: 66) and that 'reciprocity, exchange and dialogue' are at the heart of such relationships and learning (Edwards *et al*. 1998: 10). At the core of the Reggio Emilia pedagogy is the human being as knowledgeable and the process and art of pedagogy; not just the teaching of predetermined and pre-identified measurable outcomes. These ideas are well summed up by Boyd *et al*. (2006: n.p.) who state that 'Relational pedagogy equips learners to become partners in their own education, but it also recognises that building relationships without improved student learning does not constitute good pedagogy'.

What makes the Reggio Emilia approach so special and inspirational is that it invests in teachers' reflexive, reflective and creative attitudes and immediate responses to and support for individual children's needs (discussed by Luff, Chapter 6). It invests in 'dialogue, reflection and creation' for children to reach 'ownership' of their outputs (see the hourglass process in Sachs, Chapter 5) be it the birthday present for Ciara or a child's own clay sculpture. To borrow from Bernstein's concept of invisible pedagogy, Reggio Emilia has developed a certain pedagogic genre, where the intended aims, outcomes and competencies are weak and largely unknown to the learner, while the tacit knowledge of all those involved in the process is valued, since it has a deep, shared understanding and acceptance (see Georgeson, Chapter 10; Payler, Chapter 11). Neither the teacher nor the atelierista made any explicit references to what was learned and taught. It is left to children to identify the relationships between what they do and what they learn. The children themselves are the points of reference.

Relational pedagogy: bridging dichotomies

It is often argued that Reggio Emilia is process-oriented rather than pre-set goal-oriented, a feature it shares with the *Te Whāriki* curriculum of New Zealand (see Peters, Chapter 2) and, to some extent, with High/Scope principles. In the latter, the child is the decision-maker and responsible for their own actions. Independence and autonomy are fostered through key experiences determined by the child in the (now famous) plan–do–review system. The High/Scope curriculum 'emphasizes adult–child interactions, a carefully designed learning environment and a plan–do–review process that strengthens initiative and self-reliance in children. . . . Teachers and students are active partners in shaping the educational experience' (High Scope 2007).

The process/outcomes arguments raise the question as to what education is for. This question has been long and extensively debated but it remains more relevant today than ever before. Giroux (2003), referring to the North American context, argues that education has become a private economic good that focuses on decontextualised skills and on a learner who is self-reliant and separate from others. In its publication *Human Capital*, the OECD reinforces this argument by identifying education as an economic good (Keeley 2007). It argues that education contributes to economic growth and prosperity which, in turn, requires and demands more education. For this, education has become highly focused on skills and competencies that clearly serve the market economy by producing skilful, competent and productive workers.

These process/outcomes dilemmas reflect, according to Goldberg, the philosophical commitment of Western society to rational, self-interested, self-maximising and self-providing individuals (cited in Keating 2007) and this belief has changed and shaped 'the ways we see ourselves, other people, and the world' (Keating 2007: 25). In reality, however, we are more than ever interconnected and interdependent. In today's global society, we are interconnected at many different levels and systems: ecological, economical, linguistic and social (Herd

2004). There is a related demand for the development of global competencies which are defined as the learner's ability 'to understand the interconnectedness of peoples and systems, to have a general knowledge of history and world events, to accept and cope with the existence of different cultural values and attitudes and, indeed, to celebrate the richness and benefits of this diversity' (ACIIE and The Stanley Foundation 1996: 2).

Such interconnectivity requires relational worldviews where individual and collective integrity and respect are maintained (Herd 2004). We may appear to be separate but our connections are deep, and for this we cannot avoid responsibility for each other (Keating 2007). The implication for education is that it should focus on processes which, according to Giroux (cited in Peters, Chapter 2), emphasise equity, justice, critical learning and active citizenship rather than knowledge transmission. Transmission of knowledge or, in early childhood, readiness for the next phases of education is not enough, because knowing about or knowing something do not equate with practising/doing something. Kay and Bath (Chapter 3) argue that relational pedagogy, by focusing on real problem-solving situations that take place in democratic and less authoritarian relationships in schools and settings (demonstrated in the above observations), embraces active learning and citizenship.

The dialogical nature of relational pedagogy

For some time, progressive educators have strongly opposed and criticised education systems that focused on knowledge transmission that is disassociated and removed from the learner's experience. Freire (1998) saw such education as a tool for the domination and assimilation of learners in powerful ideologies and as a means of learners' distrust of their own experience, ability, wisdom, intuition and transformative powers. Freire argued for an education that is rooted in, and shaped by, the interplay of the learner and the teacher as well as their respective social, cultural and political positions (Margonis 1999). For this, he placed dialogue at the heart of the education process.

Dialogue (from the Greek word Διάλογος, Δια meaning through/between and λόγος meaning word) implies reciprocal and multi-voiced exchanges of ideas that direct the path of learning. In an educational system where learners and teachers often come from distinctly different positions (e.g. experiences, ideas, values, culture, language, ethnicity, class), there is a need for them to find a basis upon which to build their relationship and, as Margonis (1999) points out, to create educational experiences in which the intentions of both are recognised.

To develop such a relationship perhaps we should remind ourselves of the use of dialogue by Socrates, whose teachings were based on the principle of 'ignorance'. He proclaimed: 'One thing I know, I know nothing', and that was the fundamental principle of his teachings. He removed himself from any existing knowledge and preconceived ideas to avoid the interference of personal implicit interpretations and to allow his students to articulate explicitly their thinking. His technique – known as 'Μαιευτική' (midwifery) – is well illustrated in the work of Belenski *et al.* (1997: 217), who argue that teachers should assist learners 'in giving birth to their own ideas, in making their own tacit knowledge explicit and elaborating it'. As with Socratic dialogues, this means that ideas and values which inform the practice of our time should be interrogated and critically examined in order to give credence to our tacit knowledge and values. Borrowing from Socratic teaching, we should remind ourselves that scientific knowledge and techniques are of limited value if we do not know ourselves and we have not established relationships with others.

The dialogical dimension of relational pedagogy challenges teaching as a technical act. It resists the imposition of a priori beliefs of who the learner is or should be and as such challenges the functional and societal requirements of education and sets out the ethical grounds of education (issues raised and discussed by Goouch, Chapter 12). It requires teachers to re-examine their attitudes and allows them to understand their students. Such understanding enriches and transforms the teachers too, and it makes 'thinking with' possible. It enables teachers to show appropriate respect to their students as co-travellers in the learning journey rather than trying to mould or remake them in the image of dominant discourses (Margonis 1999). To borrow from Taylor (cited in Bergum 2003), relational pedagogy is reflected in dialogue that renegotiates narrative and social power.

Relational pedagogy beyond the classroom

The dialogic foundations of relational pedagogy signal a significant change in the conceptualisation of early years practice and bridges dichotomies and polarised discourses such as child-centred/initiated versus adult-centred learning, and learning processes versus outcomes/competencies-based education. To paraphrase Keating (2007), binary (either/or) thinking and dualistic models (us against them) are of little value to either learners or students. Instead we need a theoretical and pedagogical model that invests in our connectivity and interconnectivity as human beings. The dialogic underpinnings of relational pedagogy have shifted the debate from oppositional and bidirectional debates to relational discourses which acknowledge a matrix of human experience rather than individual experience that is separated from its context.

Relational pedagogy, understood as the lived in-between space and time of the learner and teacher and as a matrix of human experience, echoes Bronfenbrenner's (1979) argument that learning and development are determined by the complex and dynamic inter-relationships within and between the micro and macro systems over time. Bronfenbrenner (1979: 47 and 54) argued that 'relations with other people' as well as the 'interconnections among home, school and neighborhood' constitute the building blocks of human development.

In this context, early childhood practice and children's welfare cannot be understood without considering the social, cultural, historical and political context and the relationships among and between different contexts (for instance, early years settings and families – issues discussed by Einarsdottir and Gardarsdottir in

Chapter 16, and Brooker in Chapter 9) as well as collaboration with other services. In England, these understandings of human development are reflected in the *Every Child Matters* agenda which places emphasis on integrated services to ensure that all children succeed in reaching its five broad outcomes: staying safe, being healthy, enjoying and achieving, making a contribution, and avoiding poverty and hardship (DfES 2003). These, at first glance, seem to be a world away from supporting the development of relational pedagogy but, as Brooker emphasises, 'Teachers . . . now have collective responsibility . . . for all aspects of a child's, and the family's, well-being' (2007: 12). It is to be hoped that, as the transition to this way of thinking progresses, the concepts and reality behind relational pedagogy will become more prominent.

Similarly, the new English *Early Years Foundation Stage* (EYFS) curriculum, alongside its emphasis on learning and development, which highlights *sustained shared thinking* as a vital component (Sylva *et al.* 2004), also stresses the importance of *positive relationships* (for example, included here is respecting each other, professional relationships, communication, positive interactions and listening to children) and *enabling environments* (examples from this section include learning journeys, working together, the emotional environment and community) (DfES/DCFS 2007).

How these outcomes will be achieved is as much an issue of structures and systems being in place as the result of our pedagogy. In the English context, for example, both the *EYFS Curriculum* (DfES/DCFS 2007) and the *Key Elements of Effective Practice* document (DfES 2005) provide opportunities for early years practitioners to generate relational pedagogy processes and thinking, rather than just focusing on profiling and learning outcomes. The requirements of these documents entail a pedagogy that plays an important mediating role in safeguarding best outcomes for children by being both person-centred and process-oriented, by considering the specific contexts (at micro and macro levels) and by acknowledging time as an important factor. A pedagogy that offers the lenses and filters by which policy, statutory regulation and guidance, and practice may be critically examined, critiqued, questioned and appropriated to meet the needs of all and every individual child (Papatheodorou 2007b).

Developing relational pedagogies and getting to know our learners is an issue of equal opportunity. Derald Wing Sue (cited in Keating 2007: 28) argues that it is a myth to believe that 'fair treatment equates equal treatment with fairness, whereas differential treatment is considered discriminatory or preferential'. In reality such beliefs 'mask disparities and inequalities and allow actions that oppress groups that are not in the mainstream'. To counteract these beliefs it is important to invest in relational pedagogy as the social capital (Keeley 2007) and the building blocks for healthy development (Shonkoff and Phillips 2000). The relationships we develop and establish within and beyond the classroom allow us to identify the needs of all and each individual learner to provide the differential treatment and support to place everyone on an equal footing for the learning journey for life.

The contentious place of relationality in education

Relational pedagogy, however, claims an ambiguous and often controversial place in educational systems (Insley and Lucas, Chapter 13). Being informed by and developed from 'cues received from the children' rather than from 'knowing what is needed' (Brooker, Chapter 9), relationality conflicts with and challenges dominant rationality and outcome-based discourses. The underpinning element of care and the affective and emotional foundations of relationships make them a contested issue, too. However, early years professionals need to face the challenge of reclaiming and affirming the relational foundations of their pedagogy because 'without opportunities to develop the capacity for relational knowing, teachers and teacher educators will never be able to teach their students to develop such capacities' (Gallego *et al.* 2001: 261). Teachers using relational pedagogic strategies become great teachers because they learn as much from their students as their students learn from them, equipping learners to become partners in their own education for life (Boyd *et al.* 2006).

Indeed, the English government document *Key Elements in Effectice Practice* recommends that practitioners should develop, demonstrate and continuously improve their relationships with both children and adults (DFES 2005). However, the focus of such development should not just be on learning and teaching about relationships, but also on engaging actively in relationships; an insight captured vividly by a student who participated in the SPELLS (Story Playing for Emotional Literacy and Learning Support) project. The student reflected:

> It [the discussion] allowed me to build a strong bond with the children, learning what their strengths and weaknesses were and how I could help improve them . . . through practising discussion with children, I relaxed around them in a professional manner and found that this helped my communication skills with them.
>
> (Papatheodorou 2005)

This quotation exemplifies how we can empower children and, in turn, be empowered as unique and self-respected individuals and professionals. We maintain personal agency and integrity and sustain relational autonomy (Keating 2007) with Farren's 'web of betweenness'. We transform uniqueness and individuality into a harmonious *weness*.

It should be noted, however, that relational approaches to learning are not easy either for teachers or learners. Several reasons may count for this, but top-down, prescribed, (measurable) outcomes-and-competence-based curricula, quality assurance and inspection policies first come to mind. This is true as much in early years settings as it is in higher education. Whereas in the first case, the young learners are open to all kinds and types of pedagogical approaches, in the latter case, students are further disadvantaged. My research with colleagues has clearly demonstrated that our students arrive in early childhood courses with limited confidence and trust in their own knowledge and experience and, as a consequence, are reluctant and uncertain in engaging in relational approaches to learning. Against the backdrop of institutional systems, which are based on compartmentalised (modular) teaching, learning and assessment practices, it takes confidence from both tutors and students to engage with and sustain relational approaches to learning (Papatheodorou 2005; Papatheodorou *et al.* 2007).

Relational pedagogy: an alternative pedagogy

This chapter has discussed the overlapping ideas about relational pedagogy and provided a systematic synthesis to identify its implication for early childhood education. In general, relational pedagogy is understood as the empowering force for knowing ourselves (in whatever capacity: learner, teacher, policy-maker and implementer) and others; for making sense of others and making sense of ourselves because of others. Relational pedagogy is about individuality and the collective consciousness that is shaped and transformed in time and place. Relational pedagogy is about understanding and appreciating local and cultural imperatives and conditioning, and about developing global communicative competencies. It is about relationships which leave room for 'not knowing' so that those involved in the learning process come to know without loss of self-esteem.

Relational pedagogy bridges the false dichotomy between outcomes-based and processes-oriented pedagogical praxis. It articulates and makes explicit the underpinning principles of processes and their importance for achieving outcomes that have personal and collective relevance, meaning and use. In the fast and speedily changing world in which we live, relational pedagogy offers an alternative to school-readiness (Anning 2005) which was based on the notion of a rather static or slowly changing world, where yesterday's knowledge and tools had greater relevance and longevity for future generations. Relational pedagogy offers the tools for attending to, unpacking, deconstructing and reconstructing cognitive and social relationships for learners to become reflective, critical, meaning-making and active citizens of today's and tomorrow's world. It enables us to face the unpredictability of our own lives and the global events that affect us in many different ways, either directly or indirectly.

We cannot afford to allow the new generations that come through our classes and settings to face tomorrow's world with today's tools. However, we can allow them to face their future in the knowledge that we have instilled in them, and equipped them with, the reflexive, reflective and creative aptitude that will enable them to develop new tools fit for the purposes and the world they will inhabit. We have a responsibility for future generations to do so because, despite our elaborated scientific knowledge, we cannot predict and determine society's destiny. Relational pedagogy underwrites the development of a society's future citizens. It is not something that society and educational systems can or should ignore (Boyd *et al.* 2006).

We know from Plato, Rousseau and contemporary theorists that, as human beings, we strive to make sense of our ontological existence – who we are and who we will become. The latter may, to a large extent, depend upon and be determined by the aims and objectives of educational settings and policy-makers but pedagogy has a vital role to play. As educators of the very young, we should remind ourselves that 'what we leave behind is not what is engraved in stone monuments, but what is woven into the lives of others' (Pericles (495–429 BC) to his troops).

References

ACIIE and The Stanley Foundation (1996) *Educating for the Global Community: A Framework For Community Colleges*. Available online at: http://www.stanley foundation.org/publications/archive/CC2.pdf (accessed 25 October 2007).

Alexander, R. (2000) *Culture and Pedagogy: International Comparisons in Primary Education*. Malden, MA: Blackwell.

Anning, A. (2005) Play and legislated curriculum. Back to basics: an alternative view. In J. Moyles (ed.) *The Excellence of Play* (2nd edn). Maidenhead: Open University Press.

Belenski, M.F., Clinchy, M.B., Goldberg, N.R. and Tarule, M.J. (1997) *Women's Ways of Knowing*. New York: Basic Books.

Bergum, V. (2003) Relational pedagogy: embodiment, improvisation, and interdependence. *Nursing Philosophy*, 4: 121–128.

Bertrand, Y. (1998) *The Ordinary Hero*. Madison, WI: Atwood Publishers.

Boyd, R., MacNeil, N. and Sullivan, G. (2006) Relational pedagogy: putting balance back into students' learning. *Curriculum Leadership: an Electronic Journal for Leaders in Education*, 4(3). Available online at: http://www.det.wa.edu.au/lc/pdfs/Relational Pedagogy.pdf (accessed 9 March 2007).

Bronfenbrenner, U. (1979) *The Ecology of Human Development. Experiment by Nature and Design*. Cambridge, MA: Harvard University Press.

Brooker, L. (2007) Changing the landscape of early childhood. In J. Moyles (ed.) *Early Years Foundations. Meeting the Challenge*. Maidenhead: Open University Press.

Brownlee, J. (2004) Teacher education students' epistemological beliefs. Developing a relational model of teaching. *Research in Education*, 72: 1–17.

Bruner, J. and Haste, H (1987) Introduction. In J. Bruner and H. Haste (eds) *Making Sense. The Child's Constructions of the World*. London: Methuen.

DfES (2003) *Every Child Matters* (Green Paper). London: HMSO.

DfES (2005) *Key Elements of Effective Practice*. Nottingham: DfES Publications.

DfES (Department for Education and Skills)/DCFS (Department for Children, Families and Schools) (2007) *Early Years Foundation Stage*. Available online at: http://www. standards.dfes.gov.uk/eyfs/ (accessed 12 November 2007).

Edwards, C., Gandini, L. and Forman, G. (1998) (2nd edn) Introduction: Background and starting point. In C. Edwards, L. Gandini and G. Forman (eds) *The Hundred Languages of Children: The Reggio Approach – Advanced Reflections*. Greenwich, CT: Ablex Publishing Corporation.

Farren, M. (2006) How am I developing and sustaining the use of collaborative online learning environment in higher education through a web of betweenness and a pedagogy of the unique? Paper presented at BERA Annual Conference, University of Warwick.

Forman, G. and Fyfe, B. (1998) Negotiated learning through design, documentation and discourse. In C. Edwards, L. Gandini and G. Forman (eds) *The Hundred Languages of Children: The Reggio Approach – Advanced Reflections* (2nd edn). Greenwich, CT: Ablex Publishing Coorporation.

Freire, P. (1998) *Pedagogy of the Oppressed* (new revised 20th Anniversary edn). New York: Continuum Publishing.

Gallego, M.A., Hollingsworth, S. and Whitenack, D.A. (2001) Relational knowing in the reform of educational cultures. *Teachers College Record*, 13(2): 240–266.

Giroux, H.A. (2003) *The Abandoned Generation: Democracy Beyond the Culture of Fear*, Basingstoke: Palgrave Macmillan.

Gold, L. (2005) An introduction to relational pedagogy: relationships at the heart of learning. Paper presented at the Third International Conference on New Directions in Humanities, Cambridge, 2–5 August.

Herd, D. (2004) *Globalisation: The Dangers and the Answers*. Available online at: http://www.opendemocracy.net/globalization-vision_reflections/article_1918.jsp#six (accessed 25 October 2007).

High Scope (2007) Curriculum. Available online at: http://www.highscope.org/Content.asp?ContentId=1 (accessed 12 November 2007).

Keating, A. (2007) *Teaching Transformation. Transcultural Classroom Dialogues*, New York: Palgrave.

Keeley, B. (2007) *Human Capital. How What You Know Shapes your Life*, Paris: OECD.

Lewis, A. and Norwich, B. (eds) (2005) *Special Teaching for Special Children?* Maidenhead: Open University Press.

McCaleb, S. (1995) *Building Communities of Learners: A Collaboration Among Teachers, Students, Families and Community*. Hillsdale, NJ: Lawrence Erlbaum Associates.

Malagguzi, L. (1998) History, ideas, and basic philosophy: an interview with Lella Gandini. In C. Edwards, L. Gandini and G. Forman (eds) *The Hundred Languages of Children: The Reggio Approach – Advanced Reflections* (2nd edn). Greenwich, CT: Ablex Publishing Coorporation.

Margonis, F. (1999) *Relational Pedagogy Without Foundations: Reconstructing the Work of Paulo Freire*. Available online at: http://www.ed.uiuc.edu/EPS?PES-Yearbook/1999.asp (accessed 9 October 2007).

Meek, M. (1996) *Developing Pedagogies in the Multilingual Classroom: The Writings of Josie Levine*. Stoke-on-Trent: Trentham.

Moyles, J. and Liu Hua (1998) Kindergarten education in China: reflections on a qualitative comparison of management processes and perceptions. *Compare*, 28(2): 155–170.

Moyles, J., Adams, S. and Musgrove, A. (2002) *SPEEL: Study of Pedagogical Effectiveness in Early Learning*. London: DfES. Report No. 363.

Papatheodorou, T. (2005) Story Playing for Emotional Literacy and Learning Support (SPELLS): an affective curriculum for young children. Poster session at the 5th Warwick International Early Years Conference, Warwick, UK.

Papatheodorou, T. (2007a) *Seeing the Wider Picture: Reflections on the Reggio Emilia Approach*. Available online at: http://www.tactyc.org.uk/pdfs/Reflection_Papatheodorou.pdf (accessed 25 October 2007).

Papatheodorou, T. (2007b) Difference, culture and diversity; challenges, responsibilities and opportunities. In J. Moyles (ed.) *Early Years Foundations: Meeting the Challenge*. Maidenhead: Open University Press.

Papatheodorou, T. and Lahiff, A. (2005) Developing the Early Years Professional: Preliminary Findings of the Portfolio of Evidence. Paper presented at the 15th EECERA Conference, Dublin, Ireland.

Papatheodorou, T., Such, C. and Luff, P. (2007) Co-constructing knowledge – facilitating graduateness? Paper presented at the self-organised symposium on Making Learning Visible at the 17th EECERA Conference, Prague Czech Republic.

Shonkoff, J.P. and Phillips, D.A. (2000) *From Neurons to Neighborhoods. The Science of Early Childhood Development.* Washington, DC: National Academy Press.

Sylva, K., Melhuish, E.C., Sammons, P., Siraj-Blatchford, I. and Taggart, B. (2004) The Effective Provision of Pre-School Education (EPPE) Project: *Technical Paper 12 – The Final Report: Effective Pre-school Education.* London: DfES/Institute of Education, University of London.

Vygotsky, L. (2002) *Language and Thought.* Cambridge, MA: The MIT Press (edited and revised by Alex Kozulin).

Part I

Culture, environment and adult–child relationships

Introduction

[Relational pedagogy] . . . invests a dialectical relationship between learner and teacher and acknowledges the particular cultural, social and structural context where such relationships can develop. (See Chapter 1)

As has been explored in Chapter 1, teaching and learning – and the pedagogical relationships between adults and children – are complex interactions set in a specific political, social and cultural climate. The context can be any number of settings or institutions, each with its own ethos and environment. In relational pedagogy terms what is important is how the pedagogical relationships between adults and children are conceived and experienced by all, and how the culture, ethos and environment supports and shapes reciprocal understandings. Relational pedagogy is about self-awareness and awareness of other people but this does not happen in a vacuum: aspects such as the curriculum, the community setting, family structures, political environments and culture all affect individuals' views of themselves.

As an example, the climate and culture of a school is movingly written about by Short (2007: 102) when she describes the transformation in her daughters when they were moved from an outcomes-driven school to one whose ethos was grounded in respect for children and adults and the development of optimal confidence and self-esteem, fostered through good adult–child pedagogical relationships. David (2007: 144) also points out, citing Anderton, that 'further advances in research are indicating that it is loving interactions with familiar, significant others (children as well as adults) which stimulate the production of certain brain-influencing chemicals in the blood stream'. This claim makes yet another crucial link for us all in considering relational pedagogy. David (2007: 145) importantly goes on to say that practitioners:

must be capable not only of examining those endogenous (within the child/ intra-child) and exogenous (outside the child – contextual or environmental) processes, they must also be able to analyse whether or not social policies are informed by that knowledge.

The curriculum, too, is a part of this cultural mileau as it provides the content in which learning together can occur. This is why it is vital to develop curricula which embed the principles of young children as competent and enthusiastic learners with inbuilt dispositions towards learning such as that in the Reggio Emilia preschool settings. These curricula must also be sufficiently flexible and open-ended that practitioners can support and include all children in generating learning and development.

In this section, the five chapters cover a range of issues already alluded to above – and much more! In Chapter 2, Sally Peters from New Zealand writes about responsive and reciprocal relationships being at the heart of the famous *Te Whāriki* curriculum. She emphasises that 'careful reflection reveals the value and nature of knowing ourselves as well as our learners, in order to achieve empathy, care and respect in educational encounters'. This theme is also reflected in Chapter 3, in which Janet Kay and Caroline Bath explore the extent to which early child-hood students can develop concepts of participatory and actively negotiated citizenship through relational pedagogic processes. Large groups of students were involved in individual reflections, debates, role play and sharing of ideas through group discussions. As the pedagogy developed, the students showed a significantly higher level of awareness of their own roles and responsibilities in terms of supporting and promoting children's rights, consulting and listening to children, respecting children, being a citizen and community participation.

In Israel, as Tal Ben-Tov explains in Chapter 4, the issue is one of how the awareness and sensitivity of caregivers (with little academic background) may best be fostered in relation to the social/emotional components of children's learning. Through case studies, she is able to conclude that careful reflection reveals the value and nature of knowing ourselves as well as our learners in order to achieve empathy, care and respect in educational relationships. She explains relational pedagogy in terms of 'connected teaching', the connection between personal knowledge/beliefs (focus on the self) and scientific knowledge (focus on theory). Tal Ben-Tov emphasises that connected teaching requires mutual respect between student, peers and teachers, situating learning in student experiences and using reflection as a key element in a constructivist approach. She also stresses the importance of individuals' 'ways of knowing'; that is, their epistemological beliefs and how these structure and affect practice and reflection.

We journey to South Africa in Chapter 5 with Jill Sachs who uses the metaphor of a journey to offer readers an insight into the importance of inspiration, self-knowledge, creativity and the expressive arts in the training and development of early childhood teachers in South Africa and the particular culture of the student participants. She outlines the development of the *Caversham Hourglass Process* which consists of *Reflection* (self-exploration); *Dialogue* (active listening in order to contribute and affirm); *CreACTion* (combining collaborative attitudes with creative actions) and *Ownership/Legacy* (being in the present, recognising the past, and taking responsibility for the future). The training programme requires that students work in groups: collaboration, cooperation, sharing and mutual ownership being underpinning values through which enduring supportive relationships are established.

This section concludes with Chapter 6 by Paulette Luff, who emphasises observation as a tool for developing relational pedagogy. She refers to both the type of documentation and recording made by adults in the Reggio Emilia preschools and stresses the connections and understandings that can be developed and exchanged in the context of shared practices and making meaning from observations. From her own research she is able to assert that informal observational practice is very meaningful and enhances relationships with children, families and colleagues. It can form the basis for thoughtful, shared reflections on care and teaching and a foundation for informed action to offer social and emotional support, facilitate playful learning and provide a cognitive challenge.

As may be seen, there is much in Part I to start us off on the road to understanding more about relational pedagogy and its many facets in the context of culture, environment and adult–child relationships.

References

David, T. (2007) Birth to three: the need for a loving and educated workforce. In J. Moyles (ed.) *Early Years Foundations: Meeting the Challenge*. Maidenhead: Open University Press.

Short, E. (2007) Somebody else's business – a parent's view of childhood. In J. Moyles (ed.) *Early Years Foundations: Meeting the Challenge*. Maidenhead: Open University Press.

2 Responsive, reciprocal relationships

The heart of the *Te Whāriki* curriculum

Sally Peters

Teaching is a complex activity and many different views co-exist about pedagogy and the goals of education. This chapter considers issues surrounding relational pedagogy and the role of responsive, reciprocal relationships in teaching and learning. Examples are drawn from the New Zealand context, where relationships are central to the early childhood curriculum, and have gained increasing recognition in school contexts.

Introduction

This chapter explores the theme of relational pedagogy and considers its implications for learning in the twenty-first century. Examples are provided from the New Zealand context, where the early childhood curriculum, *Te Whāriki* (Ministry of Education 1996b), is based on reciprocal and responsive relationships, and teachers have been exploring what this means for practice. The importance of relational pedagogy for school contexts is also discussed. The intention is to stimulate reflections on pedagogy. Internationally we share many similar concerns, and exploring other people's journeys can help us to examine our own practice.

Learning in the twenty-first century

There are many different paradigms in education. This is particularly evident in the current interest in relationships, which sits alongside a drive for testing and accountability. Giroux (2003) clarified the key debates in America around the purpose of education, and we can see similar issues in English and New Zealand contexts.

Reflecting on the question 'What kinds of learners do we value in the twenty-first century?' it is useful to consider Giroux's (2003) discussion, centred on:

- learners who achieve well in high-stakes standardised tests;
- learners who engage with knowledge with thoughtfulness and critical analytical skills.

Looking first at learners who achieve well in high-stakes standardised tests, Giroux (2003) noted that this approach treats schools like a pseudo marketplace and students as consumers. Education is for the private good and the focus is on skills-based learning, individual consumerism and individual success. Schools become testing factories, with targets or goals to achieve. In this context, teaching tends to focus on 'closing the gaps' and increasing student achievement in relation to the goals or targets. Curriculum may become narrow, looking largely at the material to be tested, and, Giroux claims, ignores cultural diversity and the relevance of learning to students' lives. Students may be encouraged to separate themselves from others.

Although focused on the North American context, Giroux's (2003) descriptions resonate with Edwards and D'Arcy's (2004: 150) assertion that national testing of the individual performance of pupils, public performance league tables for schools, and personal performance standards for teachers reduce learning to teach to 'an ability to follow a lesson plan', a situation they claim that renders both teachers and pupils 'powerless in the processes of curriculum delivery' (ibid.).

In contrast, Giroux (2003) notes that when what is valued are learners who engage with knowledge with thoughtfulness and critical analytical skills, education is seen as for the public good. There is a focus on equity, justice, social citizenship and critical learning, and classrooms become a site of critique, critical exchange and social transformation. Pedagogy may be viewed as a 'critical practice in which students learn to be attentive and responsible to the narratives of others' (Giroux 2003: 87). It is this view of pedagogy that underpins the focus on relationships that will be explored in this chapter.

Relational pedagogy

Darby (2005) described the two important aspects of pedagogy as instructional pedagogy, which fosters understanding, and relational pedagogy, which nurtures relationships. Both are important. However, while teachers are familiar with instructional pedagogy, which is based on both teacher content knowledge and pedagogical content knowledge, relational pedagogy may require further exploration.

Bergum (2003) provides a useful definition: 'relational pedagogy is situated in the world – the reciprocal world – where we find home', and (citing Heidigger 1977), suggests that 'we must keep our eyes firmly fixed on the true relation between teacher and taught' (Bergum 2003: 128).

Internationally, considerable attention is being paid to the relationship between teacher and learner, even though the term 'relational pedagogy' is not always used. For example, in New Zealand, Carpenter *et al.* (2002) described eleven attitudes and beliefs of highly successful primary schoolteachers. The list included the following:

• that they try to understand what it is like to be the other and understand the reasons for what they see;

- they are caring and non-judgemental;
- they value and learn about cultural and ethnic difference;
- they create permeable boundaries with the community;
- they model successful learning and social interactions;
- they empower learners to take responsibility for their own learning and actions.

Similar traits were noted in Brownlee and Berthelsen's (2006) description of relational pedagogy. Klem and Connell (2004) also found enhanced academic performance when teachers knew and cared about their students and personalised the learning environment, a finding reiterated by Macfarlane (2007) in his overview of several studies from the USA and New Zealand.

Across primary, secondary and tertiary settings the relationship between teacher and student has been shown to be of critical importance for Maori and Pasifica students. Teacher empathy, caring, respect and effort were important factors in student success, and could be achieved even when the teacher did not share the students' ethnicity (Hawk *et al.* 2002; Sutherland 2004). A large-scale project by Bishop *et al.* (2003) showed that changing secondary school teacher attitudes and relationships with students had a direct influence on student achievement.

Developing relationships

Relationships are clearly important but they are not always easy. How many learners feel like Eeyore in the quotation below, as their well-meaning teachers fly past them, busy with the daily demands of centre or classroom life?

> Owl flew past me a day or two ago and noticed me. He didn't actually say anything mind you but he knew it was me. Very friendly of him I thought. Encouraging.
>
> (*Eeyore's Gloomy Little Instruction Book* 1997)

How can we develop more responsive relationships with learners? Time is clearly an important factor. Bergum (2003) described how, for nurses, patients became more '3D' over time. As teachers we will have experienced this too, as we learn more about our students. Power is also an important consideration (Bergum 2003). If we reflect on who listens, who leads, who respects, who decides and so on, it can give insights into the power relationships in our setting. When the power resides only with the teacher, the learners may remain '2D', with important aspects hidden from the teacher's view. Putting ourselves in learners' shoes can also be beneficial. Waldron (2006) spent a year as a high school pupil and drew much from the experience to inform her pedagogy when she returned to teaching.

ICT equipment can be valuable tools in helping teachers to understand more about children and their backgrounds. For example, Ramsey *et al.* (2007) described loaning cameras to children to document activities they are involved in outside the early childhood centre (e.g. an underwater picture at a swimming lesson, a visit to grandparents in India). These are then shared with teachers and children at the centre and, the authors noted, often represented a 'watershed' in children's engagement with the programme (p. 34).

It is clear that relational pedagogy requires teachers to be learners too. This is acknowledged in the Maori term *ako*, which means both to learn and to teach (Royal Tangaere 1997).

The New Zealand context

In New Zealand, the notion that warm, understanding, respectful relationships are important for learning at all levels of education is acknowledged at the heart of the early childhood curriculum *Te Whāriki* (Ministry of Education 1996b), and is increasingly being acknowledged in school settings too (see Ministry of Education 2007b). *Te Whāriki* is based on the following aspirations for children: 'To grow up as competent and confident learners and communicators, healthy in mind, body and spirit, secure in their sense of belonging and in the knowledge that they make a valued contribution to society' (Ministry of Education 1996b: 9).

The four broad principles at the centre of the curriculum are:

*   **Empowerment – Whakamana**: The early childhood curriculum empowers the child to learn and grow.
*   **Holistic development – Kotahitanga**: The early childhood curriculum reflects the holistic way children learn and grow.
*   **Family and community – Whānau Tangata**: The wider world of family and community is an integral part of the early childhood curriculum.
*   **Relationships – Ngā Hononga**: Children learn through responsive and reciprocal relationships between people, places and things (Ministry of Education 1996b: 14).

In practice, the principles interconnect and overlap (Ministry of Education 2004, Book 2: 2). Five strands, and their associated goals, arise from the four principles. The strands are:

*   **Well-being – Mana Atua**: The health and well-being of the child are protected and nurtured.
*   **Belonging – Mana Whenua**: Children and their families feel a sense of belonging.
*   **Contribution – Mana Tangata**: Opportunities for learning are equitable, and each child's contribution is valued.
*   **Communication – Mana Reo**: The languages and symbols of their own and other cultures are promoted and protected.
*   **Exploration – Mana Aotūroa**: The child learns through active exploration of the environment.

(Ministry of Education, 1996b: 15–16)

Te Whāriki is New Zealand's first bi-cultural curriculum document and it reflects the emphasis on relationships and holistic development that is evident in Maori developmental theory (see e.g. Royal Tangaere 1997). The Maori concept of mana is at the centre of the approach taken. One of the curriculum developers, Reedy (2003: 68), explained, 'the main achievement occurs in the development of the child's mana . . . having mana is the enabling and empowering tool to controlling their own destiny'.

This view is evident in assessment practices too. The *Desirable Objectives and Practices* (DOPs) require educators to implement assessment practices that are consistent with the principles of *Te Whāriki* (Ministry of Education 1996b), thus enhancing children's sense of themselves as capable people and competent learners. Assessments are also required to involve families, reflect the holistic way that children learn, and reflect the reciprocal relationships between the child, people and the learning environment (Ministry of Education 1996a).

The learning outcomes in *Te Whāriki* are indicative rather than definitive (Ministry of Education 1996b) and each setting develops its own emphases and priorities. *Te Whāriki* translates as 'a woven mat for all to stand on' (May 2001: 245). This metaphor recognises that many different views can co-exist at one time and it was chosen to encompass diverse early childhood services within a common framework. Settings create their own curriculum 'weaving' from the principles, strands and goals. This offers teachers the flexibility to be responsive to learners.

Te Whāriki in practice

A child's learning develops in multiple directions at the same time. The Ministry of Education (2004, Book 1) acknowledged that every day educators notice many things as they work with children, they recognise some of what they notice as learning, and respond to a selection of what they recognise. This chapter invites educators to reflect on what they see as learning, and how they respond to it. The two examples from Giroux (2003) at the beginning of this chapter show how different these might be.

The learning outcomes in *Te Whāriki* relate, first, to children developing 'more elaborate and useful working theories about themselves and about the people, places, and things in their lives', and, second, to learning dispositions or patterns of learning (Ministry of Education 1996b: 44). These learning dispositions (courage and curiosity, trust and playfulness, perseverance, confidence and responsibility) are discussed more fully in Carr (2001).

Carr (2001: 39) noted that 'dispositions provide the learner with a narrative (or a number of narratives) about what learning is, *and ought to be*, all about' (italics in the original). The focus on dispositions encourages an orientation towards learning goals where children persist with difficulty and strive to understand or master something new. This contrasts with performance goals, where children strive to gain favourable judgements or avoid negative judgements (Smiley and Dweck 1994). Dispositions may be thought of as verbs (rather than nouns), so that persisting (for example) is not seen as something a learner acquires, but a response that an individual engages in 'more or less frequently, or skillfully, or appropriately' (Claxton and Carr 2004: 2).

Curriculum documents clearly play an influential role in shaping what we recognise as learning. Relational pedagogy is supported by a curriculum like *Te Whāriki*, which focuses on relationships. Teacher beliefs and attitudes are important too. One of the teacher-researchers involved in a three-year Teaching and Learning Research Initiative project co-directed by the author reflected that '*relationships are central to everything we do in the centre and how we do it. It is through relationships that we believe the child's identity is confirmed. For us, that identity is the empowered child.*' This teacher noted that relationships include relating to self, others and place, and the teaching team had been reflecting on whether, for children, teachers were part place or other. Although they initially felt that teachers were part of place, careful analysis of their practice showed that some particularly effective teachers seemed to have a greater awareness of children and how to support their learning that went beyond this. It appeared that only when there was shared knowledge and understanding of each other, and a balance of power, did teachers become 'other' (Wilson-Tukaki and Davis 2006; Carr *et al.* 2008).

Assessment and relational pedagogy

'Assessments don't just describe learning; they also construct and foster it' (Ministry of Education 2004, Book 1: 3). Check-listing skills and strategies are incompatible with the principles of *Te Whāriki* and early childhood educators have focused on looking not only at the individual but also acknowledging the role of the context and the child's interactions with others (Fleer 2002; Fleer and Richardson 2004). Carr's (2001) *Learning Story* approach, documenting actions and behaviours associated with learning dispositions, has been particularly influential. This, and other narrative forms of assessment for learning, are illustrated and discussed in the *Kei tua o te pae* resource (Ministry of Education 2004). The role of ICTs in documenting learning is illustrated in the DVD *Kimihia nga pae: Seek the Horizons*, and other insights are offered in a number of the reports from Round One of the Centre of Innovation programme (Ministry of Education 2007a).

Recording, using narratives and photographs, captures some of the learning that is happening. It provides feedback to learners as they revisit the stories, and allows teachers to reflect on their pedagogy. The stories themselves become a vehicle for developing relationships, between children and teachers, teachers and families, children and families and children and their peers, as they are shared and discussed. This is a powerful tool, as Sfard and Prusak (2005: 18) suggest – 'stories once told take on a life of their own' – and stories about a person have the power to contribute to that person's narratives about themselves and about others. They offer a way of learning 'to be attentive and responsible to the narratives of others' which, as noted earlier, Giroux (2003: 87) saw as being a feature of learners who engage with knowledge with thoughtfulness and critical analytical skills.

Transition to school

The theme of the *Reclaiming Relational Pedagogy* conference (at Anglia Ruskin University in April 2007) posed relational pedagogy as an alternative to early school readiness, but relational pedagogy is increasingly recognised as important, not only for lifelong learning, but also for success in school (Carpenter *et al.* 2002; Hawk *et al.* 2002; Bishop *et al.* 2003; Klem and Connell 2004; Macfarlane 2007).

As Erickson (1985: 129) noted, social class or early childhood experiences do not 'cause' school achievement (or problems with school). Instead, *'people'* influence patterns of experience 'in specific interactional occasions' (emphasis in the original). This was evident in an in-depth study of children's experiences on school entry (Peters 2004). At the time, I recommended taking the principles and strands of the early childhood curriculum *Te Whāriki* into the first year (at least) of school in order to foreground the principles of empowerment, holistic development, family and community, and relationships, and to provide a framework to guide teachers in ensuring that children's well-being and sense of belonging were established, and that they had opportunities to contribute, communicate and explore.

Three years later we are fortunate that the new school curriculum acknowledges the place of relationships as a contributing factor in 'successful' transitions (Ministry of Education 2007b: 32), and in the development of the key competencies of relating to others, managing self, participating and contributing, thinking, and using languages, symbols and texts. 'Opportunities to develop the competencies occur in social contexts. . . . The competencies continue to develop over time, shaped by interactions with people, places ideas, and things' (Ministry of Education 2007b: 22). There is a clear alignment between the strands of *Te Whāriki* and the draft school curriculum, illustrated in Table 2.1.

Table 2.1 Alignment of the key competencies in the school curriculum with *Te Whāriki*

Strands of Te Whāriki	*Key competencies in the school curriculum*
Mana whenua – Belonging	Participating and contributing
Mana atua – Well-being	Managing self
Mana aotūroa – Exploration	Thinking
Mana reo – Communication	Using language symbols and texts
Mana tangata – Contribution	Relating to others

Source: Adapted from Ministry of Education (2006: 33).

The use of photographs and narrative assessments to document children's learning in early childhood can provide a tool for assisting these relationships to develop, such as the Reggio Emilia practices in Northern Italy (Rinaldi 2006). In a New Zealand study, Hartley *et al.* (2007) describe how Gaurav, a child with English as an additional language, said very little in his early childhood setting. Nevertheless, he was a capable and confident learner and this learning was documented and celebrated through stories and photographs in his portfolio. When Gaurav moved on to school he took his portfolio with him. His teacher was able to learn about his interests and prior learning and connect with them. The teacher also noticed that other children often wanted to look at Gaurav's portfolio with him, and soon it became 'the most read book on the shelf'. Gaurav used the portfolio to form relationships within the classroom, with relief teachers, and with new children as they joined the class. Other children soon began to bring their portfolios to school and to share them with teachers and classmates, providing important literacy artefacts, as well as supporting relationships. The school and kindergarten teachers started to ensure that new children brought their port-folios on their school visits. The schoolteacher wrote stories during the visits that could be shared back at kindergarten, so that in the weeks before children started school, the stories moved between settings. The kindergarten teachers noted:

> What we saw was that the portfolio supported an environment for friendship and communication using mutually interesting artifacts and cultural tools. The means of being understood, providing opportunity for talk between child and teacher and between children, some for whom English is an additional language. By valuing the portfolio and using the portfolio to get to know the interests and personality of the child the relationship between the kindergarten and the school has changed beyond our expectations.

This work is being explored in more detail in a Centre of Innovation research project.

Conclusion

For more than a decade the early childhood curriculum in New Zealand has prioritised responsive, reciprocal relationships and teachers have been explor-ing ways of fostering these in practice. Developing effective relationships takes time and effort. Careful reflection reveals the value and nature of knowing ourselves as well as our learners, in order to achieve empathy, care and respect in educational encounters. Digital photographs and narratives to document learning can play an important role in supporting shared understandings of what is valued (see Luff, Chapter 6).

Relational pedagogy clearly has an important role in school settings too. The new school curriculum in New Zealand offers exciting possibilities for develop-ing and supporting relational pedagogy but, as I noted at the beginning of this chapter, teachers are still working in contexts where different paradigms co-exist, and there is by no means consensus on some of the issues raised. My intention has been to invite reflections on practice. 'Children's learning is embedded in their reciprocal relationships with the world, with people, places, and things. The world shapes their learning as in turn, their learning shapes and changes the world' (Ministry of Education 2004, Book 1: 5). What kinds of learners do we hope they become, and what is our role in achieving this aim?

References

Bergum, V. (2003) Relational pedagogy. Embodiment, improvisation and interdependence. *Nursing Philosophy*, 4, 121–128. Accessed online at: http://web.ebscohost.com. ezproxy.waikato.ac.nz:2048/ehost/results?vid=2&hid=8&sid=fa3f68f0-d823-4d74-9c52-ca6e88cfa939 per cent40sessionmgr8 (accessed on 16 October 2007).

Bishop, R., Berryman, M., Tiakiwai, S. and Richardson, C. (2003) *Te kotahitanga: The Experiences of Year 9 and 10 Maori Students in Mainstream Classrooms*. Wellington: Ministry of Education.

Brownlee, J. and Berthelsen, D. (2006) Personal epistemology and relational pedagogy in early childhood teacher education programs. *Early Years*, 26(1): 17–29.

Carpenter, V.M., McMurchy-Pilkington, C. and Sutherland, S. (2002) Kaiako toa: highly successful teachers in low decile schools. *Set*, 2: 4–8.

Carr, M. (2001) *Assessment in Early Childhood Settings*. London: Paul Chapman.

Carr, M., Peters, S., Davis, K., Bartlett, C., Bashford, N., Berry, P., Greenslade, S., Molley, S., O'Connor, N., Simpson, M., Smith, Y., Williams, T. and Wilson-Tukaki, A. (2008) *Key Learning Competencies Across Place and Time: Kimihia ara tōtika hei oranga mo tō ao*. Teaching and Learning Research Initiative Final Report. Hamilton, NZ: Wilf Malcolm Institute of Educational Research.

Claxton, G. and Carr, M. (2004) A framework for teaching learning: the dynamics of disposition. *Early Years: Journal of International Research and Development*, 24(1): 87–98.

Darby, L. (2005) Social science students' perceptions of engaging pedagogy. *Research in Science Education*, 35: 425–445.

Edwards, A. and D'Arcy, C. (2004) Relational agency and disposition in sociocultural accounts of learning to teach. *Educational Review*, 56: 147–155.

Eeyore's Gloomy Little Instruction Book (1997) London: Methuen.

Erickson, F. (1985) Qualitative research methods. In M.C. Wittrock (ed.), *Handbook on Research on Teaching* (3rd edn). New York: Macmillan.

Fleer, M. (2002) Sociocultural assessment in early years education: myth or reality? *International Journal of Early Years Education*, 10: 105–120.

Fleer, M. and Richardson, C. (2004) Mapping the transformation of understanding. In A. Anning, J. Cullen and M. Fleer (eds) *Early Childhood Education: Society and Culture*. London: Sage.

Giroux, H.A. (2003) *The Abandoned Generation: Democracy Beyond the Culture of Fear*. Basingstoke: Palgrave Macmillan.

Hartley, C., Boyce, F., Gibbs, N., Ritzema-Bain, E., Carr, M. and Peters, S. (2007) *Finding the Magic and Taking it to School*. Paper presented at the Australian Research in Early Childhood Education Conference, Melbourne.

Hawk, K., Cowley, E.T., Hill, J. and Sutherland, S. (2002) The importance of the teacher/student relationship for Maori and Pasifica students. *Set*, 3: 44–49.

Klem, A.M. and Connell, J.P. (2004) Relationships matter: linking teacher support to student engagement and achievement. *The Journal of School Health*, 74(7): 262–273.

Macfarlane, A. (2007) *Discipline, Democracy, and Diversity: Working with Students with Behavioural Difficulties*. Wellington: NZCER Press.

May, H. (2001) *Politics in the Playground*. Wellington: Bridget Williams with NZCER.

Ministry of Education (1996a) Revised statement of desirable objectives and practices (DOPs) for chartered early childhood services in New Zealand. *The New Zealand Gazette*, October.

Ministry of Education (1996b) *Te Whāriki: Early Childhood Curriculum*. Wellington: Learning Media.

Ministry of Education (2004) *Kei tua o te pae, Assessment for Learning: Early Childhood Exemplars*. Wellington: Learning Media.

Ministry of Education (2006) *The New Zealand Curriculum Draft for Consultation*. Wellington: Learning Media.

Ministry of Education (2007a) Round One – Six Centres of Innovation. Accessed online at: http://www.minedu.govt.nz/index.cfm?layout=index&indexid=8304&indexparentid =8303 (accessed on 16 October 2007).

Ministry of Education (2007b) *The New Zealand Curriculum*. Wellington, NZ: Learning Media.

Peters, S. (2004) *Crossing the Border: An Interpretive Study of Children Making the Transition to School*. Unpublished Ph.D. thesis. University of Waikato.

Ramsey, K., Sturm, J., Breen, J., Lee, W. and Carr, M. (2007) Weaving ICTs into Te Whāriki at Roskill South Kindergarten. In A. Meade (ed.) *Cresting the Wave: Innovations in Early Childhood Education* (pp.29–36). Wellington: NZCER Press.

Reedy, T. (2003) Toku rangatiratanga na te Mana-Mātauranga 'Knowledge and power set me free . . .'. In J. Nuttall (ed.) *Weaving Te Whāriki: Aotearoa New Zealand's Early Childhood Curriculum Document in Theory and Practice*. Wellington: NZCER.

Rinaldi, C. (2006) *In Dialogue with Reggio Emilia*. London and New York: Routledge.

Royal Tangaere, A. (1997) Maori human development learning theory. In P. Te Whaiti, M. McCarthy and A. Durie *Mai i rangiatea. Maori Wellbeing and Development*. Auckland: Auckland University Press with Bridget Williams Books.

Sfard, A. and Prusak, A. (2005) Telling identities: in search of an analytic tool for investigating learning as a culturally shaped activity. *Educational Researcher*, 34(4): 14–22.

Smiley, P.A. and Dweck, C.S. (1994) Individual differences in achievement goals among young children. *Child Development*, 65: 1723–1743.

Sutherland, S. (2004) Art rooms: sites of empowerment and success. *New Zealand Journal of Teachers' Work*, 1(1): 16–22.

Waldron, D. (2006). My year as a high school student. *Educational Leadership*, 63(6): 63–65. Accessed online at: http://web.ebscohost.com.ezproxy.waikato.ac.nz:2048/ ehost/results?vid=2&hid=4&sid=77ee5305-bb6a-4c98-a518-baed3d0dc169per cent40 sessionmgr2 (accessed 16 October 2007).

Wilson-Tukaki, A. and Davis, K. (2006) *Relating Stories. Working Paper 3*. Key Learning Competencies across Place and Time. Kimihia te ara tōtika hei oranga mo tō ao. TLRI Project. Hamilton: University of Waikato Wilf Malcolm Institute of Educational Research.

3 From Rome to Athens

Active learning and concepts of citizenship for higher education

Janet Kay and Caroline Bath

This study explores the development of concepts of citizenship and participation in undergraduate early childhood studies students through the evaluation and modification of a module that examines young children's rights in a global context. The chapter outlines how the teaching and learning strategies have sought to inform students' sense of social responsibility and also how different pedagogical approaches have impacted on their learning about democratic concepts.

The methodology of the evaluation was defined as action research, as the process was intended to inform change and improve practice. The evaluation is a single case study reflecting a particular incidence. The main findings reflect emerging new perspectives on participation and citizenship and different outcomes for young and mature students. The links between pedagogical approach and content for effective learning also emerged, with an emphasis on the benefits of active and interactive learning and multimedia approaches.

Introduction

> We begin to think where we live.
>
> (Williams 1958)

The theme of citizenship has many different interpretations. The extent to which we can regard citizenship referring to a purely legal status, in the Roman tradition, is contested by the Aristotelian concept of citizenship which encompasses ideas of civic virtue and reasoned debate. This study aims to explore the development of the latter interpretation of citizenship in the context of undergraduate students in the UK higher education sector who are studying early childhood. The development of these concepts of citizenship for the students has been tracked through the evaluation and modification of a second-year teaching module which examines young children's rights in a global context. The key theme of this study is to explore the influence of the content and pedagogy within the module on students' perceptions of their own citizenship and community participation. It also suggests how different pedagogical approaches to the education of these students have a significant impact on their learning about democratic concepts.

The subject of citizenship, in the guise of 'Personal, social and health education and citizenship' (PSHE), was added to the English school curriculum in the new millennium in an attempt to tackle what was identified as 'worrying levels of apathy, ignorance and cynicism about political and public life' (Citizenship Advisory Group 1998: 8). *The Crick Report* (Citizenship Advisory Group 1998) comprised the final report of the corresponding advisory group which was presented to the Secretary of State for Education and Employment. However, Osler (2000: 7) argues that it failed to problematise notions of neighbourhood and community affairs, and Davies and Kirkpatrick (2000) identify a social welfare agenda alongside a simultaneous market agenda which constructs students as consumers with rights. These criticisms suggest that The Crick Report lacked teeth in terms of commitment of democratic participatory ideals.

Callan (1997: 221) points out a lack of inevitability about the development of citizenship in our society. The rise of global capitalism feeds a tendency for individual and group interest to favour political arrangements that dominate others. This makes it imperative that citizenship has the social commitment of an educational aim to develop the values and skills associated with public deliberation. Callan's (1997) vision of political education follows a model of justice in which autonomy is foregrounded along with a deep commitment to others, so that justice is only meaningful with their reciprocal engagement. This is a view of citizenship which implies the participation of learners. However, the detailed scheme of work for Key Stage 4 (QCA 2002) reveals a perspective in which learning *about* social issues, such as car crime, arguably interferes with developing the confidence and skills needed *for* participation itself.

The DfES funded a longitudinal study by Cleaver *et al.* (2005) which aimed to assess the short- and long-term effects of citizenship education on the knowledge, skills, attitudes and behaviour of pupils and to determine factors influencing the effectiveness of citizenship education. It concluded that there were still a number of areas in which citizenship education is making little impact. For example, only small numbers of students were actively involved in opportunities to participate in school policy development, over 70 per cent of teachers had not received training in delivering the citizenship curriculum and little or no consultation had taken place with students about how and what would be delivered. In addition, many students did not understand what citizenship means and they had little interest in participating in traditional forms of civic life.

Two key factors within these findings may to some extent explain the limited impact of citizenship education in schools. The first is that schools and teachers were found to use a limited range of teaching and learning activities that encouraged active learning, and that traditional teaching and learning continued in classrooms at the expense of discussion and debate. The second is that genuine opportunities for democratic participation in schools are limited; for example, opportunities for students to have a direct influence on running the school.

With reference to the first point, Stasiulis (2004: 296) suggests that citizenship should not be seen as a single entity but be viewed as multidimensional:

> as an unstable set of social relations actively negotiated and contested between individuals, states, other political communities, territories, and between the realms of the private and public.

The concept of an actively negotiated citizenship is in direct contradiction to the idea of a formally taught curriculum, with students receiving predetermined knowledge and concepts from teachers on topics and issues which have not been negotiated with them. The approach to teaching and learning in citizenship education in schools seems to have remained embedded in the pedagogical tradition, whereas concepts of reflexivity and developing critical debate are more typical of andragogical approaches often found in post-compulsory education. The second point also begs the question as to whether schools, as they are currently conceived of, can actually effectively deliver citizenship education. Smith (2001) reviews Dewey's work on democracy and education, and argues that schools need to be democratic in their relationships between students and teachers in order for citizenship education to take place. Smith (2001) also cites Winch and Gingell (1999), suggesting that for democratic values to be central to schools, there needs to be less evidence of authoritarian relationships within them.

However, Harkavy (2006) points out, with regard to American universities, that often the rhetoric of higher education exceeds its performance. This means that even though universities may aspire to the promotion of a democratic mission in the education of future citizens, nevertheless there are many obstacles which prevent this from happening. In contemporary terms, these focus on the aim by universities of commercialisation which 'powerfully legitimizes and reinforces the pursuit of economic self-interest by students' (Harkavy 2006: 14). This then suggests to students that they undertake a course solely for the purpose of career and credentials. Since this situation also matches a 'utilitarian' approach identified by Jones and Thomas (2005) in British universities, it would suggest that the difficulties outlined by Cleaver *et al.* (2005) that schools face, in involving students in decision-making, may also have some relevance for higher education. This is to acknowledge that active approaches to teaching and learning have also to be extended into policy areas in universities for them to be properly effective with regard to citizenship education. Thus, we can see that participatory notions of citizenship coincide best with the aims of learning in a democratic society which involves the development of the Aristotelian concept of practical reason through active debate *at all levels* of an institution. In this way reason evolves through dialogue with others.

This theme of deliberation in the context of higher education is taken up by Nixon (2004). He discusses the idea of a 'new Aristotelianism' which aims to tread the line between the Socratic idea of negative wisdom and Aristotle's moral emphasis on taking the 'right action' (p.115). Whereas negative wisdom suggests the interrogation of false assumptions, taking the right action implies civic engagement and the practice of goodness. However, the concept of a new Aristotelianism argues that these two approaches to life may be combined through the understanding that a virtuous life is achieved in the face of unpredictability. This is a model which supports the connection between pedagogy and the themes of citizenship which this project aimed to make. Learning *about* citizenship in the Roman sense of knowing one's duty is the predominant picture of citizenship which students learn through the statutory school curriculum. However, this cannot equate with the idea of *practising* citizenship through engagement with others in the pursuit of learning about others. It was the latter picture which this study is exploring; namely the extent to which pedagogical practices, which require higher levels of student debate and deliberation, can be equated with different types of learning.

Methodology

The purpose of our study was to explore the pedagogy on a second-year BA Early Childhood Studies module in one English university in order to determine the extent to which the students' concepts of participatory citizenship developed throughout this course. The purpose was also to gather data to improve the effectiveness of the teaching and learning processes on future delivery of the module: hence the links with relational pedagogy.

In a study of this type, the methodology needed to fit with the theme of participatory democracy and, therefore, to reflect the voices of the participants. This necessitated working within an interpretive paradigm to ensure that the participants' perspectives were foregrounded. The methodological strategy involved was a case study, both as the process and also as the product of the inquiry (Stake 2003). A case study approach is relevant to this study because 'the case study aims to understand the case in depth, and in its natural setting, recognizing its complexity and its context' (Punch 1998: 150).

An action research approach was used, as the process was intended to inform change and improve practice. Kemmis and McTaggart (1988) define action research as 'collective self-reflective enquiry, undertaken by participants in social situations to improve the productivity, rationality and justice of their own practices, as well as their understandings of those practices' (Punch 1998: 169). Action research approaches encompass this simultaneous data-gathering and development on a 'feedback loop' where change is informed by data-gathering and further data is then gathered on the changed actions (Punch 1998: 143).

Evaluations concern themselves with how things work and gather information about 'both processes and outcomes' (Ritchie 2003: 29). The processes explored were the teaching and learning on the module and the outcomes were the extent to which the students' understandings of participatory citizenship were enhanced by their learning on the module. However, Ritchie (2003: 29) also argues that evaluations can 'examine the nature of the requirements of different groups within the target population'. In this case, the requirements of the part-time students who are mature employees within early years contexts and settings were contrasted with the full-time students who had less experience and were mainly younger.

The sample of the study was as follows:

- *Phase 1* – Cohort 1 = 100 full-time students in groups of 25 (Semester 1, 2005/2006)
- *Phase 2* – Cohort 2 = a single group of 25 mature part-time students (Semester 2, 2005/2006)
- *Phase 3* – Cohort 3 = 100 full-time students in groups of 25 (Semester 1, 2006/2007)

Methods

In order to gather the 'multiple accounts', evaluation of the pedagogical approaches on the module was achieved through students participating in a series of open-ended group work exercises within groups of 25. These exercises gave students the opportunity to express and discuss their views with peers and to record their unique perceptions of the teaching and their own learning on the module, therefore providing the multiple accounts. The exercises were as follows:

1 Individual reflections on their own learning of the module content and the teaching and learning process.
2 Discussion in groups of four on what they had learned from the module.
3 Individual reflections on how they learned best and which learning experiences influenced their learning most.
4 Discussion in groups of four about how they learned best and then these ideas linked to what they had learned (from the first exercise).
5 Findings recorded by each group on a poster and shared with the whole class.
6 Discussion in new groups of four on how their learning affected their understanding/behaviour in respect of one of the following:

   - choices and/or lifestyle;
   - views on rights;
   - roles and responsibilities as a citizen in the community.

7 Findings recorded by each group on a poster and shared with the whole class.
8 Whole group discussion on what citizenship meant to the students.

Minor changes were made to the pedagogy on the module to reflect the findings of Phase 1. These changes for Phase 2 focused on extending the existing use of discussion, small group work, multimedia approaches and independent research as key learning strategies.

The third phase of data-gathering followed more extensive revisions to the pedagogy in response to a number of issues which came out of the earlier findings and literature review. The programme was altered for Phase 3 to include content focusing on linking what the students had learned about rights and citizenship and practitioners/students' own roles in early years settings in the UK. The teaching and learning strategy throughout the module also included more debates, sharing of information and ideas through the 'jigsaw' method of small group work in seminars, role play, and exercises to develop group work skills (e.g. listening skills, live conferencing debate on specific issues and more focus on 'unpicking' the meaning of selected readings).

Data analysis

Analyses were ongoing with analysis of the data from the first phase informing the second and third phases. As Wolcott (1994) suggests, description, analysis and interpretation are ingredients of the analytical process, which may be used in different balance and combination as required. Data from the group work were analysed by coding the content into themes and measuring the extent to which each theme was represented. The emergence of themes initially arose from existing theoretical concepts but also included 'local categories' provided by the students themselves (Coffey and Atkinson 1996). The coding process expanded the data and led to further questions to be asked at the next phase, incurring both clarification and reclarification. The data and theory were therefore dynamically interwoven, meaning that while the theory illuminated the data, the data also generated theory in terms of new 'takes' on established ideas (Coffey and Atkinson 1996).

In Phase 1, the findings about the most successful methods identified by the students for learning about different aspects of the content of the module included:

* working in small groups (for different purposes) was the most successful learning method for developing ideas and concepts;
* lectures (which were mainly mini-lectures as part of a seminar session) were identified as the key method for learning about theory;
* videos were identified as central to learning about cultural differences.

Findings about what concepts of citizenship students felt they had developed included:

* increased awareness of issues about rights;
* knowledge of rights in different cultures/national contexts;
* awareness of own relative privileges;
* awareness of own roles and participation as consumers and professionals;
* maintained notions of citizenship based on dutiful concepts (Roman) (e.g. social rules and requirements, social responsibility, rights).

In Phase 2, findings about the most successful methods identified by the students for learning about different aspects of the content of the module were very similar to the first phase. Findings about what concepts of citizenship students felt they had developed included some differences from Phase 1:

- increased political and media awareness;
- need to listen and consult with children in their care;
- significance of their own role/participation as consumers, workers and citizens;
- concepts of citizenship were significantly more participatory than the groups in Phase 1.

In Phase 3, findings about the most successful methods identified by the students for learning about different aspects of the content of the module were very similar to Phases 1 and 2. However, this cohort placed a much greater emphasis on developing their learning processes as well as learning about content. They emphasised having developed understanding and awareness of, and skills in, group work, discussion and debate, listening, time management, use of reading, research skills, presentation of work, and sharing and respecting a range of views. This cohort also showed a significantly higher level of awareness of their own roles and responsibilities in terms of supporting and promoting children's rights, consulting and listening to children, respecting children, being a citizen and community participation.

This cohort expressed much clearer and stronger views on their role in promoting children's rights and participation than the similar Phase 1 cohort (*'It is our job to empower children'*). Many articulated that they needed to do this through work placements but also through community involvement and awareness that these issues were current and relevant (*'on the doorstep'*). However, some also showed awareness of wider responsibilities for community involvement (being part of a student community; being part of a Western culture with the power to influence change). There were also more comments about changed perceptions of the world around them (*'It has influenced the way we view society'*), perception of rights and inequalities in access to these. Finally, many more students expressed the view that there were different perceptions about the issues they were studying and not a single answer to the questions they might ask about these issues (*'Whose rights? Adult or child?'*).

Discussion

The findings confirmed that the module was a good vehicle for exploring and developing concepts of participatory citizenship for these students. The best teaching and learning methods varied for different learning purposes but, overall, active methods, especially group work which involved sharing ideas and reflections and co-constructing meaning from these, were the most successful. The links made between the pedagogical approach and types of content that informed planning for Phase 3 of the module resulted in students recognising learning processes as a type of learning and showing higher levels of recognition of their own need for participation than the similar cohort of Phase 1 students.

Younger students from Phase 1 appeared to identify citizenship as more dutiful than participatory when compared to the Phase 2 mature students. However, the Phase 1 students often identified participatory concepts and practices but did not necessarily identify them as 'citizenship'. When asked directly about notions of citizenship, the more dutiful concepts came to the fore. This suggests that developing participatory notions of citizenship for these students requires a process of connection-forming between what students already identify as successful teaching and learning strategies with overt notions of participatory democracy. This connection-forming seems to have taken place more for Phase 3 students, possibly due to the changes to the pedagogy to support this development. Nixon (2004) appears to suggest that this connection-forming can be achieved by prac- tising citizenship through engagement with others in the pursuit of learning about others; a pedagogical approach which the young children's rights module incorporated to a greater extent in Phase 3.

Therefore, although, as the selected literature suggests, post-16 contexts may promote the areas outlined for a participatory notion of citizenship more frequently than schools do, clearly a more determined effort is needed in higher education for students fully to consolidate links between pedagogy and citizenship. Mature students often have an advantage of greater life and work experience to draw upon than the younger students but this does not mean that we can be complacent about the inevitability of the development of a participatory Athenian view of citizenship. For instance, Shulman (2003) suggests that the time for this under- standing to occur may be determined by educational opportunity as much as by age: he says that 'students of all ages develop the resources needed for their continuing journeys through adult life' (p.viii) in the critical period of university education. Thus, for mature students also, the messages of a participatory approach to citizenship education need to be more overt.

Nevertheless, this study does suggest that we need to think harder about how to enable the younger students, who are closer to the 'Roman' school experiences of citizenship, to become engaged in an interactive style of learning that enables links between styles of pedagogy and citizenship to become meaningful to them while they are at university. Harkavy (2006: 33) suggests that giving a 'very high priority to actively solving strategic, real world, problems in their local community' may be one way to advance this.

However, it may be that, at the same time, we have to challenge the values universities are promoting which contradict democratic values. Harkavy (2006: 121) expresses conviction in the idea that 'a sustained, massive, many-sided campaign to denounce university hypocrisy' is the tool that will produce the necessary discomfort to change behaviour in American universities.

Certainly in the context of our students in a British university, this study would suggest that active learning and teaching methods need to extend into areas of political awareness and activity for the connection of these methods with active citizenship to be nurtured further.

References

Callan, E. (1997) *Creating Citizens*. Oxford: Clarendon Press.

Citizenship Advisory Group (1998) *Education for Citizenship and the Teaching of Democracy in Schools: Final Report of the Advisory Group on Citizenship* (The Crick Report), 22 September. London: Qualifications and Curriculum Authority.

Cleaver, E., Ireland, E., Kerr, D. and Lopes, J. (2005) *Citizenship Education Longitudinal Study: Second Cross-sectional Survey 2004*. London: DfES.

Coffey, A. and Atkinson, P. (1996) *Making Sense of Qualitative Data*. London: Sage.

Davies, L. and Kirkpatrick, G. (2000) *The Euridem Project*. London: Children's Rights Alliance for England.

Harkavy, I. (2006) The role of universities in advancing citizenship and social justice in the 21st century. *Education, Citizenship and Social Justice*, 1(1): 5–37.

Jones. R. and Thomas, L. (2005) The 2003 UK Government Higher Education White Paper: a critical assessment of its implications for the success of the widening participation agenda. *Journal of Education Policy*, 20(5): 615–630.

Kemmis, S. and McTaggart, R. (1988) *The Action Research Planner*. Geelong: Deakin University Press.

Nixon, J. (2004) Learning the language of deliberative democracy. In M. Walker and J. Nixon (eds) *Reclaiming Universities from a Runaway World*. Buckingham: Open University Press.

Osler, A. (ed.) (2000) *Citizenship and Democracy in Schools*. Stoke: Trentham Books.

Punch, K.F. (1998) *Introduction to Social Research: Quantitative and Qualitative Approaches*. London: Sage.

Qualifications and Curriculum Authority (QCA) (2002) *A Scheme of Work for Key Stage 4 Citizenship*. London: Qualifications and Curriculum Authority.

Ritchie, J. (2003) The applications of qualitative methods to social research. In J. Ritchie and J. Lewis (eds) *Qualitative Research Practice*. London: Sage.

Shulman, L.S. (2003) Foreword. In A. Colby, T. Ehrlich, E. Beaumont and J. Stephens (eds) *Educating Citizens: Preparing America's Undergraduates For Lives of Moral and Civic Responsibility*. San Francisco, CA: Jossey-Bass.

Smith, M. (2001) Education for democracy. Available online at: http://www.infed.org/biblio/b-dem (accessed 12 August 2007).

Stake, R.E. (2003) Case studies. In N.K. Denzin and Y.S. Lincoln (eds) *Strategies of Qualitative Inquiry* (2nd edn). London: Sage.

Stasiulis, D. (2004) Hybrid citizenship and what's left. *Citizenship Studies*, 8(3), 295–304.

Williams, R. (1958) *Culture and Society*. London and New York: Columbia University Press.

Winch, C. and Gingell, J. (1999) Key concepts in the philosophy of education. *International Review of Education*. 46(3–4): 351–352. London: Routledge.

Wolcott, H. (1994) *Transforming Qualitative Data. Description, Analysis and Interpretation*. Thousand Oaks, CA: Sage.

4 Ways of knowing – connected teaching

The caregiver's voice

Tal Ben-Tov

This chapter will focus on the process of learning and self-awareness of a group of Israeli caregivers who participated in the guiding programme *Learning to Live Together* (Gat and Tzur 2004). The starting point of this research was my experience as a student and a guide (tutor) in the programme. It was developed to address the distressing situation in Israeli daycare where crowded conditions mean that caregivers must cope daily with a range of emotional expressions and social behaviours arising from children's intensive exposure to such conditions.

The *Learning to Live Together* programme aims to:

1 Increase the caregivers' awareness and sensitivity to the social emotional components of the group setting and teach them ways of identifying daily experiences which present opportunities for children's social learning.
2 Increase the caregivers' awareness about the attitudes, beliefs and expectations of adults regarding toddlers' social behaviour, in general, and aggression, in particular.
3 Highlight relevant issues from developmental theory on young children's emotional and social behaviour and help caregivers to acknowledge their role in these processes by implementing their professional knowledge in the field.

The study is based on multiple case study methodology. Participants in the study are caregivers who are already employed in daycare settings, most of whom do not have any previous experience of study beyond high school.

In this chapter, I will report and discuss two key findings from the pilot study:

1 Connected teaching.
2 Ways of knowing and their practical implications for the training of caregivers.

Introduction

In recent years, there has been growing recognition among parents and professionals of the important role of caregivers and their influence on the care which toddlers and young children receive outside the home (Lamb 1998). This is evident from the large number of studies that have investigated the role of caregivers and their influence on various aspects of child development (Clarke-Stewart 1993; Rosenthal 1994, 2003; Lamb 1998; Kyle 2003). At the same time, limited research has been conducted to study the role of the caregiver in the emotional socialisation of toddlers in group situations (Ahn 2005). Although extensive research has been undertaken on the role of parents (e.g. Saarni 1999; Denham 2001), very little has been written on the role of caregivers in daycare centres in the context of guidance programmes.

Research in this area is of vital importance for the facilitation of child development, in general, and the socialisation of emotions and relationships, in particular. This is because large numbers of toddlers and young children spend many hours outside the home and in different settings where caregivers, like parents, are required to manage the emotional and social climate in which children learn about emotions and relationships (Ahn 2005). This chapter reports on a pilot study conducted to inform research that addressed the learning processes and self-awareness of a group of Israeli caregivers who participated in a guiding programme entitled *Learning to Live Together* (Gat and Tzur 2004).

The Israeli context

In the Israeli context, it is important to note that government policy regarding the care and education of the very young sets standards for daycare which actually present obstacles to the creation of an appropriate social and emotional climate. For example, there are large groups of children with an adult–child ratio that is unacceptably low, compared with international standards of quality (e.g. NICHD 1999). Furthermore, the prevailing salary policy and work conditions in Israeli daycare centres lead to the employment of caregivers who lack any formal education and whose training for this work is either minimal or non-existent (National Council on Child Welfare in Israel 2001). This is so despite international research showing that the dimension of pre-service and in-service training is a predictive factor in care quality in daycare centres (Burchinal *et al.* 2000; Darling-Hammond 2000). Studies dealing with the training of caregivers have placed little emphasis, first, on the socialisation of toddlers and, second, on the training process itself. In fact, very little is known about the nature of the learning process in training programmes or about how this process mediates between the learning and the professional work of the caregivers (Brownlee and Berthelsen 2006: 17).

Within this context, this chapter focuses on the processes of learning and self-awareness of a group of Israeli caregivers who participated in the guiding programme, *Learning to Live Together*. This research starts from my personal experience as a student and a guide on this programme. As Klutter *et al.* (2001) write, in teaching educators the 'how' (the process) is no less important than the 'what' (outcome). The learning process gave me personal and professional insights and allowed for the construction of new knowledge integrating with my own previous personal and professional knowledge.

The guiding programme: *Learning to Live Together*

In Israel, there are programmes dealing with conflict resolution and prevention of violence but these are mostly appropriate for school-aged children (Heller 1996). There are few programmes for children attending preschools and only one programme for daycare centres; that is, *Learning to Live Together*. While reviewing programmes in the literature, I found that intervention programmes in the area of emotional and social development appropriate for young children tend to offer concrete activities. Some examples include:

- Non-violent communication – the language of the giraffe. This is a programme which uses animals as metaphors for non-violent communication.
- The 'conflict cloud' – a drama game for conflict resolution (see www.gov.il/preschool/mashehutov).

What characterises these programmes is that they deal directly with children in a group while the responsible adult (i.e. the educator) leads the programme without relating to his or her own knowledge, beliefs and feelings about the topic and without integrating the topic into the complex everyday life of the educational setting. Thus, the role of the caregiver in this area is neglected yet again.

Learning to Live Together (Gat and Tzur) provides an alternative to these types of programme. It was developed at the Hebrew University of Jerusalem to address the distressing situation in Israeli daycare where crowded conditions mean that caregivers must cope daily with a range of unacceptable emotional expressions and social behaviours arising from children's intensive exposure to such conditions. It aims to:

- Increase the caregivers' awareness and sensitivity to the social emotional components of the group setting and teach them ways of identifying daily experiences which present opportunities for children's social learning.
- Increase the caregivers' awareness about the attitudes, beliefs and expectations of adults regarding toddlers' social behaviour, in general and aggression, in particular.
- Highlight relevant issues from developmental theories on young children's emotional and social behaviour and help caregivers to acknowledge their role in these processes by implementing their professional knowledge in the field.

The content involves the interpersonal elements of children's behaviour in group situations and includes pro-social behaviours, social rejection, verbal and physical violence, expressions of remorse and anger, loss of control, helplessness, and tears and distress. The reactions of the adults to these situations stem not only from their acquired reservoir of knowledge but also from beliefs, values, accumulated personal life skills and experience, all of which is the focus of this programme (Tzur 2002). The programme also includes theoretical and research knowledge about a variety of relevant developmental processes such as the development of empathy in the early years, social understanding, self-control and regulation of emotions (Corasaro 1997; Howes 1998; Hoffman 2000). The programme is applied to groups of up to 20 daycare centre caregivers. It lasts for six months with meetings once every two weeks.

A note on terminology

At this stage, it is important to clarify and define the terms '*guidance programme*' and '*guide*' which I use to refer to the training programme and the trainer, respectively. Professional literature in English uses the term 'supervision' to indicate training and it means oversight and supervision. On the other hand, the Hebrew term, translated into English as 'guidance', contains the root word of 'path' and suggests that the guidance or training is a process, a journey shared equally by the trainer and the trainee, a journey that may also have surprises as well as obstacles (Zilberman 1995). As Mara (2005: 139) argues, learning leads to 'meaning making [that] is intimately connected with experience'. Metaphorically, we can relate to the trainer as a guide leading a journey and as a role-model for the trainee.

Another interpretation is to see the guide as someone who knows the direction and the final objective but, like the trainee, is an active traveller and is open to errors and surprises (Karon 1995). This corresponds with the theory from social work of a 'parallel process'. Kadushin (1992) proposes that patterns of processes tend to repeat themselves in various levels of relationships so that each set is reflected in another. I use the term '*guidance programme*' to reflect the process of acquiring a world view and the term '*guide*' to refer to the person who guides this process.

Researching the *Learning to Live Together* programme

Since the aim of the study is to examine the process of learning and the self-awareness of Israeli caregivers participating in the *Learning to Live Together* programme, I decided to do so by focusing on their voices. I conducted a pilot study, which is the focus of this chapter, in order to (1) shed light on issues to which the study might lead, and (2) clarify the focus of the study (Shkedi 2003).

I made contact with a women's organisation in order to access caregivers who attended the *Learning to Live Together* programme. The caregivers who attend this programme do not choose to participate and they are not financially compensated or advanced professionally by doing so; participation in the programme is compulsory in order to maintain their jobs. Entry into the organisation initially presented many difficulties. Despite the promises and the real desire for transparency, changes took place at the last minute, which, first, meant the increase of participants in the programme beyond the desired number and, second, the selection of the interviewees by the director of the daycare centre. Within these restrictions, for the pilot study I interviewed two caregivers chosen by the director of the daycare centre and decided to distribute questionnaires to all caregivers who took part in the programme (26 caregivers in total).

The interviews

The two interviews took place at the daycare centres while the toddlers were napping. The interviews were open-ended in order to relieve tension and create a comfortable atmosphere. The caregivers are not used to so much attention or to being listened to in their daily lives. Furthermore, they were clearly anxious to say the 'right thing'. In order to overcome this bias, I used an open-ended ethnographic interview, which is similar to a friendly conversation (Sabar 2001). It is informal and spontaneous rather than defined or prestructured. The interview is a conversation with an objective. It is a simple, flexible and direct tool for the understanding of human beings' perceptions (Robson 1993). Since this was a preliminary informative study and I was given only one opportunity to conduct the interviews, I found that this was the best way to understand the caregivers' learning experiences. Each interview lasted for about one-and-a-half hours.

The interviews were conducted as a conversation that developed from two requests:

1   Please tell me about your background, work experience, and previous studies.
2   Please tell me about your learning processes during the programme.

Further questions arose as I listened to the respondents' comments and responses.

Interviewees' backgrounds

Hanna (H) is 45 years old and has been working in the daycare centre for 17 years with groups of 1- to 2-year-old toddlers. Before working in daycare she worked as an assistant to a kindergarten teacher and commented *'Everything I know I learned from her'*. When that kindergarten closed Hanna went to the employment office where she was referred on to a seven-month caregivers' course. Since then she has been working in the daycare centre.

Sarah (S) is 50 years old and has been working at the daycare centre for 18 years. When her children grew up, she felt bored at home. A neighbour referred her to the nearby daycare centre. She began working there with no training apart from her *'many hours of motherhood'*. Over the years, she has participated in short in-service courses that the centre has suggested, such as children's literature, contact with parents, feeding and hygiene.

Questionnaires

I used data from 26 questionnaires developed by Beer (2006). As a guide in the programme, I took part in the planning of the questionnaire but I was not involved in its final design. The questionnaire contains questions that follow the sections of the programme and relate to (1) the influence of the group, (2) the development of empathy, (3) learning to play together, and (4) conflict resolution. There are 24 closed questions where the caregivers have to choose between four options ranging from 'very little' to 'very much'. In addition, there are five open-ended questions regarding the contribution of the programme to their work.

Data analysis from the pilot study

This chapter is based on the findings of the interviews and the analysis of the responses in the open-ended questions. The analysis of the data from the interviews and the questionnaires was a reflective process using open coding (Shkedi 2003). This analysis enabled me to gain initial insights about the care-givers' learning processes and self-awareness, and to clarify the focus of the planned study. The emerging issues of this analysis are discussed below.

The source of knowledge

The interviews with the caregivers revealed that studying in the programme raises the question, 'What are the ways of knowing?' These caregivers reflect different stages in ways of knowing.

Hanna: In the first meeting, which was a long time ago but I can't forget it, we were given stones; everyone had to write on one side of her stone how many years she had been working with children, including years as a mother, and on the other side we were asked to write what we feel is important about what happens in the group. At first it didn't seem relevant but then the guide surprised me. She added all our years of experience on the board and it came to a really large number – over 500.

Sarah: The programme refreshed things for me. I knew them, but I didn't know how significant they were.

Relating to authority

Relating to authority in the daycare centre is very noticeable. The centre is a hierarchical organisation. Each classroom has someone in charge. Each centre has a director and each director has an inspector who then has someone with greater authority overseeing her. The caregivers are at the bottom of the totem pole of educational leadership in the centre, even though they are the ones who come into direct contact with the children.

Hanna: I learned to detach. There is what I think and there is what I am told to do. Already 15 years ago at my caregivers' course I realised that I have to go with the flow, even though sometimes I am not happy with it.

Hanna: Sometimes in the programme I wanted to get up and tell the director how much time we spend in class on holidays and creative work, and then we have no energy left to deal with what is really important – getting along in a group. I didn't have the nerve to do it.

Sarah: I can now explain to the director what I am doing and why. She also studied with us so she knows what I am talking about.

Relevance – 'It happened to me today at the centre'

The caregivers talk about how the contents of the programme are relevant to what goes on every day at the centre and what they experience on a daily basis.

Hanna: When we were talking about conflicts, the whole group learned through the story of the child in my group . . . [*she laughs*] . . . for everything the guide said I could come up with an example of what happens to me in the centre with this boy. Even the videos we saw showed behaviour like his were the same age. It is a terribly difficult age because they do not have a clear language.

Sarah: All this work about crying is taken from our lives.

The group support

The caregivers mention the group as a safe place and a source of learning and pleasure.

Sarah: Everyone in the group had their own place in the limelight.

Hanna: There was no fear. I felt safe to describe, to bring up incidents, to say that I have a child who cries a lot . . . I wasn't afraid that I shouldn't say it. . . .

Hanna: I heard stories that were similar to what happens to me. So that is also comforting . . . you know . . . shared sorrows.

Attitude of the guide

Both the questionnaires and the interviews related to the guide's behaviour as a significant element in the programme's learning process.

Sarah: She has patience for everyone. Sometimes there were stories that were not really relevant, but she listened and answered and suggested new directions.

Hanna: She never rejected what I do. She kept on connecting it to the stones. I mean, I know and I have the right to decide: sometimes she suggested something new. She called it another tool for the 'tool box'.

Implementation of the programme in the Centre

The caregivers related to the question of how they can implement what they learned at the Centre.

Sarah: I now look at the big picture. How everyone is behaving. I relate to the group, not just to individual children – how they look – how an audience is created.

Hanna: Sometimes it seems that they are calmer. I arrange small groups of children. I see to it that there is space. I talk a lot . . . sometimes I think that I will lose my voice . . . I have lots of new things to say that I can use.

Discussion

The aims of this pilot study were to clarify the focus of my research and shed light on issues related to caregivers' awareness of their learning processes. The findings allow for the emergence of two themes that were particularly prominent: ways of knowing and connected teaching. In search of an appropriate lens through which to view these findings, I will use the conceptual framework suggested by Brownlee and Berthelsen (2006) which includes the work of Baxter Magolda (1992, 2004) and Belenky *et al.* (1986).

Ways of knowing

The first concept refers to a person's beliefs about questions such as: What is knowledge? What are its sources and boundaries? How is it created and how certain is it? Empirical investigations of these epistemological beliefs have been conducted in various branches of psychology and education under a range of labels (see Burr and Hofer 2002) and are described as the position on a continuum of epistemological development from simple to more sophisticated beliefs. These beliefs collectively form ways of knowing.

Belenky *et al.* (1986) studied a group of 135 women from different socioeconomic backgrounds and different levels of education. Their findings indicate an intertwining of beliefs about self with beliefs about authority and knowledge. There are five stages of the ways of knowing:

1 *Silence*: the process of attempting to find a voice; a growth from being silent to finding a voice and being assertive.
2 *The listening voice*: received knowledge that focuses on listening to the voices of others.
3 *The inner voice*: subjective knowledge that involves a quest for self, a knowing of self by gaining an awareness of attitudes and values.
4 *The voice of reason*: procedural knowledge that enables examination and comparison to occur along with a sense of connectedness.
5 *Integrating the voices*: constructed knowledge that involves the successful integration of information from the various ways of knowing and an ability to

incorporate the wisdom of experience into practice realities (McDrury and Alterio 2003: 118–119).

The work of Belenky *et al*. (1986) has strengths for this study for the following reasons. In their work, they include women from lower socioeconomic backgrounds and women with no academic background. The silence position, which is the first position in Belenky *et al*., may be identified with the caregivers' low professional image. This issue connects with their findings about authority and knowledge. The development of voices relates to the aim of this research, as the voice of caregivers is rarely heard in the literature of early childhood education. Belenky *et al*. (1986) emphasise the development of a genuine voice, which is part of the focus of this research.

The second concept – connected teaching (Belenky *et al*. 1986) or relational pedagogy (Baxter Magolda 1992) – refers to the connection between personal knowledge/beliefs (focus on the self) and scientific knowledge (focus on theory) and encourages more sophisticated ways of knowing. Connected teaching requires mutual respect between student, peers and teachers, situating learning in student experiences and using reflection as a key element in a constructivist approach to learning (Brownlee and Berthelsen 2006: 24).

The data emerging from the analysis of the findings in my pilot study reinforce data from other studies on the connection between ways of knowing and teaching and learning. Schommer (1994) found that ways of knowing relate to students' persistence, active inquiry integration of information and ability to cope with complex and ill-structured domains. We can say that relationships and the development of social and emotional ability are areas containing complex problems (Howes and Holli 1999). From my experience as a guide in the training programme, one of the aims is to offer the caregivers new ways or additional professional tools with which to understand complex phenomena. For example, conflicts regarding property, so typical among toddlers and young children, are not necessarily an expression of a means to reach a realistic goal (the object), but rather mainly a search for social contact (Caplan *et al*. 1991).

In addition, in an as yet unpublished study, Brownlee and Berthelsen (2006) found that caregivers who possess more complex ways of knowing lean towards a more constructivist approach to learning and develop more open and democratic relationships even with very young children. An expression of the integration of ways of knowing may be seen in the data when, in the description of Hanna's résumé, she mentions an external source of knowledge for learning her profession: '*Everything I learned came from her*'. She describes her opinion of authority and it is clear that, even though she has opinions and beliefs of her own, she silences them and acts as she feels she is required to do. In the programme, she relates to the guide as a main source of knowledge – '*She gave me tools and words*' – and she accepts the material learned in a one-dimensional manner without doubting or questioning it. We can say that Hanna has reached the second stage according to Belenky *et al*. (1986) where the knowledge is received from an external source. We can also see the first stage of silence in the face of authority: '*I wanted to say so but I didn't dare. . . .'* *'I have learned to detach'*. In contrast, Sarah expresses more complex ways of knowing in which she recognises her own inner knowledge, the silent knowledge (Polani 1958) as a source. When introducing herself she relates to her years as a mother as a source of knowledge. She distinguishes between knowledge and the refreshing of knowledge, and from this we can understand that she also sees herself as a source of learning. She feels it is important that everyone has the chance to express themselves – *'Everyone in the group had their turn in the limelight'* and she says about herself that she has the ability to talk in public. According to Belenky *et al.* (1986), it seems that Sarah is in the stage of subjective knowledge where the learner's inner voice can be heard. From my experience as a guide in the programme, I believe that we took for granted people's ability to integrate personal knowledge with acquired knowledge when the guide's viewpoint is constructivist. The findings of this study show that one must relate to the reality in which learners have different ways of knowing and prepare accordingly. In order to integrate personal knowledge with theoretical knowledge, the learners must be able to recognise themselves as a source of knowledge.

Baxter Magolda (2004) stresses that one of the most significant processes for developing complex ways of knowing, where the learner sees him or herself as a source of knowledge, is to validate that knowledge when it is at the simple stage. An example of this is found in the words of the caregiver who mentions the stones representing her life experience and the knowledge she has acquired in this field.

Since this study was meant to focus on the topic of future research, we must take into account that there was no comprehensive investigation of the caregivers' ways of knowing, for example, through a special interview for that purpose. However, the data indicate that investigating this area can clarify the meaning of the learning process for the caregivers. The data from this pilot study shed light on the significance of the group and the relationship between the guide and the group and between the members of the group themselves. According to Belenky *et al.* (1986) and Baxter Magolda (1992), the creation of a non-threatening learning environment that includes and allows self-expression can enable the learners to connect to the knowledge they have inside themselves. This is supported by Marion (2006) and Bishop and Lunn (2005) regarding emotional needs that must be met, support of the adult learner and starting the learning with what the learner knows rather than with theoretical content.

The voices of the caregivers heard in these data reflect differences in ways of knowing. The research literature is ambiguous about the factors affecting the development and the stages of ways of knowing. Although research exploring changes in and development of ways of knowing is currently limited (Tickle *et al.* 2005), evidence suggesting that ways of knowing can be nurtured through a professional development programme has also emerged (Howard *et al.* 2000); through creating a 'safe' environment that includes encouraging trust and validation of the learner.

When guiding the caregivers, we need to take into account at which of the different stages of the ways of knowing each caregiver is. We must make room for the voice of each caregiver as it reflects different ways of knowing and provide an appropriate response to each of them. The validity given to each voice will later enable development of a transition to more complex ways of knowing. Research shows the development of ways of knowing in studies for higher academic degrees (Schommer 1994). At the same time, both in the Israeli reality and in other contexts, the caregiver population is not one that has higher degrees and so connected teaching as a method of validating, respecting and enabling the construction of new knowledge is important. Learning in a group enables the caregivers to air their emotions, share dilemmas and learn from their peers and, based on the parallel process theory (Kadushin 1992), one can hope that the relationships built up between the guides and the caregivers and among the caregivers themselves will be expressed also in how the caregivers treat the children. As one caregiver in this study said: '*When you hear a kind word you have the strength to pass it on . . .*'.

Furthermore, caregivers have attitudes and opinions about how things should be handled and they need to learn from the daily experiences at the daycare centre. It is important to encourage caregivers' autonomy, which can develop by listening to the clear inner voice without being afraid of authority. We need to take into account that some of the caregivers are not interested in dealing with their past childhood memories. Sometimes this is due to harsh experiences, and we need to understand that the choice of silencing the past is a path to development that must be respected throughout the guiding process (Belenky *et al.* 1986). In this sense, this learning process validates the learners at any stage of their ways of knowing, maintains an atmosphere of respect, and focuses on relevant issues. This process can help caregivers understand their practice through finding their authentic voice in teaching toddlers how to live together in a group framework.

References

Ahn, H.J. (2005) Teacher discussion of emotion in child care context. *Early Childhood Education Journal*, 32(4): 237–245.

Baxter Magolda, M.B. (1992) *Knowing and Reasoning in College. Gender-related Patterns in Students' Intellectual Development*. San Francisco, CA: Jossey Bass.

Baxter Magolda, M.B. (2004) Evolution of constructivist conceptualization of epistemological reflection. *Educational Psychologist*, 39(1): 31–42.

Beer, T. (2006) *The Role of The Adult: Developing Social Emotional Competence in Young Children*. Unpublished Ph.D. thesis, Jerusalem: Hebrew University.

Belenky, M.F., Clinchy, B.M., Goldberger, N.R. and Tarule, J.M. (1986) *Women's Ways of Knowing: The Development of Self, Voice and Mind*. New York: Basic Books.

Bishop, A. and Lunn, P. (2005) Exploring attitudes and perceptions of early years practitioners without qualified teacher status to a university training course. *Research in Education*, 74: 1–8.

Brownlee, J. and Berthelsen, D. (2006) Personal epistemology and relational pedagogy in early childhood teacher education programmes. *Early Years*, 26(1): 17–29.

Burchinal, M.R., Roberts, J.E., Riggins, R., Zeisel, S.A., Neebe, E. and Bryant, D. (2000) Relating quality of center child care to early cognitive and language development longitudinally. *Child Development*, 71(3): 339–357.

Burr, J.E. and Hofer, B.K. (2002) Personal epistemology and theory of mind: deciphering young children's beliefs about knowledge and knowing. *New Ideas in Psychology*, 20: 199–224.

Caplan, M., Vespo, J., Pederson, J. and Hay, D.F. (1991) Conflict and its resolution in small groups of one- and two-year olds. *Child Development*, 62(6): 1513–1534.

Clarke-Stewart, A. (1993) *Daycare*. Cambridge, MA: Harvard University Press.

Corasaro, W. (1997) *The Sociology of Childhood*. Thousand Oaks, CA: Sage.

Darling-Hammond, L. (2000) How teacher education matters. *Journal of Teacher Education*, 51(3): 166–173.

Denham, S.A. (2001) Dealing with feelings: foundation and consequences of young children's emotional competence. *Early Education and Development*, 12(1): 5–15.

Gat, L. and Tzur, H. (2004) *Learning to Live Together*. Guide book. Jerusalem: Hebrew University Press (in Hebrew).

Heller, A. (1996). *Changing the School Violence: What Works. NASSP Bulletin 80*. Jerusalem: Keterpress Enterprises (in Hebrew).

Hoffman, M.L. (2000) *Empathy and Moral Development: Implication for Caring and Justice*. Cambridge: Cambridge University Press.

Howard, B.C., McGee, S., Schwartz, N. and Purcell, S., (2000) The experience of constructivism: transforming teacher epistemology. *Journal of Research on Computing in Education*, 32(4): 455–466.

Howes, C. (1998) The earliest friendship. In N.A. Bukowski, A.F. Newcomb and W.W. Hartup (eds) *The Company They Keep: Friendship in Childhood and Adolescence*. New York: Cambridge University Press.

Howes, C. and Holli, T. (1999) Peer relations. In L. Butler and C. Tamis-Le Monda (eds) *Child Psychology: A Handbook of Contemporary Issues*. Philadelphia, PA: Psychology Press.

Kadushin, A. (1992) *Supervision in Social Work*. New York: Columbia University Press.

Karon,T. (1995) *Supervision in Psychotherapy*. Jerusalem: Magnus Press (in Hebrew).

Klutter, F.B., Lodewijks, H. and Aaarnoutse, C. (2001) Learning conception of young student in final year of primary education. *Learning and Instruction*, 11: 485–516.

Kyle, I.J. (2003) Agency and ethics: family daycare providers' perspectives on quality. In A. Mooney and J. Statham (eds) *Family Daycare: International Perspectives on Policy, Practice and Quality*. London: Jessica Kingsley.

Lamb, M.E. (1998) Nonparental child care: context, quality, correlates, and consequences. In W. Damon, I.E. Sigel and K.A. Renninger (eds) *Handbook of Child Psychology. Vol.4: Child Psychology in Practice*. New York: John Wiley.

Mara, R. (2005) Teacher beliefs: the impact of the design of constructivist learning environments on instructor epistemologies. *Learning Environments Research*, 8: 135–155.

Marion, T. (2006) The importance of interpersonal relationship in adult literacy programmes. *Educational Research Quarterly*, 30(2): 30–40.

McDrury, J. and Alterio, M. (2003) *Learning Through Storytelling in Higher Education: Using Reflection and Experience to Improve Learning*. London: Kogan Page.

National Council on Child Welfare in Israel (2001) Annual Report.

NICHD Early Childcare Research Network (1999) Child outcomes when child care center classes meet recommended standards of quality. *American Journal of Public Health*, 89(7): 1072–1077.

Polani, M. (1958) *Personal Knowledge*. Chicago, IL: University of Chicago Press.

Robson, C. (1993) *Real World Research*. Oxford: Blackwell.

Rosenthal, M.K. (1994) *An Ecological Approach to the Study of Child Care: Family Daycare in Israel.* Hillsdale, NJ: Lawrence Erlbaum.

Rosenthal, M.K. (2003) Family daycare in Israel: policy, quality and the daily experiences of children. In A. Mooney and J. Statham (eds) *Family Daycare: International Perspectives on Policy, Practice and Quality.* London: Jessica Kingsley.

Saarni, C. (1999) *The Development of Emotional Competence.* New York: Guilford Press.

Sabar, N. (2001) *Genres and Traditions in Qualitative Research.* Tel Aviv: Dvir Press (in Hebrew).

Schommer, M. (1994) Synthesizing epistemological belief research: tentative understanding and provocative confusions. *Educational Psychology Review,* 6(4): 294–319.

Shkedi, A. (2003) *Words of Meaning: Qualitative Research – Theory and Practice.* Tel Aviv: Ramot University Press (in Hebrew).

Tickle, E.L., Brownlee, J. and Nailon, D.L. (2005) Personal epistemological beliefs and transformational leadership behaviors. *The Journal of Management Development,* 24(8): 706–719.

Tzur, H. (2002) *The Beliefs and Knowledge of Family Daycare Providers Concerning Social Behavior of Toddlers.* Unpublished Ph.D. thesis, Jerusalem: Hebrew University (in Hebrew).

Zilberman, Y. (1995) *Kelim Shluvim – about Supervision.* Available online at: www.gov.il/preschool/mashehutov (accessed 1 March 2007).

5   Nurturing inspiration

A journey in South Africa

Jill Sachs

Using the metaphor of a journey, my practical, participative workshop and this chapter aim to give participants an insight into the importance of inspiration, self-knowledge, creativity and the expressive arts in the training and development of early childhood teachers in the South African context. The journey will allow participants a view of the historical landscape of early childhood development (ECD) in South Africa and will take them to visit five early childhood classrooms across the province of KwaZulu Natal. At each stop-over, the unique challenges of teachers in the different contexts will be highlighted and the innovative approaches and methodology of the Caversham Centre will be used in the presentation of the workshop.

Introduction – beginning the journey

The journey begins in England, at Anglia Ruskin University, where spring is touching the countryside with green and where blossoms are budding. The destination is South Africa, the southern-most country on the vast African continent. This specific journey will end in KwaZulu Natal, a province of South Africa located on the east coast.

South Africa is a 13-hour flight from London and our travelling participant initially lands at O.R. Tambo International Airport in Johannesburg and then takes a connecting flight to Durban on KwaZulu Natal's coast. It is a beautiful province bordered by the craggy Drakensberg Mountains in the west and the wide sandy beaches of the sparkling blue Indian Ocean in the east. It is autumn in South Africa and the veld is gradually turning to a rich brown and yellow. A car journey of just over an hour northwest from Durban International Airport takes our traveller to the Caversham Centre.[1]

Situated in the beautiful midlands of KwaZulu Natal, the Caversham Centre is a non-profit organisation which has a proud history of 22 years of contribution to many lives through its creative arts-based interventions. Implicit to all programmes offered by the Centre is the belief in the transformational power and influence an individual can have in the lives of others. Making a meaningful and relevant contribution is the ultimate goal. The early childhood teacher training programmes, known as the early years education (eYe) courses, are just one of the many programmes offered by the Caversham Centre and will be the focus of exploration on this specific journey.

Preparing for the journey

The suitcase

Any journey being undertaken requires preparations to be made, items to be packed into suitcases, which may turn out to be essential or merely additional weight. Combine this with the vital ingredient of a willingness to embrace change, an open-minded curiosity and a sense of excitement and anticipation.

Despite the stories of crime and violence, the majority of South Africa's population is generous in spirit and as warm and friendly as the African sun. The smells, sights, sounds and textures of this complex and modern South Africa are as varied and unique as its people. This diversity is also reflected in the settings and provision for early childhood development. Some of these settings are in sophisticated modern cities while others can only be accessed after a two- to three-hour journey on rudimentary roads through sparsely populated terrain. In accessing remote locations, those coming from abroad may find the orthodox suitcase an encumbrance and prefer a backpack. They will certainly be astounded when meeting a traditional Zulu woman on the road who, with grace and skill, simply balances the suitcase on her head and confidently strides forward.

The vehicle

As important as the selection of the suitcase, is the choice of the vehicle to undertake this journey. With the varied terrain that this journey covers, the stalwart Land Rover has been selected. To many, the Land Rover is synonymous with success and prestige but it has been chosen for its rugged reliability, with four wheels working interdependently carrying passengers safely across even the most challenging terrain.

The map

In order to gain a deeper understanding and appreciation of this inspirational journey, a map is required, an overview of the territory which recognises those areas already experienced and those still to be visited. South Africa, with all its sunshine, warmth, beauty and rich natural resources, is a country emerging from the dark past of apartheid and it is important to understand some of the country's history in order to appreciate the present context of early childhood teacher training.

Recognising the past

The year 1994 saw the end of apartheid with the first democratic elections for all citizens of the country. While great strides have been made since then, problems of poverty, inequality, HIV and AIDS, crime and violence are still prevalent. In 1994 the term 'ECD' was not yet in official use. The country spoke of early childhood Educare and the term was limited to include children from birth to 6 years of age. Prior to 1994, the government had yet to recognise the critical importance of the early years and its impact on the future success not only of individuals but also of society. At that time, ECD was a low priority on the political agenda and consequently little funding was expended. It was also regarded as unimportant 'women's work', and a service that only professional working mothers might need. Thus the limited government funding available was directed to advantaged communities, leaving poorer communities seriously unresourced.

However, confronted by the high repetition and failure rates in the first year of formal schooling (as great as 25 per cent[2]) the importance of the years up to the age of 9 was recognised and the more inclusive term early childhood development (ECD) was developed.

The impact of apartheid policies was further seen in the inequality of ECD provision. According to the National Education Policy Investigation (NEPI) (1992) only 9 per cent of children aged from birth to 6 attended Educare services and the allocation of services was largely on a racial basis, with 33 per cent of white children having access to some form of preschool provision in comparison with about 7 per cent of black children. There were large disparities in provision between urban and rural areas with access rates lowest in heavily populated rural regions where children on farms were the worst off. Furthermore, subsidisation was targeted at middle- to upper-class preschools where the teacher received a salary, whereas teachers of children from poor and working-class families received little or no subsidy.[3]

Prior to 1994 the racial policies of the apartheid government had resulted in separate Departments of Education, Welfare and Health for whites, blacks, coloureds (a term used in SA to refer to those of mixed heritage) and Indians. In ECD planning, policies, implementation and management, there was no common legislative framework and provision was characterised by fragmentation. The narrow education focus was solely on preparing children for school, while welfare focused on providing custodial care, and health accepted responsibility for pre-natal/post-natal care with little emphasis on toddlers and older children.[4] In this plethora of governmental systems the vast majority of children were excluded, with many only having protection for very basic health and safety needs. The majority of ECD centres/services remained unregistered and employed untrained staff. The ECD non-government organisation (NGO) sector took up the challenge, making committed efforts to put in place systems for accreditation of non-formal teacher training.

Early childhood teacher training

NEPI research (1992) describes how the disparities and conflicting educational approaches were mirrored in teacher training, with very few institutions catering for black students. Admission to institutions that did offer ECD training was also gender biased, with men being excluded. Many provinces favoured the teacher-directed, group teaching approach that was based on 'school readiness' and a remedial background. Some teacher training colleges, notably in KwaZulu Natal, favoured the child-centred, process-orientated, play-based, participatory, more progressive and democratic approach.

These disparities were reflected in preschool classrooms: most professionally qualified teachers were 'white' women allocated to the relatively low number of preschools reserved for 'whites only'; the majority of 'black preschool children were taught by teachers with informal NGO training. This critical NGO training was plagued by dependence on uncertain donor funding, resulting in variable quality training and the non-recognition of qualifications. At this time the most frequently heard cry from the field was, 'We need certificates that mean something!'

Redressing the past

Since 1994 the South African government has embarked on a number of initiatives, including the National Pilot Project (1996–2000),[5] the resultant White Paper 5 on Early Childhood Education (2001)[6] and the National ECD Conditional Grant (2001–2004). Concurrently the first steps to redress the disparities in qualifications were taken with the establishment of the National Qualifications Framework (NQF).[7] The NQF may also be likened to a map with a starting point, the opportunity to collect credits along the way, to keep these credits and gradually compile a qualification. It provides all South Africans with a step-by-step progression from a very basic Level 1 qualification, which requires the completion of Grade 9, the General Education and Training Certificate (GETC), to a Level 4, which requires obtaining a matriculation, to a Level 5 and then on to a Level 6 or first degree. It provides the opportunity to study part-time, continue to work and still systematically acquire the credits needed. Each qualification has set requirements which are laid down by SAQA, the South African Qualifications Authority.[8] Before a service provider can be accredited to offer training, that provider is required to go through a rigorous process to ensure that all the stringent requirements are met.

This then provides the background to the map of ECD in South Africa and helps contribute to a deeper understanding for our *travelling participants* to recognise the impact of the past and its impact on Caversham's approach to developing innovative models that address the diversity and needs of the early childhood teachers it trains.

Being in the present

In 2006 the Caversham Centre received accreditation for its early childhood teacher training programmes meeting the stringent requirements of the South African Sector Education and Training Authority (SETA)[9] and now offers in-service, part-time training which continues to prove itself in the training of students in three KZN locations: Durban, Pietermartizburg and Kwambonambi. Programmes are steeped in creativity and each session is designed to promote personal development, to increase knowledge, and to develop relevant skills.

Starting out

Visiting classes

Continuing the metaphor of a journey and beginning at the Caversham Centre, the travelling participants will visit five of the early childhood teachers who are involved with Caversham eYe programmes, so gaining insight into the different contexts and challenges in which they work.

Over 350 kilometres from Caversham, in a deeply rural setting, Phumzile teaches a reception class in a primary school. Her school has no running water, only two pit latrines and very few teaching resources. Her class comprises sixty-two 5 to 6-year-old Zulu-speaking children who come from poor families where traditionally food was harvested from home gardens. However, the community is now facing difficulties with many able-bodied adults either seeking work in cities or being ill with HIV and AIDS, leaving the elderly to care for and raise the children.

By contrast Sandra, a Caversham facilitator, teaches and trains in an urban girls' school with light, airy classrooms, special child-sized toilets, and access to a resource centre, library, and fully equipped indoor and outdoor play areas. Her reception year class comprises twenty-six 5- to 6-year-old girls from Muslim, Hindu and Christian backgrounds. The challenges she faces include parents who have demanding careers and are competitive and ambitious for their children, anxious that they 'succeed' by obtaining highly sought-after places at independent schools. In many cases these parents lack the time or energy to devote to their children's upbringing.

On the other hand, from a converted garage in a lower income suburb, Gaynor and Vani offer early childhood education and care to children from four different ethnic backgrounds, three different faiths and three different home languages. The school, which occupies a small space, is simple but well equipped, although crowded with fifty-six children aged from 2 to 6. One of the major challenges here is the non-payment of school fees and uncertainty of enrolment as parents seek the cheapest option for their children.

Hildah teaches a group of six 5-year-old children at a well-resourced special needs school for the deaf. The school is located in a leafy suburb and caters for children from the ages of 3 to 18. Her class is well resourced but she is faced with the challenge of teaching children with either no or very little hearing who have three different home languages, and many of whom live at some distance from the school, making contact and parental support difficult.

The final stop on this journey is with Sue, Caversham's Zululand Regional eYe Manager, who manages, teaches and trains at a rural school located in a small town in Zululand. The school is very well resourced with well-equipped indoor areas and a large indigenous garden, which includes a perma-culture and pet area. One of the challenges Sue faces is that the majority of the children travel to school by taxi, often leaving their homes at 5 a.m., resulting in very little parental contact. The medium of instruction, requested by the parents, is English, although the home language of the children is isiZulu.

The majority of early childhood teachers that Caversham enskills experience the challenge and excitement of providing an excellent learning programme for children from diverse cultural backgrounds including different languages, religions and customs, in a variety of settings, with a range of resources as articulated in the examples given above. This requires creativity and innovation.

For all these teachers, particularly those from disadvantaged communities, the HIV and AIDS pandemic is a challenge of daunting proportions, as it impacts deeply on both the teacher and the children who live in tension as family members get ill and die. Family life is disrupted and children often experience neglect, fear, confusion and isolation. Frequently children have to take on adult roles with inappropriate responsibilities. The personal development component of Caversham's eYe teacher training courses helps to inspire teachers to find additional depths of patience and compassion and to develop the problem-solving skills required to provide the loving care and support these children need.

Despite the ending of apartheid and the predominant goodwill of the majority of South African people, crime and violence are still widespread with the resultant insecurity, fear and anxiety regarding personal safety and the safety of possessions. Caversham's eYe teacher training programme helps provide skills in developing collaborative partnerships by establishing networks between the ECD class and the community, thus lessening risk and engendering a spirit of courage and resilience.

Visiting Caversham early years education (eYe) training

Caversham eYe courses are held in venues called Caversham CreACTive™ Centres housed in schools. During a visit to a training session, an observer would see a session of approximately 20 participants, seated in groups of four to six. The workshop style is interactive, participative, creative and stimulating with group work and dialogue being key components. The knowledgeable and experienced facilitator is well prepared with training materials and student support materials in the form of a file, notes and so on, and has clear outcomes to be achieved during the session. Learning materials have been developed by Jill Sachs and her team of ECD specialists and each session has three core components: fostering personal development as an individual and as a professional ECD teacher; increasing knowledge of early childhood; and developing competencies and skills to offer a professional education programme.

Caversham programmes, including the early years education (eYe) programmes, use a highly effective transformational model called the *Caversham Hourglass Process* that has been developed over the past three years. It consists of *Reflection* (pausing with the intention of self-exploration); *Dialogue* (the art of active listening in order to contribute and affirm); *CreACTion™* (combining collaborative attitude with creative action) leading to *Ownership/Legacy* (being in the present, recognising the past, and taking responsibility for the future). The *Caversham Hourglass Process*© is used to give structure to each workshop session and supports presentations of information or teaching. The sequence, in which the elements of the process are offered, however, depends on the outcomes which are planned and the composition of the group. Thus there is a clear framework for each session but enough flexibility to allow for the organic nature of the process.

Unpacking the Caversham early years (eYe) teacher training programmes

Unpacking the Caversham eYe teacher training programmes is seen in the context of the many and varied parts of Caversham Centre's contribution. This contribution is evident in Caversham's Vision Statement – *Inspiration in the Individual and the Individual as Inspiration* – as well as the hourglass logo which symbolises the complementary interdependence of time, transition, transformation in individuals, families and communities when viewed as *Container and Conduit*. It recognises the indispensable role each must play in taking ownership/responsibility for establishing a balance between receiving and filling our lives, and making a contribution and leaving a worthwhile legacy.

To accommodate the need for ECD teachers to improve their qualifications, Caversham eYe programmes are offered on a part-time basis, with students attending workshop sessions and then applying the learning in an early childhood setting. This enables students to study and teach simultaneously. Recognising the past and taking cognisance of the present, Caversham has designed its courses to meet the particular need for a high-quality, practical, relevant, professional qualification which equips the teacher, both personally and professionally, to offer the very best in education and care to the children he or she teaches. The Caversham eYe teacher training programmes are offered at NQF Level 5, which is the level just below a first degree. The majority of NGOs are involved in early childhood teacher training at NQF Level 4 which is the minimum qualification recognised by the Department of Education.[10] Many teachers are eager to learn and improve their qualifications by obtaining a Level 5, then proceeding to complete a degree. This then is the niche into which Caversham's eYe courses fit – a comfortable place as it also supports Caversham's underlying philosophy that it is an organisation that works in collaboration, not in competition, with others.

At present, Caversham offers three early childhood courses which include:

THE SCOPE COURSE

A one-year, part-time course, offered over 20 sessions, specifically designed to equip preschool teachers and/or supervisors/principals with the knowledge and skills required to set up, plan for, present and evaluate an excellent ECD programme for young children aged 2-and-a-half to 6 years. The course also includes theories and approaches in child development, assessment and reporting, administration and team work.

THE THREE LEARNING PROGRAMMES FOR THE RECEPTION YEAR

A 10-month (13-session) course, specifically designed to enable a reception year teacher, who already possesses a qualification in ECD, or a professional teacher's qualification, to plan, prepare, present, assess and evaluate a high-quality literacy, numeracy and life skills programme for the reception year (Grade R) in line with the policy requirement of the National Curriculum Statement.

USING ARTS AND CULTURE-BASED METHODOLOGIES FOR LEARNING

In this six-module programme the child is seen as the greatest resource, rehearsing and modelling qualities of questioning, reflection, problem-solving, creating and re-creating. The course is specifically designed to focus on the individual's intrinsic resources to create fresh ways of thinking, doing and seeing the world. It engages teachers in an exploration of 'heart, head, hand and spirit'. The course offers the opportunity for the student to explore herself or himself as a creative being within the context of the rich cultural diversity in South Africa. It also provides knowledge about the importance and development of creativity and teaches skills necessary to offer a range of visual arts-based activities, including drawing, painting, modelling, collage, group work and print-making.

Student requirements for undertaking a Caversham eYe course journey

Reflecting the Caversham logo of the hourglass, Caversham accepts students who are dedicated to learning how to 'fill the container' that will enable them to contribute. Students, whose ages range from the early twenties to the late forties, have a personal passion for making a contribution to the lives of young children, their families and communities. They are required to have the minimum of a matriculation, a Grade 12 school-leaving certificate, and a foundational knowledge and skills in ECD practice. They undertake to attend all the sessions and to participate wholeheartedly, share willingly, complete all assignments and other assessment tasks and to create a personal testimony in a tangible form of the relevance of their personal journey on the course.

Assessment requirements

Contents of 'backpacks of evidence'

Outcomes-based assessment is conducted on an ongoing basis and evidence includes keeping a journal, completing written assignments, creating a personal testimony, observations of learners, planning of sessions in the learning programme and interviews. A final assessment of the competence of the student in implementing the learning is conducted in the classroom.

Our journey ends

Learning from Caversham eYe programmes

The very essence of the Caversham early childhood teacher training programmes is reflected in the wise statement made by Pericles (495–429 BC) to his troops: 'What you leave behind is not what is engraved in stone monuments but what is woven into the lives of others' (source unknown).

From feedback derived from interviews, questionnaires and testimonials, as part of internal evaluation systems, the *Caversham Hourglass Process*© (Reflection, Dialogue and CreACTion™, leading to Ownership and Legacy) has provided an effective personal development component to the holistic training of early childhood teachers.

The face-to-face contact and consequent relationship between the facilitator and students, as well as students with students, is one of the central elements of success of the Caversham eYe training. Using the interactive workshop style, where students work in groups with collaboration, cooperation and sharing and mutual ownership as underpinning values, enduring supportive relationships have been established.

Creativity is about embracing change, enabling individuals to become catalysts for change, overcoming challenges through problem-solving, and empowering through cultivating opportunities to contribute. The arts as a basis for unique expression may be used to create bridges of deeper understanding of self and the relevance of this to others. This reflects the essential African philosophy of *Ubuntu* – 'I am, because of others'.

When dealing with the enormity of challenges that are faced in a developing democracy, it requires the individual to begin with the basic building blocks of their own uniqueness and the power of relationships. It is about igniting the spark within the individual teacher that can transform a classroom into an exciting, innovative laboratory of questioning and learning. An inspired teacher is an inspiration and makes a contribution, is a catalyst for change, and is an indispensable community resource.

One of the significant challenges facing Caversham is in making its excellent quality programmes affordable to students from disadvantaged backgrounds. A number of innovative ways are currently being explored but the necessity for sustainable, predictable funding is crucial to help grow the next generation of creative catalysts, thereby building a strong and vital legacy that is instilled in our children. In them rests the truth that this journey never ends, that our perceived destination is but a point of departure.

A 'take home' souvenir

This is an extract from *A Return to Love: Reflections in Principles of a Course in Miracles* by Marianne Williamson (1992: 190–191):

> Our deepest fear is not that we are inadequate. Our deepest fear is that we are powerful beyond measure. It is our light not our darkness that most frightens us. We ask ourselves, who am I to be brilliant, gorgeous, talented and fabulous? Actually, who are you not to be? You are a child of God. Your playing small does not serve the world. There is nothing enlightened about shrinking so that other people won't feel insecure around you. We are all meant to shine as children do. We were born to make manifest the glory of God that is within us. It's not just in some of us, it's in everyone. And, as we let our own light shine, we unconsciously give other people permission to do the same. As we are liberated from our own fear, our presence liberates other.

Notes

1 www.cavershamcentre.org.
2 National Education Policy Investigation 1992: 15.
3 Ibid.: 17–19. From Lategan (1991 and 1992) (NEPI working papers).
4 Department of Education 2001b.
5 Department of Education, 2001a.
6 Department of Education, South Africa 2001.
7 http://www.acts.co.za/ed_saqa/index.htm.
8 http://www.saqa.org.za/.
9 http://www.etdpseta.org.za/.
10 http://www.sace.org.za/article.php?parent=6&article_id=25.

References

Chisholm, L. (ed.) (2004) *Changing Class: Education and Social Change in Post-apartheid South Africa*. HSRC Press. Accessed online at: http://www.hsrcpress.ac.za/product.php?productid=1937&cat=0&page=1 (accessed 6 March 2007).

Department of Education South Africa (2001) *Education White Paper 5 on Early Childhood Education: Meeting the Challenge of Early Childhood Development in South Africa*. Pretoria: Government Printer. Accessed online at: http://www.education.gov.za/dynamic/dynamic.aspx?pageid=326&dirid=3 (accessed 6 March 2007).

Department of Education (1996) *Interim Policy for Early Childhood Development*. Pretoria: Government Printer. Accessed online at: http://www.education.gov.za/dynamic/dynamic.aspx?pageid=326&dirid=3 (accessed 7 March 2007).

Department of Education (2001a) *Report on the National ECD Pilot Project*. Pretoria: Government Printer. Accessed online at: http://www.education.gov.za/dynamic/dynamic.aspx?pageid=326&dirid=3 (accessed 7 March 2007).

Department of Education (2001b) *Report on National ECD Policies and Programmes*. Pretoria: Government Printer. Accessed online at: http://www.education.gov.za/dynamic/dynamic.aspx?pageid=326&dirid=3 (accessed 7 March 2007).

Department of Education (2002) Revised *National Curriculum Statement Grades R to 9 (Schools) Policy*. Pretoria: Government Printer. Accessed online at: http://www.education.gov.za/Curriculum/GET/GETstatements.asp (accessed 7 March 2007).

Education and Training Development Practices Sector Education Training Authority (n.d.) Accessed online at: http://www.etdpseta.org.za (accessed 7 March 2007).

Gerber, R. E. (n.d.) *The NQF and SAQA. An Introduction*. Bureau for Educational Support. Port Elizabeth: Port Elizabeth Technikon. Accessed online at: http://tutor.petech.ac.za/educsupport/html/probsolv/index.html (accessed 7 March 2007).

National Education Policy Investigation (NEPI) (1992) *Early Childhood Educare. A Work of the NECC Early Childhood Research Group*. Cape Town: Oxford University Press.

National Education Policy Investigation (NEPI) (1993) *The Framework Report and Final Report Summaries. A Project of the NECC*. Cape Town: Oxford University Press.

Office of the President (1995) *South African Qualifications Act. No.58*. Pretoria: Government Printer. Accessed online at: http://www.acts.co.za/ed_saqa/index.htm (accessed 11 March 2007).

Porteus, K. (2004) The state of play in early childhood development. In L. Chisholm (ed.) *Changing Class: Education and Social Change in Post-apartheid South Africa*. HSRC Press. Accessed online at: http://www.hsrcpress.ac.za/product.php?productid=1937&cat=0&page=1 (accessed 11 March 2007).

South African Qualifications Authority (n.d.) Accessed online at: http://www.saqa.org.za/ (accessed 11 March 2003).

South African Council of Educators (n.d.) Accessed online at http://www.sace.org.za/article.php?parent=6&article_id=25 (accessed 11 March 2007).

Williamson M. (1992) *A Return to Love: Reflections on the Principles of a Course in Miracles*. London: HarperCollins. Accessed online at: http://skdesigns.com/internet/articles/quotes/williamson/our_deepest_fear/ (accessed 11 March 2007).

6   Looking, listening, learning and linking

Uses of observation for relational pedagogy

Paulette Luff

This chapter considers the role of skilled and careful observation of young children in fostering relational approaches to young children's care and education. Here relational pedagogy is defined as work with children which recognises that human relations are of paramount importance, both within care and education settings and beyond. The connections and understandings exchanged and developed in the context of shared practices and meaning-making are also central to this relational approach to caring, learning and teaching. In the light of this, the first section of the chapter discusses the potential of observation as a pedagogical tool and then highlights inadequacies that have been identified in this area of early childhood professionals' practice. The second section draws on evidence from a collective case study of 11 newly qualified childcare and education workers, employed in three different early years settings.

Findings from this research indicate that informal observant practice is very meaningful and enhances relationships with children, families and colleagues. However, this is not often reflected in the formal documenting of observations, which are focused upon monitoring the progress of individuals and therefore have limited use in developing children's care and learning. Finally, proposals are made for a move towards more inclusive and collaborative ways of working, drawing inspiration from models of excellence in order to maximise the potential of child observation as a tool for relational pedagogy.

Introduction

Observation is a vital element in most human relationships. Attending to another person, often automatically and unknowingly, noticing their facial expressions, being aware of their body language, tone of voice and general behaviour, provides valuable clues about how they are feeling and how to respond. We recognise that a colleague who comes into the office looking pale and tired will appreciate help and support rather than a list of questions and demands! We tune into the feelings of our partners, children, friends and colleagues in order to build up these important relationships and foster harmony in our domestic and professional lives. Bruner (1996) theorises that this endeavour to come to know each others' minds is a uniquely human characteristic, which can form the basis for interactive and inter-subjective approaches to pedagogy. In this chapter, I propose that careful observation, focused upon social understandings and meaning-making, can be an invaluable way of getting to know and understand babies and young children. If practitioners then share and discuss insights gained from observations with one another, with parents and with the children themselves, relationships can be built, and knowledge gained which may then enhance every child's care and education.

Background

Susan Isaacs' (1930, 1933) diary records of children at her Malting House school modelled the use of narrative observations of play and interactions as part of a quest to know more about children's thinking and to understand their feelings and relationships. Capturing the detail of babies and children's daily lives is, similarly, central to the methods of close observation devised by Bick (1964) for the training of psychoanalysts. This Tavistock model of observation recognises the place of emotion and the significance of relationships for both the observer and the observed (Miller 2002). When used in the training and continual professional development of social workers, it has been shown to be a valuable tool for developing accurate empathy with clients and improving the quality of assessment and care planning (Trowell and Miles 1991; Trowell *et al.* 1998; Tanner and Le Riche 2000). This approach has also been found to be a useful tool for researching the experiences of babies and young children in nurseries (Elfer and Selleck 1999) and for developing practice with children under 3 (Elfer 2005). In another example of a relational method of observation, utilised to get as close as possible to children's experience, ethnographic, participatory observation techniques are used. By adopting the 'least adult role' (Corsaro 1985), an adult researcher plays alongside 3 to 6-year-olds in a Danish nursery in an effort to appreciate and articulate the children's perceptions of their everyday lives (Warming 2005). All these methods of observation acknowledge the subjectivity of the observer, and the mutual, relational influence of the observer and the observed, within the specific context in which the observation occurs. These methods are not widely used in early childhood settings but there are observation techniques, in current use, which share similar qualities in capturing the subtleties and complexities of observational encounters, particularly when we seek inspiration from international icons (Gammage 2006).

The municipal infant toddler centres and preschools of Reggio Emilia have become world renowned for excellence in early childhood care and education. The projects which give expression to the hundred languages of children, and the work of the atelieristas in promoting the children's creativity, are immediately apparent. Yet this is underpinned by an impressive pedagogy of listening and the processes of pedagogical documentation, which offer inspiration and challenge to early childhood practitioners internationally. The term *child observation* is not used, and has even been decried, as the antithesis of pedagogical documentation (Dahlberg *et al*. 1999), since it implies a normalising and technical approach to teaching focused on the achievement of predetermined learning outcomes. In contrast, written documentation of children's activities, transcriptions of conversations and examples of work in progress are used to explore and interpret children's meaning-making, and to identify clues for fostering and extending learning. Displaying and discussing the documentation allows for the involvement of parents, children and members of the wider community to participate in open dialogues about classroom work (Rinaldi 2006).

A second, relevant example may be found in the *Basic Development Curriculum*, on offer in the early years of some primary schools in the Netherlands. The educational objectives for this holistic approach are represented in a circular diagram (Janssen-Vos 2003) with well-being, curiosity and self-confidence at the centre, aspects of personal and social development in a middle circle and specific motor, cognitive and language skills around the outer circle – a very different design from the compartmentalised, linear progression, via stepping stones to early learning goals, indicated in earlier English curriculum guidance (QCA/DfEE 2000). Teachers have a challenging double role to play within the *Basic Development Curriculum* as they both participate in, and reflect on, the activities and interactions with children (Van Oers *et al*. 2003). Logbooks are used for daily planning, general observation and reflection; and observations of individual children, engaged in play activities that are meaningful for them, are recorded in diaries and portfolios. These are complex and demanding tasks (Fijma 2003) but, through collaborative work with 'innovators', teacher educators and academic researchers, teachers are given systematic assistance in learning to use these logbooks and diaries, which has been shown to boost their confidence and raise the quality of observations (Van Oers and Holla 1997). Van Oers (2003) describes this approach to observation and documentation as the creation of developmental narratives for and about the children; a storying of learning and structuring of experiences so that they can be revisited. This narrative understanding is also at the heart of the *Learning Story* method (Carr 2001).

The familiar process of parents and practitioners exchanging informal observations about children at the beginning and end of the day, common in most early childhood settings, is formalised in a learning story approach to documenting learning (Cowie and Carr 2004). These learning stories record, reflect and promote learning outcomes, in accordance with the strands of the *Te Whāriki* curriculum: well-being, belonging, communication, contribution and exploration (New Zealand Ministry of Education 1996). As in the *Basic Development* model, these learning outcomes are not prescriptive stepping stones and performance goals (Dweck 1985) linked to specific skills and knowledge within subject areas but, instead, emphasise each child's participation and the development of positive dispositions and attitudes towards learning. Observation, in this *Learning Story* approach, is structured according to the requirements and opportunities in different local settings and is focused upon describing children's achievements. Observations are discussed and interpreted collaboratively and, along with photographs, work samples and comments from teachers, parents and the child, form part of the documentation which then becomes the basis for decisions about the next steps for learning (Carr 2001).

Each of these three international examples illustrates the potential of thoughtful and observant work with children as the basis for building relationships with them, working in partnership with colleagues and children's families and together building understandings which enable reflective, responsive care of the children and thoughtful, exciting opportunities for learning. In England, similarly engaged and collaborative observation practices also exist. The development of 'possible lines of direction' (PLOD) charts at Pen Green (Whalley 1993) has provided a fruitful example of ways in which records of children's play can be made, interpreted in the light of schema theory (Athey 1991) and then used as a basis for planning a curriculum to provide for the children's dominant interests. New media, particularly digital photography, have enhanced the possibilities for capturing and recording children's play as it occurs and using this as a means of celebrating and reflecting upon their learning. Exemplars of effective practice include work at Wingate Community Nursery School (DfES 2006; Miller 2006), and at Fortune Park Children's Centre (Driscoll and Rudge 2005). In both of these cases, written observations and other representations of the children's experiences are skilfully utilised to construct shared understandings of educational processes.

Vygotsky (1978, 1997) argued that human activities and interactions, including cognitive processes, are mediated by cultural tools. While these tools can be as simple as 'casting lots, tying knots and counting fingers' (Vygotsky 1978: 127), extending human ability to make decisions, remember something or perform simple arithmetic, the term also refers to more complex symbol systems, including spoken and written language, which are powerful tools for the shaping of human intellectual abilities. Kozulin (2003), following Vygotsky, emphasises the potential use of such symbolic tools in education. Child observation may be viewed as a pedagogical tool, mediating and supporting the thinking and actions of childcare and education workers (Cowie and Carr 2004) and also, in turn, promoting their awareness of children's developing use of cultural tools, and the impact of these upon their learning (Dijk 2003; Egan 2003).

There is, however, evidence that English practitioners find difficulty in using observation of children as a tool to inform their professional work. The *Study of Pedagogical Effectiveness in Early Learning* (Moyles *et al.* 2002) identified observation and formative assessment, linked to a cycle of recording and planning, as an area in which training was needed, and this was borne out by the *Children at the Centre* report (OfSTED 2004) which confirmed a link between accurate observations and effective planning, but found too little observation leading to limited planning and inconsistent practice, even in designated *Early Excellence Centres*. Similarly, observation and assessment of 5-year-olds in school reception classes is sometimes reduced to 'making the greatest number of ticks in the shortest possible time' (Adams *et al.* 2004: 84).

The research

The small-scale research study from which the evidence that follows is drawn arose from a desire to investigate the discrepancy between these negative findings, which draw attention to the limitations of practitioners' skills, and a strong emphasis upon child observation in training courses for childcare and education workers in England. The research took the form of a collective case study, using an ethnographic approach, to explore how 11 newly qualified early years practitioners from level three Diploma in Child Care and Education courses and equivalent National Vocational Qualification courses, working in three different early years settings, understood and used child observation during their first year in the workplace. The main sources of data were field notes from participant observations and semi-structured interviews with participants. Here some of the findings have been condensed and are discussed in relation to three themes:

1   observant practice;
2   the use of frameworks;
3   collaborative work.

Observant practice

Elfer (2005) suggests that, in their conversations, early childhood practitioners speak in lively and thoughtful ways about babies and young children, and yet this is lost when observations are documented. This contrast between informal and formal practices is also highlighted in my study. Informally, practitioners share rich information about each child's day with parents: details of play and learning; small achievements; minor upsets and concerns; and the funny things they have said or done. The formal record is more limited. For example, daily report sheets, known in one nursery as *Happy Charts*, are filled out for each child under age 2, and for some of the children over age 2 whose parents request it. These have the potential to be a wonderful daily diary, capturing highlights, giving information and forming the basis for dialogue between the nursery staff and each child's parents. However, if filled in by a busy worker during five minutes grabbed while the children sleep, they rarely record anything special or significant. Instead, these day sheets are often limited to lists of provision: the activities on offer; daily menus; and the number of nappy changes. Although they are produced for each named child and are valued by parents, the records are often very similar and could even be interchangeable.

Similarly, I frequently witnessed observant fostering of progress in which adults were responsive and facilitative to children, adjusting their expectations sensitively and thoughtfully according to their perceptions of children's abilities and potential. For example, when H (working in a school reception class) takes a group of 5-year-olds to practise letter formation, she puts a gripping device on Phoebe's pen, draws dots for Tom to trace, gives Jack a dot to start on, pointing out the direction in which he should form the letter, and watches as Katy carefully does the task without help. Likewise, S (in the garden of the nursery where she works) supervises 4-year-old Saffron on a climbing wall, standing close by, making suggestions about where she should place her hands and feet, encouraging and reassuring her until she is able to climb up, over and down this play equipment by herself.

There are many instances of this gentle support of progress but they are rarely made explicit, captured in planning, or articulated in children's records. Some practitioners openly express a reluctance to document their understandings, claiming: 'I just notice what's going on without doing observations. I notice things anyway and don't need to write it all down' (H) or admitting 'Practical stuff I love but I hate written work. Like, I have got patience with children but I hate it when I've got to write' (C). Others see the value of close observation to deepen knowledge and understanding: 'You actually focus on that child rather than look-ing all around the room and so you notice much more' (S) but feel constrained by lack of time to document and reflect upon what they have seen: 'The observa-tions are fine, its time that's the problem. . . . We do it at sleep times, times like that but sometimes, like last week when there were staff missing, then you get no time at all' (M).

The use of frameworks

Despite pressures of time, all the new practitioners in the study are conscientious, hard-working, and very aware of their responsibilities to uphold standards of care (Sure Start 2001), and to implement the *Birth to Three Matters* framework (DfES 2002) and the *Curriculum Guidance for the Foundation Stage* (QCA/DfES 2000). They all use published English government documents as a means to inform curriculum plans and take pride in keeping up-to-date records of the children's progress. In all three settings, practitioners record children's achievements by noting observed behaviours on sticky labels (e.g. 'Chose book, said it was her favourite story about Postman Pat. Pointed to pages saying Pat and Jess'). These notes are signed, dated and later transferred to record folders as evidence of the child having met relevant learning outcomes. A main motivation for this careful record-keeping seemed to be anxiety about external scrutiny and compliance with quality assurance procedures, rather than a desire to celebrate achievements and to learn about the children's experiences.

As indicated in the brief discussion of pedagogical documentation in Reggio Emilia above, such attention to mapping observed behaviours according to specified learning outcomes has been widely criticised as leading to a limited, restrictive view of children and of learning (Dahlberg *et al.* 1999; Carr 2001; Drummond 2003; Fleer and Richardson 2004). Fleer and Robbins (2007) suggest that, while sociocultural theories are increasingly influential in early childhood education, observation and assessment practices remain within traditional developmental and constructivist frameworks that fail to take into account the immediate environment, relations between individuals and the activities in which they are engaged, and the wider social and historical context. In the approaches to observation discussed in the first part of this chapter, the role of the observer is not to identify what a child can and cannot do but, rather, to analyse why the observed behaviour may have occurred, to seek a deeper understanding of the child and of learning processes, and to consider what further opportunities to provide. For English practitioners, this demands more reflective, flexible and creative ways of using guidance documents. Dewey (1972) offers inspiration here, using the metaphor of a nautical almanac guiding a sailor to illustrate the usefulness of a rule book (such as a curriculum document) as the basis for thoughtful and skilful action.

Collaborative work

This reflection and professional action should not be a lone endeavour. All the examples of effective pedagogical uses of observation, discussed in the first part of this chapter, involve shared, interactive processes. The participants in the research study showed considerable skill in relating to colleagues and to students on work placements in their settings, as well as to the children and their carers. D's description of coming to terms with the, then new, *Birth to Three Matters* framework (DfES 2002) provides just one example of this supportive, collaborative work:

> 'After we did it on the two training days, and then we came back, K and I were talking about it and it was so confusing we had to go right the way back again and then gradually come through it and it's just taken a little while to get going in the right direction.'

The children also demonstrate pro-social behaviour and identify strongly with their nursery groups. When I visit they tell me about the staff and the other children, informing me who is off sick or away on holiday and asking me the whereabouts of children who are absent. In a small (36-place) nursery, this sense of community is fostered at shared playtimes and mealtimes. For example, when 13-month-old Henri makes attempts to feed himself using a spoon, his key worker calmly supports him in this task during several lunchtimes until he can eat his food independently – an achievement then noted, discussed and praised by several of the older children and reported by them to his mother and older siblings when they come to collect him.

This sense of community and collaboration is less apparent in processes of observation and record-keeping. While potentially valuable for building rela- tionships with each child and family, the operation of key worker systems also seems to lead to individuals taking responsibility for documenting progress and making independent decisions about children's care and learning. Nutbrown (2002: 77) points out that: 'watching children as they learn and understanding the significance of those learning moments are complex tasks that make high demands on all who attempt them'; and yet this challenging work is rarely shared. Despite frequent staff discussions about children, particularly regarding concerns about health or behaviour, the study found no systems in place in these early childhood settings to support and encourage the formal participation of colleagues, parents and children in talking about observations and documenting achievement.

Conclusion

In all three settings involved in the research project, sensitive and conscientious early childhood practitioners seek to do their work well and to provide positive experiences of care and education for young children and their families. The findings indicate the scope of observation as a tool for relational pedagogy while also highlighting areas for development and change in order to realise its potential. If practitioners, and their managers, value time spent looking at and listening to children attentively, discussing what is seen and heard, making links with existing knowledge and investigating possibilities for learning, then observation may become an effective tool for relational pedagogy. It can then form the basis for thoughtful, shared reflections on care and teaching and a foundation for informed action to offer social and emotional support, facilitate playful learning and provide cognitive challenges.

References

Adams, S., Alexander, E., Drummond, M.J. and Moyles, J. (2004) *Inside the Foundation Stage*. Final Report. London: Association of Teachers and Lecturers.

Anning, A., Cullen, J. and Fleer, M. (2004) *Early Childhood Education*. London, Thousand Oaks, CA, and New Delhi: Sage.

Athey, C. (1991) *Extending Thought in Young Children*. London: Paul Chapman Publishing.

Bick, E. (1964) Notes on infant observation in psychoanalytic training. *International Journal of Psychoanalysis*, 45: 558–566.

Bruner, J. (1996) *The Culture of Education*. Cambridge, MA: Harvard University Press.

Carr, M. (2001) *Assessment in Early Childhood Settings: Learning Stories*. London: Paul Chapman Publishing.

Corsaro, W. (1985) *Friendship and Peer Culture in the Early Years*. Norwood, NJ: Ablex.

Cowie, B. and Carr, M. (2004) The consequences of socio-cultural assessment. In A. Anning, J. Cullen and M. Fleer (eds) *Early Childhood Education*. London, Thousand Oaks, CA, and New Delhi: Sage.

Dahlberg, G., Moss, P. and Pence, A. (1999). *Beyond Quality in Early Childhood Education and Care: Postmodern Perspectives*. London: Falmer Press.

Department for Education and Science (DfES) (2002) *Birth to Three Matters*. London: DfES Publications.

Department for Education and Science (DfES) (2006) *Celebrating Young Children* (poster and DVD pack). London: DfES.

Dewey, J. (1972) *The Early Works of John Dewey, 1882–1898* (Vol. 3). Carbondale and Edwardsville: Southern Illinois University Press.

Djik, E. (2003) Institutional contexts and language use in classroom conversations. In B. Van Oers (ed.) *Narratives of Childhood*. Amsterdam: VU University Press.

Driscoll, V. and Rudge, C. (2005) Channels for listening to young children and parents. In A. Clark, A.T. Kjørholt and P. Moss (eds) *Beyond Listening*. Bristol: Policy Press.

Drummond, M.J. (2003) *Assessing Children's Learning* (2nd edn). London: David Fulton Publishers.

Dweck, C.S. (1985) Intrinsic motivation, perceived control and self-evaluation maintenance: an achievement goal analysis. In C. Ames and R. Ames (eds) *Research on Motivation in Education* (Vol. 2, *The Classroom Milieu*). San Diego: Academic Press.

Egan, K. (2003) The cognitive tools of children's imagination. In B. Van Oers (ed.) *Narratives of Childhood*. Amsterdam: VU University Press.

Elfer, P. (2005) Observation matters. In L. Abbott and A. Langston (eds) *Birth-to-Three Matters*. Maidenhead: Open University Press.

Elfer, P. and Selleck, D. (1999) Children under three in nurseries. Uncertainty as a creative factor in child observations. *European Early Childhood Research Journal*, 7 (1): 69–82.

Fijma, N. (2003) Mathematics learning in a play-based curriculum: how to deal with heterogeneity. In B. Van Oers (ed.) *Narratives of Childhood*. Amsterdam: VU University Press.

Fleer, M. and Richardson, C. (2004) Mapping the transformation of understanding. In A. Anning, J. Cullen and M. Fleer (eds) Early Childhood Education. London, Thousand Oaks, CA, and New Delhi: Sage.

Fleer, M. and Robbins, J. (2007) A cultural-historical analysis of early childhood education: how do teachers appropriate new cultural tools? *European Early Childhood Research Journal*, 15(1): 103–119.

Gammage, P. (2006) Early childhood education and care: politics, policies and possibilities. *Early Years*, 26(3): 235–248.

Isaacs, S. (1930) *Intellectual Growth in Young Children*. London: Routledge & Kegan Paul.

Isaacs, S. (1933) *Social Development in Young Children*. London: Routledge & Kegan Paul.

Janssen-Vos, F. (2003) Basic development: developmental education for young children. In B. Van Oers (ed.) *Narratives of Childhood*. Amsterdam: VU University Press.

Kozulin, A. (2003) Psychological tools and mediated learning. In A. Kozulin, B. Gindis, V.S. Ageyev and S. Miller (eds) *Vygotsky's Educational Theory in Cultural Context*. Cambridge: Cambridge University Press.

Miller, J. (2006) Adam's Story. *Nursery World*, 106 (4021).

Miller, L. (2002) *Observation Observed: An Outline of the Nature and Practice of Infant Observation* (videos and booklet). London: The Tavistock Clinic Foundation.

Moyles, J., Adams, S. and Musgrove, A. (2002) *Study of Pedagogical Effectiveness in Early Learning (SPEEL)*. London: DfES.

New Zealand Ministry of Education (1996) *Te Whāriki. He Whāriki Mātauranga mō-ngā-Mokopuna o Aotearoa: Early Childhood Curriculum*. Wellington: Learning Media.

Nutbrown, C. (2002) Watching and learning: the tools of assessment. In G. Pugh (ed.) *Contemporary Issues in the Early Years: Working Collaboratively for Children* (3rd edn). London, Thousand Oaks, CA, and New Delhi: Sage.

Office for Standards in Education (OfSTED) (2004) *Children at the Centre*. London: OfSTED.

Perry, R. (1997) *Teaching Practice: A Guide for Early Years*. London: Routledge.

QCA (2000) *Curriculum Guidance for the Foundation Stage*. London: DfEE.

Rinaldi, C. (2006) *In Dialogue with Reggio Emilia*. London and New York: Routledge.

Sure Start (2001) *National Standards for Under 8s Day Care and Childminding.* Nottingham: DfES Publications.

Tanner, K. and Le Riche, P. (2000) Intentional observation. In V.E. Cree and C. Macaulay (eds) *Transfer of Learning in Professional and Vocational Education.* London and New York: Routledge.

Trowell, J. and Miles, G. (1991) The contribution of observation training to professional development in social work. *Journal of Social Work Practice*, 5(1): 51–60.

Trowell, J., Paton, A., Davids, Z. and Miles, G. (1998) The importance of observational training: an evaluative study. *International Journal of Infant Observation and its Applications*, 21: 101–111.

Van Oers, B. (2003) *Narratives of Childhood.* Amsterdam: VU University Press.

Van Oers, B. and Holla, A. (1997) *The Milestone: An Implementation of Developmental Education.* Case-study Report for the European Observatory of Innovations in Education and Training. Paris/Amsterdam: INRP/VU.

Van Oers, B., Janssen-Vos, F., Pompert, B. and Schiferli, T. (2003) Teaching as joint activity. In B. Van Oers (ed.) *Narratives of Childhood.* Amsterdam: VU University Press.

Vygotsky, L.S. (1978) *Mind in Society: The Development of Higher Psychological Processes*, ed. and trans. M. Cole, V. John-Steiner, S. Scribner and E. Souberman. Cambridge, MA: Harvard University Press.

Vygotsky, L.S. (1997) The history of the development of higher mental functions. In *The Collected Works of L.S. Vygotsky*, Vol. 4. New York: Plenum Pewaa.

Warming, H. (2005) Participant observation: a way to learn about children's perspectives. In A. Clark, A.T. Kjørholt and P. Moss (eds) *Beyond Listening.* Bristol: Policy Press.

Whalley, M. (1993) *Learning to be Strong: Setting up a Neighbourhood Nursery Service for Under-fives and Their Families.* Sevenoaks: Hodder & Stoughton.

Part II

Adult–child relationships at micro level

Introduction

> [Reggio Emilia] pedagogy focuses on children's self-awareness and well-being
> acquired through, and because of, the relationships which they develop with others.
>
> (Chapter 1)

At the heart of any pedagogy is the relationship between the adult and the child in the day-to-day situation. As Gold (2005) emphasises, relational pedagogy in particular stresses inclusion and careful listening and thinking skills by encouraging receptivity in adults and helping learners to cope with not knowing. It focuses on reciprocal responsiveness to need and education as a co-creative process. Self-awareness and self-regulation, awareness of others and knowledge of the impact of interrelations are also important features and these are highlighted in Part II. It also requires the adult to have and exhibit respect for children and childhood in ways that acknowledge the value of children's contributions to the learning relationship.

There is, of course, a relationship between social constructivism (learning through interaction with knowledgeable others) and relational pedagogy, although they differ in the responsibility placed on all learners to understand themselves in that role and their own metacognition (see Merry and Rogers 2007) as well as that of those with whom they interact. To educate the child, we need to educate the adults: it is important that adults see and understand experiences such as play through the eyes of the child rather than mediating children's experiences in terms of adult expectations (Moyles 1989). In the UK, the findings of the Effective Provision of Preschool Education (EPPE) by Sylva *et al.* (2004) show that warm adult interactions with children are vital to children's intellectual development, as is 'sustained shared thinking' between adults and children, the importance of which is embedded in the need for each to understand the other's perceptions, perspectives and understandings, and requires negotiation and empathy in order to achieve a co-construction of meanings. Underlying these processes are more characteristics of relational pedagogy which chapters in this section on adult–child relationships will embrace; for example, the concepts of language and culture, open discussion, trust and shared control, self-regulation, curious and open relationships, positive learner identities, intuitive behaviours and teachers' professionalism.

'Language is . . . developed through culture and, through language, culture is realised': thus assert Eva Maagerø and Birte Simonsen, Norwegian academics (Chapter 7) who have researched language and culture in the context of 3- to 5-year-olds learning English as a foreign language. They assert that, during the process of learning English nursery rhymes, young Norwegian children increased their intercultural understanding and their potential for positive mutual relations with, and sensitivity to, children from a different culture and were more able to handle differences. This chapter links Part II with Part I.

In Chapter 8, Sue Bingham and David Whitebread present the findings of an investigation into the extent to which 3- and 4-year-olds can self-regulate their emotional and social behaviours. The need for negotiation, open discussion and the building of trust and genuinely shared control between children and adults are explored as vital components of relational pedagogy in this context. The writers emphasise that, through the process of consulting with children about their attitudes and behaviour, some of the autonomy and responsibility which adults recognise as being critical within the domain of emotional and social development of young children was handed directly to them. The consultation process also appeared very effectively to bind the children together emotionally and socially, creating a real sense of community.

Liz Brooker (Chapter 9) explores the role of the key worker and how under-3s' own preferences and prior experiences shape the children's pedagogical relationship with that adult. One of the key worker's statements – 'Just like having a best friend really' – is seen as indicating the child's own agency in constructing relationships which help that learner to experience satisfaction and to feel a sense of belonging. Liz Brooker concludes that even the youngest children can be empowered to explore and exploit all the opportunities within the setting and to develop peer relationships.

This co-construction of experiences and meanings are taken up by Jan Georgeson (Chapter 10) and Jane Payler (Chapter 11). These contributors report on a linked research project in two areas of England which drew on Bernstein's theory of pedagogic discourse. Through analysis of children's utterances, the research demonstrates that different interactional microclimates in the different settings are linked to the difference in organisation and pedagogical emphases. For example, settings that prioritise care and socialisation foster an interactive climate more favourable to the co-construction of meanings between staff and children than those which emphasise educational outcomes (see Chapter 1). This also resulted in the development of more positive learner identities and greater participatory positions by the children.

Play is the focus of Kathy Goouch's contribution (Chapter 12), the final chapter in Part II, in which she explains how high levels of curriculum and pedagogical prescription can thwart attempts to engage in the processes of relational pedagogy. In her research she has found that some teachers are able to give status to play and intuitively respond to children, so co-constructing play narratives and placing the intentions of the children at the forefront of the play. This, she feels, is an intuitive behaviour because of some teachers' implicit and embedded respect for children and childhood. She emphasises the subtlety of this effective practice, and the teachers' skills, commitment and professionalism in ensuring that play and adult support is central in children's experienced curriculum.

While some of Part II has, to a degree, overlapped with Part I, it may be seen that the focus on children in each of these chapters and the role of the skilled and professional adult in generating a pedagogy based on relationships and mutual understanding is also prominent. This adds a further dimension to our understanding of relational pedagogy and stresses the importance of self-awareness in adults and children, awareness of other people and reciprocal interactions as being at the core of well-being and self-knowledge.

References

Gold, L. (2005) An introduction to relational pedagogy: relationships at the heart of learning. Paper presented at the Third International Conference on New Directions in Humanities, Cambridge, 2–5 August.

Merry, R. and Rogers, J. (2007) Inside the learning mind: primary children and their learning processes. In J. Moyles (ed.) *Beginning Teaching: Beginning Learning* (2nd edn). Maidenhead: Open University Press.

Moyles, J. (1989) *Just Playing? The Role and Status of Play in Early Childhood Education*. Buckingham: Open University Press.

Sylva, K., Melhuish, E., Sammons, P., Siraj-Blatchford, I. and Taggart, B. (2004) *The Effective Provision of Pre-school Education (EPPE) Project. Technical Paper 12. The Final Report*. Effective Pre-school Education. London: DfES/Institute of Education, University of London.

7 Children living far away

How does one develop positive relationships with children in other cultures?

Eva Maagerø and Birte Simonsen

In this chapter the relational and cultural aspects of the project 'Polly put the kettle on: English in kindergarten' will be presented. The project was developed and completed in two daycare centres in Lillesand in southern Norway during the period 2002 to 2006 (Maagerø and Simonsen 2006; Elvin *et al*. 2007). Young children ranging in ages from 3 to 5 years were invited to use English as a foreign language twice a week in order both to learn English and stimulate their overall language skills. Language is, however, developed through culture, and through language culture is realised as well. Every time young children encounter English, they also meet a new culture. Whenever they listen to English books and stories, look at photos from the English-speaking world, sing songs and rhymes, watch films and so on, they are introduced to another way of doing and saying things. In the cultural expressions they meet at daycare centres, children are visible, and the way they play and interact is emphasised. The meeting with English is therefore also a meeting with children living far away. Through the use of cultural expressions in the project, we can observe how the interest in and relationship with children from other cultures grow alongside the increase in their cultural knowledge. We hope that the experience with another culture while very young will make children curious and open in their relationships with others in the future. In our presentation and discussion we will expand on the ideas of 'context of situation' and 'context of culture'.

The project 'Polly put the kettle on' has also been part of a larger Comenius Project, in which two daycare centres in Lillesand have cooperated with preschools in Cáceres in Spain, which have also introduced English instruction. Similarly, daycare centres in Belfast, Northern Ireland, have introduced French and Gallic. Through this collaborative effort children have made contact with children in Spain and Northern Ireland through English. This is another dimension of the development of a consciousness of, and knowledge about, children living far away, a factor which will also be briefly mentioned in this chapter.

Introduction and background

In 2002, the local authorities of Lillesand decided to give children in two of the town's daycare centres the possibility of receiving a head start in English by employing a native speaker for two 20-minute teaching sessions per week. Their primary reason for doing this was to take advantage of the fact that young children easily adapt to a foreign language, especially in the area of pronunciation, a belief supported by research (e.g. Singleton 1989, 1999). However, during the development of the project, we realised that cultural and relational aspects ought to play an important role in the instruction, and these aspects were therefore included in the list of main objectives:

* broadening children's cultural knowledge by presenting English songs, rhymes, tales, stories and riddles;
* increasing children's linguistic skills, which are important for communication and understanding in an increasingly globalised world (Maagerø and Simonsen 2006).

Knowledge as prophylaxis

Development of intercultural understanding and positive mutual relations are important aims, not only in education, but also in general society. Following the Second World War, several specific efforts have been made to prohibit further conflicts. Pairing 'friendship cities' in different countries, developing student exchange programmes and summer camps for young people are examples of this kind of work. Moreover, exchange and development programmes in the EU system have given rise to even more possibilities in this area. Friendship across borders is supposed to foster knowledge, consciousness and reflection.

In recent decades more and more people have been moving away from their homes, either deliberately or because they have been affected by war and/or environmental problems. As Giddens (2000) points out, we live in a runaway world and this fact cannot be ignored. Bauman (2000) characterises people of today as being not nation bound, but rather ex-territorial. Meeting people from other cultural backgrounds is therefore a part of most people's everyday life. Lack of knowledge about other people will often give rise to a feeling of insecurity. Prejudice (in its extreme form, xenophobia) allows no possibility of bringing the world closer to better understanding. National educational systems have a tendency of both promoting ethnocentrism and 'othering' people from outside. The Norwegian anthropologist Marianne Gullestad (2002) claims that this is a challenge of the national order. When different cultures live side by side, not only does the minority culture have to change but also the majority culture.

Are Norwegian daycare centres prepared for the world of today? The national curriculum for daycare centres points out seven special basic areas for work in these institutions. One is *Communication, Language and Text*. The recommended working method is to develop a combination of *experience, reflection and feeling*.

Foreign language is not mentioned explicitly, but we claim that the Lillesand choice of presenting English language and culture is well grounded in this formulation.

Framing and developing cultural knowledge

There is a variety of definitions of culture. To us it represents all aspects of life, the totality of meanings, rituals, ideas and beliefs shared by individuals within a group of people. Culture in this respect also includes language, values, norms and customs.

We have stated the need for different cultural experiences and intercultural understanding, and we also believe that it is important to start challenging a mono-cultural perspective and development at an early age. The children attending Norwegian daycare centres will normally not travel around exploring the world or be forced to move because of war and natural disaster. Therefore, 'the world' must come to them. In higher education this is formalised and called 'Internationalisa-tion at Home'. We regard our project as being part of the same objective, albeit directed towards much younger 'students'.

How can cultural knowledge be described, and what does it look like in practice? Cultural knowledge is the interest in and the ability to communicate with people from other cultures. Not only does it have an intellectual side, it is also closely connected with emotions and cultural sensitivity. It is a discursive phenomenon, and may therefore be developed only through processes. As Habermas has taught us, only through participation is one able to understand other people's lifeworld (Habermas 1999).

Therefore, it is a question of being aware of and being able to handle differences. Differences are important because they lead to reflection. Let us remember what Piaget pointed out; real learning comes as a result of a *disturbed equilibrium*. He made a distinction between *assimilation* and *accommodation*. However, in order to develop cultural understanding, it is not enough merely to adjust and assimilate. You have to first enter into a state of true imbalance in order to leave the process having gained new knowledge. Herlitz (1992) uses the concept *culture grammar* to explain how cultural skills depend on an understanding of people living their lives inside different paradigms.

Is English 'other' enough?

Presenting English as a *foreign* language does not provoke many protests from the general public. And yet, is it truly another culture? For instance, travelling to England from Norway by plane takes only one hour, and our countries also share common literature, films and TV programmes – therefore, is there anything new to learn? Most importantly, are English and Norwegian children different from one another? We would answer affirmatively to these questions, as we feel that an encounter with a different culture is taking place, even if we are not talking about the Masai people of Kenya or other persons living in distant countries. While the rituals we intend to study will normally not be considered 'exotic' in nature, we may perhaps find elements of this as well. Our belief is that it is wise not to start with the greatest differences, because children need to use their own points of reference in the learning process (for example, you have to know beforehand that a pig says 'nøff-nøff' in Norway in order to find it interesting and funny that his cousin in England says 'oink-oink').

Furthermore, English instruction is part of a long tradition in the Norwegian school system. Over the course of the past five decades, English as a subject has moved from being offered during sixth form 'down' to the first form as dictated by the national curriculum. Some of the arguments presented in 1992 (when there was a shift from the fourth to the third form) were the following: the need for competence in English in the work for internationalisation and peace, and the growing tourism industry in Norway. The message is obvious; it is not only a question of learning a language, but communication skills and cultural aspects play an important part as well. We believe that when children learn one additional language and one new culture, this will have an exemplary effect. When children are further able to compare Norwegian and English cultures, they will probably be more conscious, more curious and more tolerant of others.

Correspondence regarding the curriculum for daycare centres

The intent of the project was to introduce English as a topic in kindergartens. We were absolutely aware of the fact that a lot of preschool teachers would raise a critical voice, almost like 'leave those children alone!' In Norway, schools and daycare centres are based on different traditions. The working methods in Norwegian daycare centres are constructed from a variety between unstructured and structured activities; Frøbel-oriented and child-centred. The English lessons are similar to *samlingsstund*, an organised gathering led by one of the adults. However, our project is not an attempt to make daycare centres more academic. The work we do is based on the children's terms as well as on the ideals, values and working methods from these centres. It is the intention that children will attend, but deliberately and by their own choice. Provoking the accepted system of daycare centres is not our interest; rather, it is the children upon whom we wish to focus.

'We all have tea' – meeting more than one context

When Polly is present, talking to and playing with the children, different discourses are running. In the concrete context of situation the children are challenged to understand what is happening, to say *yes* and *no* correctly and to find out what she calls the different things she is showing them. But there is also a circle outside, the more general context of culture (Halliday and Hasan 1985). Every context of situation is a realisation of a context of culture, showing how things are normally done in that culture. And every context of situation also influences the culture in a dynamic way so that the culture in the depth of time is changed through daily practices. Through the current situation the children get the information of how it is to be a child in England, that England is a place where tea is a popular drink, and where postmen in the countryside drive small, red cars. Parents in the kindergartens report that their son ordered food in a convincing way at restaurants when they were on holiday in England. He communicated with people, said hello and thank you, and seemed to be much more English than his elder siblings. It is obvious that their way into English had been mediated through Polly; one of the teachers had been to a seminar in England, and when she returned, a little girl asked: 'Did you meet Polly there?'

Teddy bears' birthday as cultural action

In addition to experience that animals talk different 'languages', the children also take part in cultural events – we may call it authentic, cultural situations. Children in Norway are acquainted with outdoor activities, but the way Norwegians behave is not similar to what Polly represents. Teddy bears play an important part in children's life in England. Rhymes, songs and actions contains lots of references to them. The children in Lillesand were included both in their birthdays and picnics, and they tasted special food connected to the celebrations. The Easter Bunny was also visiting Lillesand, and the baking of special Easter cakes gave a new dimension to the Norwegian Easter.

Children's culture in all countries often has a nostalgic image, and with Polly as an adult mediator, the result could easily be a presentation of children's activities of yesterday. Our opinion was that the content must include both old and new elements. Today, English TV programmes for children are more or less common culture for all children. Fireman Sam, Postman Pat and Bob the Builder are well known everywhere. However, the national adjustments through translation provoke discussion. Why does Bob have an English wife called Wendy and a Norwegian one called Wenche?

Real children far away

A growing interest from the teachers in Lillesand, and their cooperation with the project researchers, resulted in an application to the Comenius Programme in the European Union. Since the children are very young, staff exchange seemed to be the most reasonable option. The application resulted in a two-year programme together with preschools in Cáceres (Spain) and Belfast (Northern Ireland). The period has prompted many interesting discussions and excellent relationships. To underline the educational discussions the children should be included in the process. From the very beginning an aim was to develop relationships between children in the three countries. The crucial question is, however, how this can be done. Small children are not necessarily interested in children whom they have never met, and whom they cannot play with in concrete situations. We will present some of the methods which were exploited in the project.

In the three countries, a film was produced showing the children in their daily life activities. The perspectives are really challenged when the 4-year-olds in Belfast and Spain look at the Norwegian children climbing trees and working with knives and axes to prepare a bonfire. Conversely, the Norwegian children are impressed with the nice school uniforms and how even the small children go to 'real' schools in Belfast and Cáceres, and have desks, school bags and pencil boxes. And the adults, who through their teacher exchanges in the project have visited the different places, are able to add more information from their experiences. They can relate to the names of children and places and have additional stories about the schools and daycare centres to which they have been taken. This is important, because it is not obvious that the children should take an interest in these films only because they show children. The adults' task is to create an interesting context or frame for the children, to enter into a dialogue with them about the activities going on in the film, and to help them to focus on different phenomena which are of interest from a contrastive and cultural point of view. Through a scaffolding process (Bruner 1975; Vygotsky 1978) the children's attention and interest for 'the other' is developed. In this way more and more new pieces of the big puzzle to understand their mutual world fit together.

In Spain, a special film was created. Cáceres is a town with long and strong carnival traditions. Children are an important part of the carnival event which takes place every year, and carnival is considered both as a joint celebration where adults and children can be together in a positive way, and as a means of cultural learning and learning of traditions. In order to focus on the Irish and Norwegian culture the Spanish preschool teachers wanted to make a carnival procession where the children were dressed up like children in Ireland and Norway (e.g. skiers, Nordic animals, Vikings, line dancers), and where music from the two countries played a major role. The parents were involved in making costumes and other equipment which could be a symbol of the two countries. The national flags were painted and erected on posters. This activity became so popular that costumes and songs from other countries and also their home country were included in the planning. A large number of children dressed up and went singing and dancing through the streets of Cáceres on one special day. They were organised into groups dedicated to one country similar to the parade of the opening of the Olympic Games. The parents, friends and relatives were gathered along the route to see their children. The celebration was filmed by the preschool teachers, and this film was shown in the preschools in Belfast and in the daycare centres in Norway. To see the Spanish children dressed up in familiar clothes, and hear familiar music coming from Spain, gives a strong impression which raises many questions. On the other hand, the children in Spain learned a lot about Ireland and Norway during the whole process.

Another method which was used to establish contact among the children was to send postcards, letters and parcels to each other. The contact between the children in Northern Ireland, Norway and Spain started with a Christmas present to each daycare centre or preschool. The content was typical Christmas cards from the three different countries which the teachers could use in the activities in the daycare centres or in the preschools. In Norway, Polly integrated the Christmas cards in her work with English, comparing them with her British cards which the children had seen before, and with Norwegian cards which they were used to. The same process was repeated before Easter. This means cultural learning. However, the greetings from the children were as important as the cards themselves. In all three countries children had dictated Christmas greetings (later Easter greetings) to the children in the other countries. Together with drawings and photos the box from the other countries became a personal presentation of the other children which made them curious and excited, a good point of departure in getting to know 'the other'. The drawings in particular should be emphasised. When children draw, they demonstrate a cultural expression where some of their experiences are coded into a visual meaning-making system (Maagerø 2005). The drawings were on the one hand reflecting experiences which were different from the children's own experiences, in some cases even unknown, and therefore were new and challenging. On the other hand, they were personal in the sense that real children had made them in a meaning-making system which was well known to the children receiving them. The drawings were a symmetric contact in a higher sense than films, letters and cards which needed an adult as a mediator. This may be the reason for the special interest many children showed in connection with the drawings.

It is also important to emphasise that all children in the project both received and were engaged in creating boxes with presentations of themselves. The self-presentation was an inspiration to many discussions in the different institutions. What was typical, for example, for food, activities, books and places in daily life in daycare centres in Norway? Which Christmas cards are typically Norwegian? What do children in Norway do at Easter? Again we will stress the fact that questions such as these are important in the cultural learning of the children.

In the project, contact on the internet was planned as an important activity. The idea was that children might show pictures of themselves, of their life in kindergarten or preschool, of their town, their families and so on in closed rooms and that this medium could make frequent contact possible. Writing e-mails and using a web camera was also planned. This method has been used successfully in many school projects. This part of the process failed, however, in this project. The reason was mainly the lack of equipment which led to frustration among the teachers. In order to use this method, access to the web has to be a well-integrated possibility in the different institutions so that virtually daily contact can be realised, not only something which happens every second week. A week is a long time for small children, and interest and enthusiasm disappears if there is too little continuity in an activity. However, we believe that this kind of activity should be exploited among young children and that it can be very positive in the development of contact between the children.

Conclusion

In our project we have, as we interpret it, experienced that cultural learning across borders is possible for young children in daycare centres and preschools. By learning a foreign language as the children did in the local project 'Polly put the kettle on: English in kindergarten', they meet a different culture during the learning process, both through the language itself and through the activities related to the learning process. Language is a part of a culture, and ways of saying is ways of meaning in a culture (Hasan 1996). The way we realise language in different contexts also tells us about the culture where the language is realised. The texts, pictures, cards, films, figures, songs, games and so on all tell about a culture and make children pay attention to the culture's differences and similarities. In the meeting with other cultures, this last perspective – awareness of the self – is also of great importance. We interpret this insight, however, also as a beginning development of the awareness of the 'other' and of an opening of the world to young children.

In addition to this, we believe that the meeting with the children in Northern Ireland and Spain (and with the Norwegians for the children in those two countries) through film, music, photos, cards, letters and, not least, drawings make 'the other' real. The children have learned that there are children out there with shared interests, but who also experience other things than those which we do. They are there and it is possible to be in contact with them. This, we hope, will make children curious and understanding in their attitude to people whom they meet from different cultures in the future.

References

Bauman, Z. (2000) *Savnet felleskap*. Oslo: Cappelen.

Bruner, J. (1975) The ontogenesis of speech acts. *Journal of Child Education*, 2: 1–21.

Elvin, P., Maagerø, E. and Simonsen, B. (2007) How do the dinosaurs speak in England? English in kindergarten. *European Early Childhood Education Research Journal*, 15(1): 71–87.

Framework Plan for the Content and Tasks of Kindergartens in Norway (2006) Oslo: Ministry of Education.

Giddens, A. (2000) *En løbsk verden*. Copenhagen: Reitzel.

Gullestad, M. (2002) *Det norske sett med nye øyne*. Oslo: Universitetsforlaget.

Habermas, J. (1999) *Kommunikasjon, handling, moral og rett*. Oslo: Tano.

Halliday, M.A.K. and Hasan, R. (1985) *Language, Context, and Text: Aspects of Language in a Social-Semiotic Perspective*. Cambridge: Cambridge University Press.

Hasan, R. (1996) *Ways of Saying: Ways of Meaning*. London: Cassell.

Herlitz, G. (1992) *Kulturgrammatikk*. Holmestrand: Global.

Maagerø, E. (2005) Multimodal communication in a young child's compositions. In M. Asplund Carlsson, A. Løvland and G. Malmgren (eds) *Multimodality: Text, Culture and Use*. Kristiansand: Norwegian Academic Press.

Maagerø, E. and Simonsen, B. (2006) *Polly Put the Kettle on*. Engelsk i barnehagen. Oslo: Sebu forlag.

Singleton, D. (1989) *Language Acquisition: The Age Factor*. Cambridge: Cambridge University Press.

Singleton, D. (1999) *Exploring the Second Language Mental Lexicon*. Cambridge: Cambridge University Press.

Vygotsky, L. (1978) *Mind in Society*. Cambridge, MA: Harvard University Press.

8 Teachers supporting children's self-regulation in conflict situations within an early years setting

Sue Bingham and David Whitebread

This chapter presents the findings of the first phase of an action research project with children in a Bedfordshire nursery school, the aim of which was to investigate the extent to which 3- and 4-year-olds have the capacity to self-regulate their emotional and social behaviour within conflict situations in a classroom. The objective was to trial ways in which teachers can support young children's social and emotional self-regulation.

A range of interventions was introduced into the classroom over an academic year with the objective of scaffolding the children's emotional and social learning, including special 'feelings' circle times and a range of physical props within the environment to encourage self-regulated sharing and negotiation. A climate of open discussion had been incorporated into the everyday life of the classroom from early on, and the act itself of valuing the children's input was seen to have had its own positive effect on their self-esteem, independence and effectiveness. With the objective of 'measuring' the children's perceptions of their own competence and ability to exercise emotional control within social contexts, consultations with the children were carried out focusing on a 'conflict' situation.

In line with recent work concerned with developing a pedagogy for self-regulation in young children, the project supports the view that, given the opportunity and appropriate support, 3- to 4-year-olds show a capacity for considerable emotional and social self-regulation within conflict situations. However, for this to be achieved in practice, the building of trust and genuinely shared control must be established within the classroom between educators and children.

Introduction and background

> Human relationships, and the effects of relationships, are the building blocks of healthy development.
>
> (Shonkoff and Phillips 2000: 27)

Early years teachers are pivotal in shaping a young child's first experiences of being in a society outside the family and in scaffolding their learning to adapt, cope and succeed in emotionally and socially demanding situations. The child's early learning of particular 'rules' for the classroom or school essentially becomes the basic framework for ways of behaving in general life, in any group, where the needs and desires of others as well as oneself have to be taken into account and reflected in behaviour. This chapter reports a small piece of research in one early years classroom which explored the extent to which conflict situations may be used to promote young children's social and emotional learning.

Social and emotional competence in the early years classroom requires children to develop emotional regulation, social knowledge and understanding and specific social skills. A child's capacity for emotional self-regulation is essential to social competence and acceptance among peers because the skills of emotional control are necessary for managing aggressive impulses, responding appropriately to a peer's feelings, affirming friendships and cooperating within a group. Emotional self-regulation is also important for formal learning because capacities to follow instructions, focus attention and cooperate with teachers and peers in a classroom require feelings and behaviours to be managed.

Conflicts are common in 3- and 4-year-olds' peer relations (Parker and Gottman 1989; Shantz 1987), but they are rarely terminal to relationships, and children of this age do not regard conflict as incompatible with friendship (Shantz 1989). Because cooperative play occupies an increasingly central place in social relations, preschoolers tend to regulate their squabbles so that they do not undermine the broader purposes of working together. In this respect, peer social relations appear to evoke certain types of behaviour more frequently than do family contexts. Dunn (1988), for example, examined the use of reasoned argument by 3-year-olds at home with mother and siblings, and by the same children when alone with a close friend. It was found that conciliatory, reasoned argument was more common in peer conflicts (at 22 per cent) than in domestic strife (at 9 per cent). Not only does emotional understanding with peers enhance the incentive for pro-social behaviour and reduced aggressive conduct among preschoolers, it also contributes to the quality of social skills that elicit peer acceptance or rejection and fosters the emergence of lasting friendships in early childhood (Dunn and Herrara 1997). In this sense, rather than being an entirely negative experience, conflicts between young children can be an important source of emotional and social learning.

The key objective of the action research project reported in this chapter was to support children within a particular preschool setting in exercising control over their actions specifically within situations of conflict. Interactions between the children were certainly more friendly than unfriendly, but due to the limited understanding of emotion and others' experiences of emotion at the ages of 3 and 4, and the fact that they are still emotionally labile, nursery-aged children can become 'swamped' by emotions that temporarily dominate their attention and behaviours. This can lead to dramatic short-term fluctuations and eruptions in the course of interactions with both peers and adults. Recent research has shown, however, that young children are capable of developing greater self-regulation than previously thought in a number of areas of development (Bronson 2000; Whitebread *et al.* 2005). The current project explored the extent to which 3- and 4-year-old children's emotional and social self-regulation can be enhanced by supporting them in resolving common conflict situations within an educational setting.

An example of conflict: the problem of 'lining up'

During the course of this project, a number of conflict situations were identified and worked upon. As a consequence, a particular methodology was developed which is exemplified here in relation to one situation, the problem of 'lining up'. This methodology consisted of the following elements:

- detailed *observation* and *analysis* of the conflict situation, and the children's conflict behaviour;
- *presentation of the problem to the children*;
- *consultation with the children*, leading to some proposed solutions;
- further consultation and *evaluation* with the children as to the success of the revised procedures.

Observation and analysis

Video-recordings, tape-recordings and observations were made of the lining-up routines and the types of conflict observed were categorised, including 'power struggles' (e.g. wanting to be the 'leader' of the line), 'possession disputes' (e.g. 'I was there first' or 'That's my space') and 'mild physical aggression' (e.g. pushing or barging into the line).

Analysis of the observations of these behaviours revealed that children seemed to be confused about the objective behind lining up as well as the process of doing so. Some children evidently did not realise that they were supposed to go to the end of the line, some did not understand the concept of the 'end of the line', some children seemed to think they were being sensible by 'filling in' a gap in the line, not realising that others may see this as 'pushing in', and other children simply left huge spaces within the line for no discernible reason. Moreover, it was clear that, although the children used the term 'the end of the line' quite freely in telling each other how to queue up, many children had not yet grasped the concept of finding the intangible 'end', which led to many instances of 'pushing in'.

First of all, the staff discussed some options surrounding the routine of lining up, to see what would be workable and how the children's forthcoming discussion might need to be shaped. The alternatives included not lining up at all, but allowing the children to go down the stairs individually once they were ready, lining up in smaller groups, and whether there is any real benefit to the young child in learning to line up appropriately at this age. It was agreed that although most 3-year-olds are still quite egocentric and therefore often unable, perhaps, to understand the need to respect the validity of others' needs and desires before their own, queuing is a necessary social competence with whose rules even a 3-year-old child is expected to comply in the real world (e.g. at the supermarket checkout or the ice-cream van). It was concluded that the problem of lining up presented the children with an educationally valuable social and emotional problem.

Presentation of the problem to the children

Within the 'feelings' circle time of the two weeks leading up to the 'Discussion Week', the focus had been upon 'being fair' in terms of treating other people as the children like to be treated themselves. During 'lining up' time after circle time one morning, a situation was stage-managed where the teacher commented on how many faces displaying 'negative feelings' could be seen and heard: some children in the line looked cross, some sad and some children were even shouting or crying. The question was posed 'What does this show?' One or two children said it showed that there was a problem, so the teacher asked what could be done about it. The children suggested talking about it, so everyone went back into the classroom and reformed the circle.

Consultation with the children

Analysis of the transcript of the consultation reveals that initially, the focus of the discussion time was on clarifying the objectives behind lining up. The reasons for going to the end of the line, what in fact constitutes 'the end of the line' or 'a gap' in the line, and the term 'pushing in' were all clarified through discussion.

JT: We could all go to the back of the line and if there's too much people, some people could go over there [*pointing*] so we could have a bigger line.

Teacher: Good idea, James . . . I think you said you didn't want the line to be too squashy, so we could make the line longer, with enough space for everyone. Was that your idea, James?

JT: Yeah.

Teacher: So people aren't squashed?

JT: Yeah. We could leave a gap if someone wants to be in the middle.

Teacher: Hmmm. Gaps in the line make us muddled up. Sometimes when children come out from the loo, they see a gap and go into it. They think it looks like the end of the line and they get muddled up.

IS: Then some children might tell them they are pushing in.

JT: But we don't want our friends to be squashed.

Teacher: No, we don't.

HW: How about if we just made a little space in between each person? [*General 'yes' noises*]

Teacher: Shall I write that on our page of ideas? OK. . . . Just a little space between each person in the line, so we aren't squashed.

IS: Not big gaps though.

Teacher: OK. [*Writes*] No big gaps in the line.
EMc: When we squash people we might fall over.
FC: We might fall over when we're walking. You might bump your head or get blood.
IS: I hear people saying 'Ow, that's squashy'.

In response to the issue about 'pushing in', one boy suggested having an 'end of the line person', to point out where there were gaps in the line and direct those children joining it where to stand.

JT: If you were in a line and someone took your place . . . [*hesitates*]
Teacher: If someone took your place by mistake, do you mean, James?
JT: [*Does not want to continue*]
Teacher: OK, well if someone took your space by mistake, what could we do?
ET: Tell them to go somewhere else.
Teacher: Hmm. Maybe we could just remind that person that they need to go to the end of the line. Using our words.
IS: Not the front.
Teacher: No – but how does that person know where the end of the line is?
TE: The person on the list can tell all the children where the end of the line is!
Teacher: I see! You mean the person whose name is on the list to have their turn at the end of the line can tell everyone coming to join the line 'This is the end of the line. I am the last person today!' Is that right Tim?

The children also decided that they wanted a line on the floor in the corridor, to mark where the front of the line was:

IS: Maybe we need something to show all the children where is the front of the line too. 'Cos some children can't read their names like me.
Teacher: Another good idea. I wonder what we could do?
HW: We could make a sign.
Teacher: Yes we could.
GC: We draw a line on the floor like when we do the sweeping up when it gets sand on the floor. We could use the chalk.
WD: No – chalk goes away.
Teacher: Hmm. Yes, if all the children's feet walked on the chalk line it might get rubbed off.
GC: We could use a teacher's pen so it don't come off.
FW: We could put a sticker on the place.

It was agreed that the fairest way would be take turns at being 'the leader' of the line. The children asked that a list of the class be put on the wall and the names ticked off as each child had a turn day by day, so that they could see whose turn was next:

Teacher: I wonder how we could remember whose turn is next, so we don't forget or miss anyone out by mistake?

IS: Write it down!

Teacher: Oh, I heard another good idea then . . .

IS: I said it!

HW: We could do the register!

TE: We could have one register for the front and one for the back.

Teacher: Would that be a fair way to sort it out, Tim? [*He nods*] Yes, because some people like being at the back of the line and they want their turn.

HW: And one for the middle.

Teacher: There are lots of people to go in the middle, Henry, aren't there?

HW: [*After a little while*] . . . Yes but only one leader and only one back leader.

Teacher: So, we're going to have a list of all the nursery children's names, so we can see whose turn it is to be the leader every day and we'll be able to see who has already had a turn and whose turn it is tomorrow. And another list for the back of the line. Does that seem a fair way to do it?

Evaluation

After several days of trying out the new system of lining up, a second, impromptu consultation took place in which the ideas the children had come up with were assessed in the light of their implementation. This discussion came about when one of the adults spotted the 'leader' of the line for that day walking along the line counting the children. When she asked what he was counting, he replied that he was counting 'smiley faces'! The idea of counting 'smiley faces' as a measure of the successful implementation of the new system was stunning in its simplicity and logic! The assessment of there being a problem with lining up in the first place had been to look with the children at how many faces were showing 'negative feelings' within the line-up. Counting faces showing happy feelings was a direct extension of the same idea and one which the children themselves could effect, making the measuring of success immediate and relevant.

Discussion

In line with recent work concerned with developing a pedagogy for self-regulation in young children (Whitebread and Coltman 2007), this project supported the view that, given the opportunity and appropriate support, 3- to 4-year-olds show a clear capacity for considerable emotional and social self-regulation. Key to the success of the intervention developed here was the identification, through careful observation, of a problem which was meaningful to the children and the development of a process which supported the children themselves in articulating the nature of the problem and devising strategies aimed at its resolution.

The evolution of a specific style of interaction based on trust between children and adults was the bedrock for taking the step from theory into practice in this action research project. It enabled the children to express their ideas, thoughts and feelings openly and coherently, deciding for themselves the direction and content of their work and conversation, working in partnership with adults in a climate of shared control. The 'lining-up' consultations encapsulate in microcosm the essence of independent learning; the degree of autonomy and ownership by the children of their own learning, together with the practice of adults scaffolding the learning processes for the child. It was evident that the children understood the process of consultation was to be reflective: everyone's view was important and there may not be just one 'right' answer to the problem. The ideas suggested by the children reveal a high degree of enthusiasm, originality and inventiveness.

Through the process of consulting with children about their attitudes and behaviour, some of the autonomy and responsibility which adults recognise as being critical within the domain of emotional and social development of young children was handed directly to them. The children seemed motivated by the challenge of finding a solution to the problems themselves, because they were real to them. Moreover, these conversations with children, where they, and not the adults, did most of the talking, have provided evidence of their responses to learning and to experiences. The very act of articulating ideas and understandings, of putting into words how they could go about things and what they wanted to do in the future revealed so much about their learning – what they found important and interesting, what strategies they used for making sense of the world – and even some misunderstandings.

In the process, the children learned that rules can protect as well as restrict and help a community to regulate itself. The consultation approach highlighted succinctly the relationship between individual and group self-regulation. The consultation process also appeared very effectively to bind the children together emotionally and socially, creating a real sense of community. The children also listened well to each other during each consultation process, which gave everyone time to reflect on what was being discussed. On several occasions, for example, one child endorsed and developed an idea or point of view expressed by another. Underlying the success of this whole approach, however, and perhaps most importantly, was the building of a relationship of trust and genuinely shared control between the adult educators and the children.

References

Bronson, M.B. (2000) *Self-regulation in Early Childhood; Nature and Nurture*. New York: Guilford Press.

Dunn, J. (1988) *The Beginnings of Social Understanding*. Cambridge, MA: Harvard University Press.

Dunn, J. and Herrara, C. (1997) Conflict resolution with friends, siblings and mothers: a developmental perspective. *Aggressive Behaviour*, 23: 343–357.

Parker, J.G. and Gottman, J.M. (1989) Social and emotional development in a relational context. In *Meta-emotion: How Families Communicated Emotionally*. Mahwah, NJ: Erlbaum.

Shantz, C.U. (1987) Conflicts between children. *Child Development*, 58: 283–505.

Shonkoff, J.P. and Phillips, D.A. (eds) (2000) *From Neurons to Neighbourhoods: The Science of Early Childhood Development*. Washington, DC: National Academies Press.

Whitebread, D. and Coltman, P. (2007) Self-regulation in young children. In J. Moyles (ed.) *Beginning Teaching: Beginning Learning* (3rd edn). Milton Keynes: Open University Press.

Whitebread, D., Anderson, H., Coltman, P., Page, C., Pino-Pasternak, D. and Mehta, S. (2005) Developing independent learning in the early years. *Education 3–13*, 33(1): 40–50.

9   'Just like having a best friend'

How babies and toddlers construct relationships with their key workers in nurseries

Liz Brooker

The recent growth in numbers of children entering daycare settings at a very young age has prompted concerns about the well-being of babies and toddlers. The study presented here explores the ways in which staff in one setting support young children's well-being during transitions. The data include observations of children under 3 during the first ten weeks of their attendance at a children's centre and concurrent interviews with their parents and key workers. Findings reveal the ways in which relationships are formed between small children and their key workers, and the ways in which both parents and practitioners understand this relationship. In every instance, it is the child's own preferences and prior experiences which shape the relationship with their key worker, so that the description given by one key worker – 'just like having a best friend really' – is seen as indicating the child's own agency in constructing a relationship which helps her or him to experience satisfaction and to feel a sense of belonging in the setting. Observations of the children suggest that, as a result, even the youngest children can be empowered to explore and exploit all the opportunities and affordances of their environment and to develop peer relationships which support their continued involvement in activities.

Introduction

The description 'I would say it's just like having a best friend' was offered to me in an interview with a key worker in a babies' room in response to the question, 'How would you describe the relationship you have with your key child?' The response surprised me – I had anticipated something, if not more 'motherly', then more 'adult', suggesting a responsibility of care for the child, rather than a relationship of equality and reciprocity. However, as I continued my research in this children's centre, it began to make sense. This chapter describes the ways in which relationships of care and friendship were constructed by the young children in the study and the adults who looked after them. It emphasises both the agency shown by very young children in this matter and the ways adults found to respect the children's wishes.

The chapter first discusses some key issues to be considered when children under age 3 enter group care. The impact on children's sense of identity as they encounter a new environment and new relationships, at a time when their sense of self is still evolving, needs careful consideration if positive rather than negative outcomes are to be ensured. These 'outcomes' concern the child's feelings of well-being and belonging, and inform all the supportive structures that professionals aim to provide as young children move into new settings. Meanwhile, the nature of 'care' and the caring relationship remains a contested issue (Dahlberg and Moss 2005; Tronto 1993).

The chapter goes on to discuss findings from this small-scale study of the ways in which children aged from birth to 3 establish relationships with their key worker that suit their own needs and the ways in which practitioners' expertise supports and enables this process.

Key issues in early transitions

Early relationships: early identities

Young children's construction of a personal, social and cultural identity begins at birth or earlier, and the nature and outcomes of their early interactions with caregivers have been extensively documented (Schaffer 1996; Trevarthen 1998; Woodhead 2007). The sense of self which evolves through reciprocal engagements with their caregivers enables children to understand their own separate nature and their own agency in relation to others and to the inanimate world of objects. Some infants may enter a rapidly widening circle of acquaintances during their early days and weeks of life, while others remain within a small family nucleus, but the infant's experience provides her with her earliest understanding of the world she inhabits and with continually developing hypotheses and expectations about its nature and stability (Cole and Cole 1989; Schieffelin and Ochs 1986). All children, except those in exceptionally adverse circumstances, will develop a sense of belonging within their own family environment, which is fashioned to accommodate them and which, in turn, accommodates itself to them as they grow and acquire mastery of their surroundings.

Early moves into group care

Despite cultural variations in caregiving (Rogoff 1990), children in both pre-industrial and post-industrial societies have typically spent their early years in the care of family members and, for the most part, in family homes or in the local community. Only in the past half-century has out-of-home care been offered to children from an early age and only in the past decade has it become the norm in many societies, including in the UK, where public policy now encourages mothers to enter or re-enter the workforce before their children are 3 years old. The impact of these early transitions into group care has only recently engaged researchers, although the long-term effectiveness of educational provision from the age of 3 is now demonstrated (Sylva *et al.* 2004). Public policy in this field appears to derive its rationale as much from the benefits which will flow to parents and the economy, as from the demonstrable benefits to young children. It is for this reason, and in order to assure the most desirable outcomes for babies and young children, that a focus on the quality of early relationships in group care is needed.

Care as a concept

There has been a struggle in recent years to describe the relationship between 'care' and 'education' for preschool children: grounds for the debate are still shifting. Most practitioners as well as policy-makers will agree that care and education are inseparable but that the 'caring' aspect of the provision leads the 'educating' aspect in the case of children under 3. At the same time, the whole concept of 'care' as an instrumental or technical service, in which one individual (generally older, more experienced or more competent) has responsibility for the physical needs of another, has been challenged by feminist writers such as Tronto (1993) and by those who have reconceptualised early childhood services (Dahlberg and Moss 2005). Early childhood professionals 'care' for their children in more senses than this and the relationships they construct with children are based on mutual feelings of affection and pleasure, as well as on custodial responsibilities.

The 'care' relationship, it is increasingly recognised, is a triangular one constructed for the mutual benefit of the child, the parent and the practitioner. It may include a strong emphasis on nappy-changing, feeding and sleep routines but it will also describe the ways in which the child communicates her wishes, interests and feelings – and these feelings will almost certainly include 'caring' for her main caregivers. Identifying the contributions of children to this 'triangle of care' (Hohmann 2007) allows us to move away from the idea of a service provided *by* adults *for* babies and young children towards an understanding of a co-constructed social environment.

The nature of transitions

Transitions, as Bronfenbrenner (1979: 26) has argued, involve not simply a change of location or environment but also a change of role and identity. For a young child, new roles and relationships may radically challenge some aspects of her emergent identity. The outcomes may be positive, in the form of a more multifaceted and conscious 'self' who can reflect on her existence in more than one environment and with more than one array of relationships, but such a successful outcome requires strong links and continuities to be created and sustained during the transition period. For the youngest children, the most important of these links will be the relationships established with their new caregivers.

Research on children's transitions has contributed some helpful descriptors for the outcomes which demonstrate children's *well-being*, which is understood both as a short-term goal and as a vital precursor to their longer term development. Two phrases continually recurred during the fieldwork for this study: that of Laevers *et al.* (1997), who adopt Bourdieu's and Wacquant's (1992: 127) image of children who 'belong' being like a 'fish in water'; and that of Broström (2002: 52), who describes the well-integrated child as 'feeling suitable' in her setting. These evocative phrases aptly describe the babies and toddlers who established successful caring relationships with the adults in the nursery environment.

Relationships and friendships

A number of empirical studies have demonstrated the key role of relationships in early transitions into educational settings. Transitions of this kind (such as that from preschool to school) have been described as essentially a process of relationship formation (Pianta and Cox 1999) and the links between systems, which underpin Bronfenbrenner's ecological systems theory (1979), consist in the main of human links between micro-systems. For young children, whose principal micro-systems may be home, preschool and school, these links take several forms, including visits to and from homes and settings by each of the parties involved. Research (Broström 2002; Entwisle and Alexander 1998) indicates that most nurseries, preschools and schools employ at least some of these strategies for scaffolding the transition process. With very young children, such as those in this study, a 'settling period' of two weeks or more is common, during which the child can access both her familiar and her 'new' caregivers simultaneously.

A smaller number of studies have focused specifically on the role of friendships in supporting children's transitions. With few exceptions, these studies indicate that children who make a move along with existing friends settle more easily in their new environment, suffer fewer negative feelings and 'recover' from the transition and pick up the threads of their development more quickly (Brooker 2002; Corsaro *et al.* 2003; Peters 2000). Friendship, however, is understood in these studies as an existing relationship between peers, rather than a new relationship with an adult: hence my initial surprise at the idea of an adult who aspires to be the 'best friend' of an infant who has made the transition into her care.

The study

The fieldwork for this study was conducted in an inner-city children's centre which offers extended-day childcare for children from 6 months to 5 years. Childcare is organised in three age ranges: 'babies' for children from 6 to 24 months, 'toddlers' for children aged 24 to 36 months, and 'kindergarten' for children aged 36 to 60 months.

Children who were making a transition into each of the three phases were selected for the study. Three children aged 7 to 18 months, three aged 24 to 27 months, and six aged 36 to 39 months were identified by the staff, and the parents of all the children gave written consent to their participation (the children's own consent to participation had to be judged on a daily basis by the researcher). The 'babies' moved into a suite of spaces catering for up to 12 children, where each key worker was responsible for up to three key infants, and the 'toddlers' into a parallel set of spaces catering for up to 24 children, where each key worker looked after up to six key children. 'Kindergarten' children were in key groups of ten children within larger classrooms.

Ethnographic observations, with the purpose of building a picture of the everyday life and culture of the nursery, were interspersed with more focused observations. Each of the children was observed repeatedly for periods of 15 to 20 minutes, usually by means of an unstructured narrative but sometimes using the Leuven observational format (Laevers 1994). Semi-structured interviews were conducted with the children's parents and key workers.

After all the data had been transcribed, a series of categories emerging from the observations was developed and then refined by reference to the interview transcripts. The emergent categories described a range of contributions to the children's adaptation and their construction of new relationships and a new identity in the setting. These contributory factors included the child's own actions, the behaviours of key workers and family members, and the actions of peers.

Making relationships

Observations of the children, and interviews with the adults in their lives, suggested the wide range of key worker relationships available to the child; the similarities to, and differences from, parental relationships; the contributions made to the relationship by all three participants in this triangular relationship of care; and the contribution of this relationship to the child's sense of belonging and well-being in the new setting.

'Not like a parent'

None of the key workers in this centre felt that their own *relationship* with their key children in any way resembled a parent's, although they acknowledged that their *roles* – feeding, changing, comforting, playing, getting to sleep – were often essentially similar to those of parents. Although the key workers (KW) acknowledged the intimacy of the tasks they undertook with the child, and even referred to the fact that the child might spend more of her waking hours in their care than in parental care, they still felt that there were significant differences in the relationships they formed.

> 'We are definitely not a parent: they are there for them 24 hours a day but we are just providing a service. . . . They see us as a friend, as educators, as another human being who is helping them and whom they can play with' [KW: Kindergarten].

This particular (male) key worker expresses, like many of his colleagues, what we might call the 'view from the child': key workers' responsibilities are to be available when the child needs a playmate, a comforter, a help-mate or an emotional support, rather than to be either a constant presence, or someone who can demand reciprocal attention:

'He just comes to me for comfort, if he gets upset; and sometimes if he's coming in from the garden, he'll just call my name and just check that I'm there, so I suppose it's just that bit of security . . . he doesn't spend much time with me during the day but he'll always call my name when he comes in and, if I pop my head round, I'll say "You OK?" and he'll say "Yeah" and he might go back off out again; but I do feel we've built up a good kind of relationship' [KW: Toddlers].

'I'd like to think I'm their friend. I use this quite a lot, if they're upset, I say "Would you like a little cuddle? I know my cuddle's not as good as mummy's cuddle but I can give you my cuddle now and then we'll wait and mummy will come and she'll give you a nice big cuddle"' [KW: Toddlers].

'I think if you had to put a name to it I would say it's just like having a best friend. Somebody that you can go to, somebody that you know is always going to be there for you' [KW: Babies].

All the key workers' accounts suggested that the nature of the relationships was shaped by the child's own wishes: that some children wish for more explicit and visible shows of affection and attention, whereas others prefer to maintain their independence. In this respect, it is clear that the adults' professional role requires them to be less demanding of the children themselves than a parent might be, though several acknowledged how devastating it can be to say goodbye to a child when it is time for the next transition.

Children's individual preferences

However young the children are, their key workers describe them as individuals with strong personal preferences rather than as generic 'children' for whom particular professional strategies are required. These impressions are often formed during the home visit which precedes the child's first visit to the nursery, as these extracts suggest:

'He was quite interested with what I brought, because we take a bag of toys and he was quite happy playing with the musical instruments and things like that, so that's something he appeared very keen on, so I thought if I needed anything that would be my key for Billy, that he is interested in sounds and music' [KW: Babies].

'We had quite a bit of interaction: he was interested and curious about what I had in the bag. . . . So I sat on the floor and just did some play-partnering, just to get to know him, and I had the opportunity then to talk to him as well, just about the routine of the day' [KW: Toddlers].

'He knew I was coming to talk to him about going to nursery, so he seemed quite happy to have us there and to share his toys, and he showed me his bedroom. I was interested in just seeing what Jack wanted to show me during the home visit, his kind of favourite things' [KW: Toddlers].

In the settling-in period too, respondents emphasised the importance of following, rather than leading, the child's interests. An additional member of staff is drafted into each room at this time so that the new child's key worker can observe her continuously and offer one-to-one attention as needed:

'Obviously I was with her on those days and there was more one to one, I was play-partnering her and most of the time we played in the home corner. We play-partner them for the first week' [KW: Kindergarten].

This close attention is a means to discover the child's preferences, both for activities and for personal relationships:

'He showed a lot of confidence: he quite happily explored different areas of the room, and actually he loved being outdoors . . . he was showing lots of interest in the environment.

I suppose I see myself as a security, a sort of emotional security. Davey is not a very tactile child whereas other children are, they want to be on your lap' [KW: Toddlers].

In each case the key worker, in conjunction with the child's parents, has tried to interpret their wishes and respond with the kind of relationship that meets their needs. To some extent these differences are age-related, with older children relying more on peer friendships and less on their key adult. To some extent, they reflect family and cultural experiences (as in the case of a Chinese child from a large family who was used, as her mother confirmed, to seeing to her own needs) and to some extent they reflect the child's own strategies for adaptation. As one key worker pointed out, 'They have different uses for you'. She went on:

'I think you do have different relationships, because someone like Liam especially is quite independent . . . then Hana I had to work very hard at, so that was a very different relationship' [KW: Babies].

These different 'uses' may follow different patterns: some of the children begin with a close attachment to their key worker and only gradually relinquish it, while others take time to request and construct an overtly affectionate bond. In the case of the Chinese child, her key worker reports:

'If you tried to pat her, she would push your hand away: she didn't want it. But now, if you go up to her and touch her – a little rub on her cheek or a little tickle – it really brings a smile to her face. She's got this smile, so that's a really big thing that's moved on and she'll often come and lean against my leg, or she'll bring a chair to sit beside me, and the conversation is starting to build as well' [KW: Toddlers].

Similarly for Davey who was 'not very tactile' when he started settling in:

'Davey doesn't come for that kind of attention, but just recently he has started to. He just runs up, puts his arm round my leg, and then just runs off again. I do enjoy picking children up and having a cuddle but it has to be very much on their terms . . . it's just reading the situation' [KW: Toddlers].

Children's initiatives: adults' responses

Observations undertaken over the three-month period reveal many instances of young children making overtures to adults in the setting and taking the initiative in choosing activities and pursuing relationships. Staff are adept at waiting for the child to show intentions in this way and responding to these intentions, as Liam's encounter with his key worker demonstrates:

'Liam picks up a Bob-the-builder doll as he enters the room and approaches Lillian to show her. Lillian responds with interest and he collects more soft toys, presenting them to her and awaiting her comments (e.g. "This one looks like an owl, doesn't he?"). He attends carefully to these responses and continues until they have examined several soft toys together. He continues to lead the activity and interaction for the next few minutes, jiggling up and down so that Lillian will copy him, which she does, and they end up jiggling together' [Observation: Babies].

At 8 months old, Billy can initiate a satisfying activity with another member of staff:

'Billy is sitting in a little chair sucking his toast while adults talk. Suddenly he notices Jacintha's nails (which are very long, sparkly, orange, and plastic) and starts to play with them. Jacintha offers her hand and he plays with each finger and all fingers with noisy amusement, pulling at each nail and giggling, separating each finger for a separate attempt' [Observation: Babies].

A few days later, this staff member is observed, still slightly behind and to the side of the child, unobtrusively accompanying his play without seeking to influence it:

'Jacintha deposits Billy gently on the mat by the sounds baskets. He immediately selects a long plastic-coated chain and sucks it. Jacintha sits alongside him and slightly behind; he sometimes leans towards her, otherwise is obviously aware of her presence at his side, but is independent' [Observation: Babies].

Hana: a case study

Hana has a Danish father and a Greek mother and has travelled all over Europe visiting members of her extended family during her short life. She was abroad when her home visit was booked, so her 'induction' took place on the first day of the settling-in period. On that day, in Lillian's words, 'she didn't depend on her mum, and mum said she'd been left before and she's very happy, and mum didn't foresee any problems with her'.

This did not prove to be the case once the separation process began. Lillian reported that 'Mum stayed with her for the first few days but was quite keen to go . . . but I did say we need to judge this by Hana'. In the event, Hana became increasingly distressed on parting every morning and periodically throughout the day. Lillian and her colleagues had recourse to a number of strategies for helping her to link home and nursery and providing her with resources which would comfort and reassure her, but many of these strategies required close cooperation with her family, which was not always forthcoming. One of the first problems was with the actual 'goodbyes': the nursery insists that parents always say goodbye to their child but both Hana's mother and father sometimes 'snuck out' as the staff described it, denying the child any opportunity to come to terms with their departure.

Among the transitional objects the staff find effective are favourite toys from home and family photos, and both of these were helpful to Hana, so long as her parents remembered them:

'She started asking for Bear quite a bit, which we asked mum to bring in but, unfortunately, she kept forgetting, so we ended up having to phone her, and mum would bring it in and leave it at reception, and that seemed to ease her a little bit. We'd phone her up and say she's distressed, could you bring the bear in, but you'd be going all morning, without the bear, and it just appeared at lunchtime.'

There was a long delay too before the family photos were produced, but when they were, 'It was literally just like a magic button!'

'She carried them around – she's very close to Dad – she carried his photograph around with her that day, and literally she went to sleep with the photograph in her hand; so what I did, I actually had it scanned so it was always accessible for her . . . and from then she seemed to settle in.'

Once reconciled to the separation, and reassured by the routines, Hana transformed herself into one of the most active, engaging and sociable children in the babies' area. Her relationship with Billy brought pleasure to them both – this observed moment is typical:

> 'Hana is passing Billy, who has a basket of sounds objects, and decides to stop and sit down with him. She squats and then kneels a short distance from him, and picks up two metal jar-lids, which she bangs together experimentally. She then repeats the action with more intention and pleasure and begins to interact teasingly with Billy, who looks at her with interest. She continues to bang, pause, look, tease and turn-take with Billy and both giggle' [Observation: Babies].

On another occasion Billy reaches out for her from the safety of his cushioned support in the garden and strokes her hair, while she obediently bows her head to allow him; and it was not uncommon to see the two of them simply grinning and giggling at each other – as Lillian reported, 'He seems to find Hana hysterically funny!'

After five weeks, Hana appeared fully settled and demonstrated her confidence daily in exploring all the areas, all the activities and all the resources the environment offered her. As Lillian pointed out, she had even begun to 'escape' from the babies' area: 'She also ventures over into Toddlers occasionally which is good, it shows she's not relying on the familiar adults she's got here.'

Conclusion: an ethic of care

As Dahlberg and Moss (2005: 1) affirm, pedagogy must be understood as 'a relation, a network of obligation', and the pedagogical relationship is one which requires 'infinite attention to the other'. This attention should not have the aim of making the 'other' like ourselves but should allow the other – even the small child – to develop independently as an individual with rights and desires of their own. Genuine 'ethics of care' for young children require adults to take their cue from the children: to watch and wait and respond to their preferences, rather than to 'know what they need'. When this ethical pedagogy is offered, children like Hana, Billy and Davey are able to show their caregivers the kind of care, and education, they require. We can learn from them.

References

Bourdieu, P. and Wacquant, L. (1992) *Invitation to Reflexive Sociology*. Bristol: Polity Press.

Bronfenbrenner, U. (1979) *The Ecology of Human Development*. Cambridge, MA: Harvard University Press.

Brooker, L. (2002) *Starting School: Young Children Learning Cultures*. Buckingham: Open University Press.

Broström, S. (2002) Communication and continuity in the transition from kindergarten to school. In H. Fabian and A-W. Dunlop (eds) *Transitions in the Early Years*. London: RoutledgeFalmer.

Cole, M. and Cole, S. (1989) *The Development of Children*. New York: Scientific American Books.

Corsaro, W., Molinari, L., Hadley, K. and Sugioka, H. (2003) Keeping and making friends: Italian children's transition from preschool to elementary school. *Social Psychology Quarterly*, 66(3): 272–291.

Dahlberg, G. and Moss, P. (2005) *Ethics and Politics in Early Childhood Education*. London: RoutledgeFalmer.

Entwisle, D. and Alexander, K. (1998) Facilitating the transition to first grade: the nature of transition and research on factors affecting it. *Elementary School Journal*, 98(4): 351–364.

Hohmann, U. (2007) Rights, expertise and negotiations in care and education. *Early Years*, 27(1): 33–46.

Laevers, F. (1994) *The Leuven Involvement Scale for Young Children*. Leuven: Centre for Experiential Education.

Laevers, F., Vandenbussche, E., Kog, M. and Depondt, L. (1997) *A Process-oriented Child Monitoring System for Young children*. Leuven: Katholieke Universiteit.

Peters, S. (2000) *Multiple Perspectives on Continuity in Early Learning and the Transition to School*. Unpublished paper, EECERA, London.

Pianta, R. and Cox, M. (eds) (1999) *The Transition to Kindergarten*. Baltimore, MD: Paul Brookes.

Rogoff, B. (1990) *Apprenticeship to Learning*. Oxford: Blackwell.

Schaffer, H.R. (1996) *Social Development*. Oxford: Blackwell.

Schieffelin, B. and Ochs, E. (1986) *Language Socialization Across Cultures*. New York: Cambridge University Press.

Sylva, K., Melhuish, E.C., Sammons, P., Siraj-Blatchford, I. and Taggart, B. (2004) *The Effective Provision of Pre-school Education (EPPE) Project: Technical Paper 12 – The Final Report*: Effective Pre-school Education. London: DfES/Institute of Education, University of London.

Trevarthen, C. (1998) The child's need to learn a culture. In M. Woodhead, D. Faulkner and K. Littleton (eds) *Cultural Worlds of Early Childhood*. London: RoutledgeFalmer.

Tronto, J. (1993) *Moral Boundaries: A Political Argument for the Ethics of Care*. London: Routledge.

Woodhead, M. (2007) *Changing Perspectives on Early Childhood: Theory, Research and Policy*. Paper commissioned for the EFA Global Monitoring Report 2007, Strong Foundations.

10 Co-constructing meaning

Differences in the interactional micro-climate

Jan Georgeson

This chapter draws on the findings of a research project conducted in a range of early years settings in England with the aim of investigating the development of ways in which children and staff build meanings together. The project was designed from a sociocultural theoretical perspective and drew on aspects of Bernstein's theory of pedagogic discourse as tools for analysing organisational culture. It used a combination of quantitative and qualitative analyses in the context of comparative case studies of four preschool settings in the West Midlands. Two of these settings could be characterised as having a hierarchical organisational style, while two had a more open, organic style of organisation. Two had explicitly educational aims while two prioritised care and social relationships. Through analysis of children's utterances as they looked at photographs of preschool activities, the project demonstrated that different interactional micro-climates existed in the four settings and that these differences could be linked to the difference in organisation and pedagogical emphasis. In particular, the ways in which children built up meanings together differed between the settings, and the findings suggested that settings that prioritised care and socialisation fostered an interactive micro-climate which was more favourable to co-construction than those which emphasised educational outcomes.

Introduction

Early years provision in the UK is characterised by diversity both within and between the four constituent countries. In England, the introduction of funding for preschool places between 1996 and 2004 has been accompanied by a unified inspection regime and a common educational framework. All children aged 3 years and over are now entitled to government funding for some form of preschool education but this can take place in a wide variety of settings – schools, homes, village halls, purpose-built nurseries – which span public, private and voluntary sectors and include sessional and full-day care. There is a corresponding bewilderment of qualifications held by staff working in early years settings although recent initiatives have sought to introduce clearer career paths. Therefore, although all children are working towards the same early learning goals (Qualifications and Curriculum Authority 2000), their early years experiences can differ markedly.

The research project investigated subtle differences in children's learning experience between different early years settings in England, with particular emphasis on differences in ways in which staff and children make meanings together. The project was designed from a sociocultural theoretical perspective and investigated settings as distinct subcultures of pedagogy (Payler 2005), using aspects of Bernstein's theory of pedagogic discourse (1990, 2000) as tools for analysis.

For insights into how we might trace the origins of children's understanding of how to use language in the specific context of the classroom, I have drawn on some of the concepts that have emerged from research in systemic functional linguistics (SFL). Using SFL, Hasan has carried out fine-grained analyses of children's early experiences of interacting with adults to show how everyday exchanges shape children's orientation to meaning within their own sociocultural contexts: 'through semiotic mediation in local environments we learn ways of being, doing and saying which are intelligible to others in our speech community' (Hasan 2005: 138). She has drawn attention to the implications this has for children's capacity to read their way into the practices of formal schooling. This work had been extended to show how parents' ways of interacting with their children can constitute 'semiotic preparation for schooling' (Painter 1999) and how everyday routines and practices in the early years of schooling introduce children to different pedagogic genres (Christie 2002).

To describe differences in pedagogic culture between settings, I have made use of concepts from Bernstein's theory of the pedagogic device (Bernstein 1990: 180–204, 2000: 13 and 32). This is the set of 'rules or procedures via which knowledge is converted into pedagogic communication' and pedagogic discourse 'is the set of rules for the embedding of two discourses; namely a discourse of competence (discipline specific knowledge) into a discourse of social order' (Singh 2002: 573 and 576). I have also called upon the distinction between classification and framing:

> classification refers to what, framing is concerned with how meanings are to be put together, the forms by which they are to be made public and the nature of the social relationships that go with it. . . . Framing is about who controls what.
>
> (Bernstein 1996: 27)

In the context of preschool provision, instructional discourse (ID), the discourse of competence, refers to aims, activities, assessments and outcomes associated with school subject knowledge and skills, which are encapsulated for most settings in the early learning goals. Regulative discourse (RD), the discourse of social order, refers to the often tacit understandings about relationships between actors in pedagogic institutions. Instructional and regulative discourses are described as 'embedded', signalling that, although we might tease the two discourses apart analytically, in any pedagogic exchange both are in play and operate together. According to Bernstein's analysis, strong framing generally gives rise to a visible pedagogy with explicit ID and RD, whereas weak framing gives rise to an invisible pedagogy with implicit ID and RD, 'largely unknown to the acquirer' (Bernstein 1996: 29).

The balance of the two elements of pedagogic discourse, ID and RD, can vary so that one or other element is foregrounded. Daniels shows how this can occur as a result of increasing emphasis on curriculum content, assessment and outcomes, and argues for the need for careful examination of the form of pedagogic discourse in schools (Daniels 2001). The changes in early years provision since the introduction of government funding may be seen as resulting in a similar shift in the structure of pedagogic discourse in preschool provision, particularly in the non-maintained sector. By describing settings in terms of the *balance* between instructional and regulative discourse, ID and RD will be used to distinguish between a differential emphasis on the 'acquisition of instructional (curricular content) and regulative (social conduct, character and manner) texts' (Singh 2002: 573).

The concepts outlined above were used in this project to describe systematically the difference in pedagogic subcultures between the different early years settings. Particular aspects are reported to illustrate how different structures, relationships and values were associated with differences in interactional style and, in particular, differences in the way participants responded to and supported meaning-making.

The West Midlands Project

This project was designed to compare organisational style (in terms of the relative strengths of classification and framing) and pedagogical emphasis (in terms of the balance between ID and RD) in four preschool settings from the non-maintained sector. These particular settings were selected to cover different combinations along the two dimensions of difference, to enable comparison of different preschool cultures. The settings were all from the Birmingham area, two urban and two semi-rural, two day nurseries and two community playgroups, one in each type of location. The process of researching and selecting potential settings took place between January and September 2002, and the majority of the data were collected between September 2002 and July 2003. The settings had comparably good inspection reports, and were comfortable with their aims and proud of their provision. The type of settings, their organisational style and pedagogical emphasis are outlined in Table 10.1.

The case studies were built up from observation, documentary analysis and interviews. The perceptions of staff were elicited during career biography interviews and parents' views on preschool provision were sought through questionnaires. These findings are reported in full elsewhere (Georgeson 2006), and showed that both parents and staff had awareness and approval of their own setting's particular

Table 10.1 Summary of the four settings in the West Midlands project

Name/number of setting*	Setting type	Organisational style	Pedagogical emphasis
Village Hall *1*	Community preschool	Weak classification and framing – organic, open, egalitarian structure	RD dominates – setting prioritises socialisation for children before they start school
Rocking Horse *2*	Private day nursery	Strongish classification and framing – hierarchical structure but blurred boundaries between home and school	RD dominates – setting prioritises socialisation in homely surroundings
Orchard House *3*	Private nursery school offering full daycare	Very strong classification and framing – hierarchical structure	ID dominates – high educational emphasis
Building Blocks *4*	Community preschool within charitable organisation	Mixed strong and weak classification and framing – complex organisational structure	ID dominates – high educational emphasis aimed at both children and families

Note: * Pseudonyms

organisational style and pedagogical emphasis. The motivation for the third part of the project – which is the focus of this chapter – was to find out about children's awareness of the structural and pedagogical particularities of the settings they attended. Children aged 3 and 4 were encouraged to talk about preschool activities as they looked at photographs of their own and the other settings in the project. Fine-grained analyses of the ways in which children interacted provided insights into the particular interactional style of the individual settings, including findings relevant to the issue of co-construction in interaction. The differences in children's interactional style were then related to the differences in organisational style and pedagogical emphasis.

Methods

Photographs were displayed on a laptop computer to prompt children to talk about their preschool settings. Photographs were chosen over videos because they are inherently more ambiguous and open to interpretation, and might therefore offer more scope for different interpretations to emerge. There is an increasing use of photographs in early years projects, employed as prompts to elicit children's views about their provision (Einarsdottir 2005; Smith *et al.* 2005).

The photographs included children taking part in activities and shots of the exterior, interior and outside space (where there was one) as well as photographs of displays. Staff distributed letters to parents to ask for their permission for children to be included in the final set of photographs. The letter also sought their permission for their children to take part in the sessions looking and talking about the photographs, and advised parents that these sessions would be recorded.

In each photograph session, children saw between 40 and 50 photographs of one of the other settings followed by the 40 to 50 photographs from their own setting. A session lasted for about 20 minutes. Conversations were recorded directly using a discreet digital microphone connected to the computer. Children were told that the computer was recording their voices, but they seldom showed any interest in the small microphone. Seven sessions were recorded in three of the settings but only four sessions took place in Building Blocks because there were not enough children there aged 3 and over to take part in any more sessions. Sometimes children were prompted to comment with simple questions, but generally their comments were spontaneous.

Findings from photographic activity

The children's comments were transcribed and coded using a coding scheme built up from repeated readings of the transcriptions and based in part on concepts from Systemic Functional Linguistics, notably the interdependence of the content, interpersonal and textual context in all utterances (Halliday 1985; Christie 2002). The coding scheme is best described as three separate analyses; that is, Content, Interpersonal and Ways of speaking. The coding involved all those instances where children went beyond simply labelling something or someone in the photograph, showing that they were thinking more deeply about the photographs.

The categories are based partly on Clare Painter's study of the development of language use in the context of simple day-to-day utterances within the family, and how this prepares children for the sort of thinking they will need when they start school (Painter 1999). The reliability of the coding scheme was assessed using Cohen's Kappa, in preference to a simple percentage of agreement, because it corrects for chance agreements (Hartmann 1977: 109–110). The agreement between judges was high.[1] The results reported here are drawn from the Ways-of-speaking analysis to shed light on differences in co-construction between the settings.

Ways of speaking: difference between settings

The results of the study showed that the main effect of setting was significant for the Ways-of-speaking coding.[2] The children in the four settings differed in the proportion of utterances in which they went beyond simply labelling the photographs. To investigate which codes were contributing to the overall difference between settings on proportion of Ways-of-speaking codes, further analyses were carried out on the individual codes W6 (co-constructing recall/story) and W7 (co-constructing interpretation), which were concerned with co-construction.[3] These analyses revealed statistically significant effects for code W7 ($p < 0.05$), with W6 approaching significance. A further Discriminant Function Analysis showed both codes contributing to the difference between settings, with W7 again showing the stronger effect.

The statistical analyses established both that settings differed in the extent to which children used ways of speaking that took them beyond simple labelling, and that the two co-construction codes were contributing to this difference. The next stage of analysis examined how settings differed in their use of co-construction. Figure 10.1 shows the percentage of utterances on both co-construction codes in the four settings. It is clear that setting 2 (Rocking Horse) has the highest proportion, even when the greater talkativeness of Rocking Horse children was taken into account.

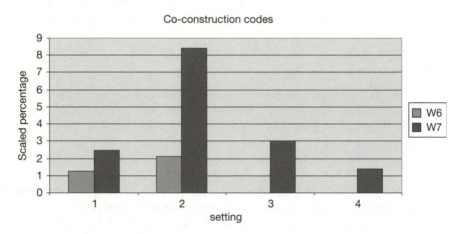

Figure 10.1 Percentage of utterances on co-construction codes in the four settings.

Taken together, the analyses described in the previous section support the conclusion that children in the four settings differed in the extent to which they used co-construction as they talked about the photographs. Differences in other aspects of interactional style, such as pronoun use, were also found in the four settings and are described elsewhere (Georgeson 2006). In this section, extracts from transcripts of children's talk from the two settings offering full daycare – Rocking Horse and Orchard House – will be analysed to illustrate the sort of differences in the ways children responded to each other's utterances.

As illustrated in Figure 10.1, Rocking Horse showed the greatest difference in the proportion of instances of co-construction. This is consistent with observations in this setting, which revealed an ethos of awareness of and pragmatic consideration

Table 10.2 Extracts from transcripts of photograph sessions at Orchard House and Rocking Horse

Orchard House	Child 1: sticking bits	Child 1: that's Chantal
	Child 2: bones	Child 2: she's making a snake
	Child 3: skelingtons [*sic*]	Child 1: pattern
		Child 2: snake
Rocking Horse	Child 1: they're shells	Child 1: it looks like oranges
	Child 2: and it looks like plates as well	Child 2: some oranges and pears
	Child 1: dinner plates	

for the needs of other people. Co-construction was less prevalent during the photograph sessions at Orchard House (Setting 3 in Figure 10.1), but the interpersonal tone at Orchard House included other notable elements such as challenge, countering and assertiveness. Instead of building on the comments of other children, children at Orchard House had a tendency to speak out in opposition to what others had said. This is consistent with the maintenance of sharp boundaries between categories that follows from its particularly strong classification. Compare the extracts given in Table 10.2, and see also Tables 10.3 and 10.4.

While the children at Rocking Horse use connecting elements ('and', 'as well'), repetition and extension to link what they want to say with what has been said before, the children at Orchard House simply present their own opinions in opposition to the previous utterances.

In addition to differences in the use of connecting elements, repetition and extension, children's responses also differed in the ways children signalled modality; that is, how they sought to qualify the truth status of the propositional content of their utterance. For example, this can be achieved by adding words or phrases such as 'perhaps', 'maybe' or 'it could be' to the sentence; this is the method favoured by staff and children at Rocking Horse. Alternatively, uncertainty can also be signalled by using a modal verb such as 'might', or by prefacing the statement with a phrase such as 'I think' or 'I expect'. Compare the extracts from Rocking Horse and Orchard House given in Tables 10.3 and 10.4.

Table 10.3 Extracts from transcripts showing use of ways of signalling modality at Rocking Horse

Picture 27 Drill	Child O: it makes it round like a circle like a teddy bear
	Child E: you turn it around like a chocolate maker
	Child O: it could be a chocolate maker
Picture 24 Sticking	Child S: it looks like you'm doing colouring, M.
	Child M: maybe I'm doing gluing
Picture 9 Girl sticking	Child D: maybe they're doing gluing
	Child K: yes, sticking, aren't they
	Child D: he's laughing at the dog
	Child K: maybe he's scratching the dog

Table 10.4 Extracts from transcripts showing use of ways of signalling modality at Orchard House

Picture 9 Girl sticking	Child BE: doing some gluing Child BR: I think she's painting *Child BE: Do you think she's painting?* Child BR: Gluing Child BR: stroking the dog, I think
Picture 11 Boy and tablecloth	Child BE: who's that there? Child BR: I bet he's putting the new pillows up, putting them there Child BE: I bet he's making a picnic Child BR: I bet he's putting that one there
Picture 24 'Doctor' play	Child B: there's C Child P: I think they're playing in the music room

The ways in which the Rocking Horse children signalled modality objectivise the point of view expressed, whereas the Orchard House children's use of 'I' + mental operation verb reflects the subjective nature of the assessment (Thompson 2004: 70). It would seem therefore that there may be differences in the way children position themselves with respect to the propositional content of the utterances.

Implications of findings

The two settings offering full daycare – Rocking Horse and Orchard House – differed greatly in their pedagogical emphasis, with Rocking Horse emphasising socialisation in a homely environment (RD) and Orchard House promoting independence and acquisition of concepts and skills related to school subjects (ID). Both showed strong classification and framing in some aspects of organisation, but Rocking Horse blurred the boundaries between home and school and between activity time and free play.

Furthermore, although the two settings could be seen as offering similar services and working towards the same outcomes in the form of the early learning goals, analysis of the way children talked to each other showed differences in the interactional climate, which could have implications for the development of pedagogical identities. Through their tendency to objectivise expressions of modality, Rocking Horse children appeared to approach the task of working out what is happening in the photographs as a collaborative project on some uncertain object 'out there'. Orchard House children subjectivised their expressions of modality with phrases like 'I bet' that demonstrated their more individual standpoint. This was consistent with the picture of more social and more individual approaches respectively in many other aspects of organisation, pedagogical emphasis and interaction in these two settings.

It could be argued, however, that the 'countering style' at Orchard House helped children to develop ways of speaking which might be useful in an educational context, particularly if their next school placement has a similarly challenging style. The countering style could also contribute to sharpening their ability to assign things to categories and so help them to learn to generalise. Painter has examined the development of children's ability to generalise through their experience of contrasts, definitions and attributes, particularly relating to the mastery of categories (Painter 1999). She argues that it is important for children to refine their understanding of category membership by reflecting on the attributes of members and non-members of overlapping sets; this helps them to acquire an understanding of superordinate and subordinate category membership, and facilitates general-isation. Settings with strong classification provide clear examples of what belongs and what does not belong, and this could help children to develop their ability to categorise and generalise, especially if they are given some guidance about category membership.

However, the weaving together of one's own and another's thoughts, which is required in the co-construction that was more evident in Rocking Horse, could be seen as requiring more sophisticated understanding of two points of view, in contrast with the 'that's wrong; this is right' rhetoric which characterised the countering exchanges at Orchard House. Painter draws attention to the importance for children's cognitive development of becoming aware of other people's ideas and integrating these with one's own thoughts:

> the ability to represent the cognitions of oneself and others can be seen as fundamental, not only for monitoring one's own learning, but for reflecting on the world of ideas and beliefs in general.
>
> (Painter 1999: 320)

It seems likely therefore that children at Rocking Horse, in their tendency to build on the comments of other children, were developing a style of thinking which could equip them well for learning through contact with other people's ideas.

Conclusions

This chapter has described differences in the ways in which children responded to each other's utterances by countering or building on what the previous speaker had said. Children in the setting that prioritised care and socialisation over educa-tion were found to be using more co-constructive ways of speaking in comparison with children from a similar setting that prioritised education. These findings contribute to the understanding of how children develop different pedagogical identities during their time in preschool provision, and this has implications for practitioners in their next settings. In order to have the confidence to join in, children need to feel comfortable with the particular style of interactions around them. A child who is used to building tentatively on her classmates' comments may find it difficult to respond to a more challenging assertive style, and vice versa.

Such distinctions between interactional styles are, however, subtle and it might not be easy for practitioners to make themselves aware of differences that operate at a tacit level. One possible route towards awareness of such distinctions is offered by explicit training in language games, such as 'yes and' and 'yes but', played by professional improvisers and recently used in training in a variety of contexts, including early years practice (Lobman 2003, 2005).

Notes

1   Mean Kappa 0.83 and s.d. 0.16, with 23/25 Kappa values lying between 0.6 and 1.00. These values may be interpreted as showing good (0.60 – 0.75) to excellent (above 0.75) inter-observer agreement (Robson 2002: 342).
2   MANCOVAs (using SPSS 10.0 software package) were carried out on each coding set, each time using the number of utterances by session and setting (SUM) as a covariate, to control for the likelihood that differences in talkativeness between settings were masking possible differences in coding profile. Results were significant at p<0.05.
3   Univariate analyses were carried out on the individual codes, using the data re-expressed as percentages of the average number of utterances per session to factor out the differences in talkativeness between settings. W7 had a high loading (0.478) on Function 1 (which accounts for most of the variance between settings) and W6 a modest loading of 0.338 on Function 2 (which accounts for most of the remaining variance), which is just above the level generally accepted as eligible for interpretation (Tabachnik and Fidell 1996: 540). This supports the interpretaion that differences in levels of co-construction contributed to the overall significant difference in Ways of speaking between the settings.

References

Bernstein, B. (1990) *The Structuring of Pedagogic Discourse*. London: Routledge.
Bernstein, B. (2000) *Pedagogy, Symbolic Control and Identity: Theory, Research, Critique*. Lanham, MD: Rowman & Littlefield.
Christie, F. (2002) *Classroom Discourse Analysis: A Functional Perspective*. London: Continuum.
Daniels, H. (2001) *Vygotsky and Pedagogy*. London: RoutledgeFalmer.
Einarsdottir, J. (2005) Playschool in pictures: children's photographs as a research method. *Early Child Development and Care*, 175: 523–541.
Georgeson, J. (2006) *Differences in Preschool Culture: Organisation, Pedagogy and Interaction in Four Selected Settings*. Unpublished Ed.D. thesis, University of Birmingham.
Halliday, M.A.K. (1985) *Introduction to Functional Grammar*. London: Arnold.
Hartmann, D.P. (1977) Considerations in the choice of interobserver reliability estimates. *Journal of Applied Behaviour Analysis*, 10: 103–116.
Hasan, R. (2005) Semiotic mediation and three exotropic theories – Vygotsky, Halliday and Bernstein. In *Language, Society and Consciousness: The Collected Works of Ruqaiya Hasan*, 1: 130–156. London: Equinox.
Lobman, C.L. (2003) What should we create today? Improvisational teaching in play-based classrooms. *Early Years*, 23: 131–142.
Lobman, C.L. (2005) (Re)learning how to play together. In *First ISCAR Congress*. Sevilla.
Painter, C. (1999) *Learning Through Language in Early Childhood*. London: Cassell.
Payler, J.K. (2005) *Exploring Foundations: Sociocultural Influences on the Learning Processes of Four Year Old Children in a Pre-school and Reception Class*. Unpublished Ph.D. thesis, University of Southampton.
Qualifications and Curriculum Authority (2000) *Curriculum Guidance for the Foundation Stage*. England and Wales: QCA.

Robson, C. (2002) *Real World Research; A Resource for Social Scientists and Practitioner-researchers*. Oxford: Blackwell.

Singh, P. (2002) Pedagogising knowledge: Bernstein's theory of the pedagogic device. *British Journal of Sociology of Education*, 23: 571–582.

Smith, A., Duncan, J. and Marshall, K. (2005) Children's perspectives on their learning: exploring methods. *Early Child Development and Care*, 175(6): 473–487.

Tabachnik, B. and Fidell, L. (1996) *Using Multivariate Statistics*. New York: HarperCollins.

Thompson, G. (2004) *Introducing Functional Grammar*. London: Arnold.

11 Co-constructing meaning

Ways of supporting learning

Jane Payler

The project described in this chapter was a qualitative study of learning processes among ten 4-year-old children in a community-run preschool and a primary school reception class in the South of England with distinct subcultures of pedagogy: preschool with an invisible pedagogy, emphasising social development, and reception with a visible pedagogy, emphasising specific learning outcomes. Multi-modal analyses of teaching and learning episodes (Kress and Van Leeuwen 2001) showed the different ways in which staff guided children's learning and meaning-making. In keeping with the findings of the West Midlands Project (Georgeson, Chapter 10, this volume) it was found that the care and socialisation-oriented preschool fostered co-construction between staff and children, whereas the educational outcomes-oriented reception class used scaffolding towards predetermined learning objectives. The reception approach appeared to result in some negative positioning of children, particularly those perceived as less able by the staff, with implications for developing learner identities. A third approach to guidance was noted in the preschool in which a predetermined learning outcome existed, but in which collaboration was emphasised, similar to proleptic instruction (Forman *et al.* 1993) fostering a range of participatory positions by the children. This encouraged children's risk-taking and legitimate peripheral participation (Lave and Wenger 1991), contributing to the development of more positive learner identities.

Introduction

In sociocultural theories of learning, the importance of the ways in which learning is mediated through interaction has long been recognised as vital to understanding learning processes in different contexts. Vygotsky's concept of the zone of proximal development (ZPD) has provided a springboard for research into how adults support children's learning. The processes involved in helping children to learn within their ZPD have been described more fully by Wood and colleagues

(1976) as scaffolding, by Rogoff (1990) as guided participation, and by Newman *et al*. (1989) as the construction zone. Work by Edwards and Mercer (1987) and Mercer (1995) has helped to identify the significance of dialogue in scaffolding or mediating learning, while Rogoff (1990) has clarified the concept of 'appropriation' as the way in which a child acts upon, understands and takes as her own information given. Rogoff describes how the process gradually emerges during a period of apprenticeship in which the child becomes more and more involved in problem-solving and decision-making.

Previous research relevant to mediating learning has highlighted the contingent and responsive nature of successful adult guidance or teaching (Wells and Nicholls 1985), its dependence on capturing or recruiting interest (Wood 1988), staying one step ahead of the learner by gradually making the task more complex and keeping within the ZPD (Bruner 1985), creating joint understanding and guiding the child to make links (Rogoff and Lave 1984; Edwards and Mercer 1987; Rogoff 1990; Mercer 1995), and the importance of noting fully the social, affective and intellectual aspects of the child's understanding (Donaldson 1978; Thornton 1995; David and Goouch 2001).

Recent work by Sharpe (2006), applying tools derived from systemic functional linguistics (SFL), goes some way towards further 'unpacking' the notion of scaffolding by examining the kinds of discourse and multi-modal strategies used in creating a scaffolded environment in a classroom. Sharpe's contribution identifies an induction genre, in addition to the macro- and micro-genres defined by Wells (1995, cited in Sharpe 2006: 213), and some of the strategies used in 'contingent scaffolding'. Aspects of contingent scaffolding appear to engender a shift from scaffolding towards a more dialogic co-construction. However, Sharpe's study was based on research with 12- to 13-year-old pupils streamed into a high achieving class; Sharpe rightly questions how far this can be generalised to other learners and learning situations.

Jordan's (2004) investigations into interactions in early years settings have led her to make useful distinctions between different guidance strategies used by adults to meet different purposes: the first, guidance for process-oriented activities and the second for pre-set goal-oriented activities. These she refers to as co-constructing understandings with children and scaffolding learning for children. In co-constructing, part of the adult's role consists of ascertaining, suggesting or jointly creating a goal with the child. While acknowledging a role for both scaffolding and co-construction, there is more possibility for incorporating the child's own ideas into co-construction: it is a shared space in which the adult and child both have a constructive role to play. Past study by Schaffer (1996) on 'joint involvement episodes' and more recent study as part of the EPPE project relating to 'sustained shared thinking' (Siraj-Blatchford *et al*. 2003: v) identify similar features to co-construction. All associate this mode of interaction with more effective early learning, Jordan's research showing that co-construction was more empowering for children and that they engaged in higher order thinking through their involvement than when the adults scaffolded learning for them (Jordan 2004: 42).

But what are the factors that help to determine whether practitioners and children are more likely to engage in scaffolding or co-construction? Georgeson (Chapter 10, this volume) reported on research suggesting that organisational style and pedagogic emphasis influenced children's styles of talk. This chapter complements the findings reported in Georgeson's chapter (see Chapter 10) by exploring guidance strategies in two different types of settings. It considers the implications of these for children's developing learner identities and the part relationships play in shaping guidance interactions. It also raises questions about whether co-construction and scaffolding are sufficient to describe the range of guidance strategies in early years pedagogy.

The South of England study

In the southern project, naturalistic episodes of teaching and learning in a reception class and preschool were analysed using a multi-modal approach to explore the different ways in which staff guided children's learning and meaning-making. Evidence here suggested that at the community-run preschool playgroup, with an emphasis on socialisation and emotional development, the patterns of interaction showed greater opportunity for children to take part in supported self-initiated dialogue akin to co-construction. However, findings in the school reception class challenged the view that fostering familiarity with such co-constructive interactive styles would offer the best preparation for school. The reception class, with an emphasis on predetermined learning outcomes, fostered greater teacher-directed interaction more akin to scaffolding towards specific learning objectives in large groups. This gave children very little opportunity to take part in co-constructed dialogue.

Methodology

The case studies of ten 4-year-old children in two settings were developed over a period of four school terms from 2002 to 2003. The studies comprised participant observation, documentary analysis, informal conversations with the children, focus group and individual interviews with staff, parent interviews, parent diaries, and extensive use of audio- and video-recording (102 hours) in the settings and homes. The video- and audio-recordings of naturally occurring interactions were made to allow detailed analysis of teaching and learning in action and the style of pedagogy identified. Here, the study was influenced by Stone's acknowledgement that there are other communicative mechanisms at work in successful guidance such as the semiotic devices of gesture, gaze and pauses.

> How can we move beyond the assumption that the 'dialogue' constituting scaffolding is verbal to develop an integrative framework capable of incorporating a broader notion of semiotic interactions in scaffolding situations?
>
> (Stone 1993: 176)

The study, therefore, employed close analysis of action, gaze, gesture, body positioning and use of objects as well as speech to set out some of the ways in which guidance is transmitted and co-created with the child. Learning and meaning-making are multi-modal and in recent years there has been a renewed interest in considering this in empirical studies, not only in relation to young children (Kress and Van Leeuwen 2001; Lancaster 2001; Wang *et al*. 2001; Matoesian and Coldren 2002; Pahl 2002; Anning 2003; Bourne and Jewitt 2003; Flewitt 2003; Kress *et al*. 2004). Since the 1960s, social psychology has contributed an enormous amount of empirical research, largely from a positivist, non-situated, experimental stance, to an understanding of non-verbal aspects of interpersonal communication (NVC) (Argyle 1988; Burgoon 1994). Researchers such as Burgoon (1994) and Knapp *et al*. (1994) however, pointed out the importance of viewing NVC as an integrated communication system.

> The traditional decomposition into separate codes leads to a piecemeal and distorted understanding of the social and communicative role of non-verbal signals. Non-verbal behaviours operate as an integrated, coordinated system in achieving particular social functions, and their importance becomes apparent when they are examined collectively.
>
> (Burgoon 1994: 238)

This is supported by the work of Kress and Van Leeuwen (2001). Instead of treating each as separate aspects to be then added together, Kress and Van Leeuwen propose a theory of multi-modal communication which concentrates on the semiotic resources. They suggest that the move away from mono-modality entails a fresh look at issues about cognition, learning and knowledge (2001: 131–132). The study in the South of England reported here aimed to contribute to this by adopting such an approach in examining some of the ways in which learning was mediated in two early years settings.

The corpus of data was analysed at four levels: ethnographic analysis of the learning environments and of children's learning over the year; broad patterns of interaction in the settings using taxonomies drawn from the data based on the functions of and participants in staff and child interactions; multi-modal analyses of the micro-processes of frequently occurring types of teaching and learning episodes; and in the fourth level of analysis, critical features already identified were used as markers to track processes and issues across the recorded data for the year. The findings reported in this chapter are based mainly on the final level of analysis, but necessarily build on the findings from previous levels.

Findings and discussion

Pedagogical styles of staff–child interaction

The ethnographic analysis of the learning environments used concepts from Bernstein's theory of pedagogic discourse to distinguish between pedagogic styles

Table 11.1 Most frequently occurring types of staff-to-child interaction (in descending order)

Preschool staff		Reception class staff at school	
Encourage	small group	**Instruct/explain**	large group
Instruct/explain	small group	**Instruct/explain**	small group
Enable	small group	**Explore**	large group
Enable	1:1	**Reinforce**	large group
Instruct/explain	large group	**Assess**	1:1
Explore	*large*	*Model*	
Reinforce	*small*	*Assess*	*small*
Concern for well-being	*small*		
= 51% of all interactions		**= 50% of all interactions**	

in the two settings. In spite of working to the same curriculum, the settings provided very different learning environments, influenced by the 'arenas' within which they operated (Kirshner and Whitson 1997). The preschool had a largely invisible pedagogy with weak classification and framing (Bernstein 1996). Its goals were to promote children's personal and social development. The analysis of the pattern of interaction in the preschool revealed that staff here spent much of their time in small-group or one-to-one interactions with children, sharing control with the children as the staff supported and extended children's interests (Table 11.1). The reception class at school had a visible pedagogy and was strongly classified and framed. The setting emphasised individual progress towards Level 1 of the English National Curriculum through a focus on specific learning objectives, with much of the teaching and learning time dominated by literacy and mathematics. Staff–child interactions in reception showed much greater adult control with less opportunity for children's initiations.

Most frequently occurring types of children's interactions

There were distinct differences in the use children made of these interactive opportunities (Table 11.2). The preschool children initiated and pursued their own goals, often supported by an adult. The reception children were more likely to be responding or listening to the teacher, often in large groups, with far less opportunity to participate in co-construction (see Table 11.3 below).

These findings were supported by observation and by the detailed micro-analysis of teaching and learning episodes. Although the data presented as evidence here show discrete instances, it is pertinent to note how the styles of interaction became a routine part of the children's experiences in the settings and shaped their relationships with the staff. This echoes Stone's identification of two aspects of the interpersonal relationship involved in guidance: those of the immediate qualities of an interaction and the more enduring, developing dimension over repeated interactions as the relationship forms and colours (and is coloured by) each new interaction (Stone 1993).

Table 11.2 Most frequently occurring types of children's interactions (in descending order)

Preschool children	Reception class children at school
Parallel activity	**Taking part in large group non-routine activities**
Selecting and using resources for own goals	**Responding positively to adult requests**
Taking part in small group activities	**Selecting and using resources to achieve adult-set or closed**
Offering information to adults	Contributing in unison in large groups
Exploring possibilities	Contributing alone as requested in small
Responding to adult requests	groups
Large group routine	Small group activity
	Parallel activity
= 50% of all children's sample interactions	**= 52% of all children's sample interactions**

Multi-modal strategies for co-construction between staff and children

At preschool, the analyses revealed co-construction between staff and children using a variety of multi-modal strategies. This is illustrated by Table 11.3 in which we can see Jill (the practitioner), Henry and Lloyd building on each other's verbal contributions during the conversation, while Henry makes a construction influenced by Lloyd.

In the school reception class, the teacher was more likely to be scaffolding the children's learning towards specific learning outcomes, often in large groups, and rarely took part in co-constructive dialogue with the children. In addition, in the small group sessions supported by the teacher, multi-modal micro-analysis revealed scaffolding by the teacher which appeared to result in some negative positioning of children, particularly those perceived by staff as of 'below average' ability. The episode of teaching and learning from the reception class related below serves as an exemplar of the interactive style in reception. The episode is reported in narrative form for reasons of space, but is illustrated with outline tracings of video stills to show the multi-modal nature of the interaction and analysis.

Scaffolding in the reception class at school – Tom positioned as an unsuccessful learner

In reception in January 2003, the teacher worked with Paul, Tom and Lawrence on the mat during the numeracy hour small-group work session. This was a group of 4-year-old children who, in school, were finding it difficult to fully grasp the connection between written numerals and quantity, and to count objects reliably up to five (Tom) and up to ten (Paul and Lawrence). This became a priority for mathematics work with the group. The teacher instructed the group in a clear, firm

Table 11.3 Co-construction at preschool

	Time	Jill's actions	Jill's speech	Henry's actions	Henry's speech	Lloyd's actions and speech
3 8	10.35.23	Elbow on table, hand to mouth. Head turns to H briefly. Points at H with finger to emphasise agreement. Gaze back to L, head resting in hand.	Have you ever been in a windmill – Lloyd – Have you ever been in a windmill J>H Is there Yes there is you're right And there's a windmill in – Um let me see – Trumpton too But I don't suppose you watch Trumpton It's not on telly anymore	Begins a new construction, fixing pieces with greater ease now.	There's a windmill in the Telly-tubbies	Yeah
3 9	10.35.36	Points to L with finger, emphasising words. Eyes wide in explanation, eyebrows raised. Indicates rotating movement with finger and hand.	J>L No Actually Thomas the Tank Engine's got a different sort of mill a watermill hasn't he	Gaze to L and back to own construction.	I've never heard of it	

4 0	10.35.44	Hand across chin, gaze to L. Knitted brow as if thinking and listening intently.	#Has it got a windmill as well	Concentrating on his construction. He is involved in making a copy of the shape that L had produced. Brief gaze up to L and his construction.	Yeah yeah and he's got a different one# Yeah he's got something that takes water up and he's got a windmill (indicates rotating movement with arms)
4 1	10.35.57	Emphasises points made with finger. Indicates circular movement with finger. Indicates direction of the movement described with finger.	Yes I think you're right I know there's a watermill there because I remember seeing it The other day I happened to turn the TV on and Thomas the Tank Engine happened to be on and I thought Oh I haven't seen that for such a long time The waterwheel was going round and Thomas was going along the railway track	By this time H has half constructed a copy of L's model. Gaze down to construction, still building, looks intent.	

voice and with a serious facial expression. This was to be work that required attention. She set the scene for the task as an individual activity in which each child independently was to follow the teacher's instructions. 'Now you get out for me two multilink and put them together. No, you're not listening. You've got your one. I want you to get two multilink and put them together . . . 1, 2' (she counted out two multilink in her own hand), 'and put them together in a tower. Go on, you do the same.'

Tom took a brick and looked hesitant. He gazed at the teacher and at the other children, clearly unsure. The teacher noticed and took two of his multilink bricks, one in each of her hands, and showed them to him, saying firmly, 'One, two' (Figure 11.1). She put them both on one of her hands, palm flat, and held them out to Tom. 'You count them.' Tom pointed one at a time to each brick, mumbling the words, clearly unsure. He said 'Three'. The teacher repeated firmly to him 'One, two. Put them together' (at which point she demonstrated joining the two bricks), 'and make a tower.' Tom gazed to the bricks placed in front of him on the floor, positioned as illustrated in Figure 11.2. At that point the teacher became aware of Paul's apparent lack of compliance. She took both of his hands in hers and, putting

Figure 11.1 Teacher counting out two bricks for Tom (Reception: 9 January 2003).

Figure 11.2 Tom's two towers.

Figure 11.3 Refocusing Paul's attention.

her face directly in front of his with her gaze to his, said firmly, 'Look at me. Listen to what Miss Green is asking you to do, okay?' (Figure 11.3).

The atmosphere created was one of rather tense work. The teacher then directed the group to 'Take out three multilink. Count them out.' She demonstrated again by putting three bricks one by one in her hand: 'One, two, three.' She looked at Tom and said, 'You should have three in your hand, three in your hand, one, two, three. Put them together in a tower.' Tom again looked hesitant, glancing frequently at the teacher and at her tower, while handling two bricks uncertainly. The teacher noticed his uncertainty and took his two bricks from him, held them out in her hand in front of him and asked, 'How many are there?' in a firm voice. Tom tried to count them. His voice was unclear, but he did say 'Three'. The teacher shook her head slightly to indicate that he had made a mistake, but then turned her attention to Paul who was not making the correct tower either. She turned back to Tom and said, 'One, two.?' She took another brick and added it, saying emphatically, 'Three. Put them together in a tower.' Tom took them and hesitantly put two of them together, forming the pattern illustrated in Figure 11.4. This was different to the teacher's model, illustrated in Figure 11.5.

Figure 11.4 Tom's four towers. *Figure 11.5* The teacher's model of towers.

Tom then turned his gaze from his model to the teacher's model and towards the other children's efforts. He looked unsure, shifting his gaze and wringing his hands and fingers silently until the teacher noticed his mistake and asked, 'Where are the three I gave you a few minutes ago, Tom? The three I just gave you, what have you done with them?' Tom gazed uncertainly at the teacher and at his bricks (Figure 11.6). She re-formed his towers to match her own, counting aloud again in demonstration. The activity continued in the same manner to a five-brick tower. Tom remained confused and unquestioning, but attempted to follow the teacher's instructions. The teacher continued to demonstrate and correct Tom's efforts, supporting his actions almost to the extent of completing the task for him, something the teacher commented on when reviewing the video-tape.

Figure 11.6 Tom's uncertainty.

Finally, Tom appealed first to me, calling to me over the teacher's head as her attention was focused on someone else (Figure 11.7), and then to the LSA who was working with another group, holding up a brick and asking, 'What shall I do with this?' He did not question the teacher or try to explain or defend his decisions about where to place the bricks. He looked relieved when it was tidy-up time.

Tom clearly found the task very challenging and undoubtedly had difficulty in counting reliably. However, I suggest that there was something in the tone of the interaction relating to the activity, the non-verbal communicative strategies used and the words the teacher chose which made it more difficult for Tom to communicate where his difficulty lay. This in turn hampered the teacher in supporting him in a way that would help to circumvent his difficulties, so that the outcome

Figure 11.7 Tom asking for advice.

contributed to Tom's self-image as a successful, rather than unsuccessful, learner. What is also of interest here is how the detail of this episode had become part of a usual way of interacting, part of the relationship between Tom, Paul and the teacher in school, further contributing to Tom's reluctance to speak out.

The findings appear to challenge the view that co-construction in the early years may form a useful preparation for later schooling given that children in this study at least were rarely likely to co-construct once at school. The findings of the study in the South are in line with previous research showing the specific and characteristic nature of school discourse (Sinclair and Coulthard 1975; Willes 1983; Mercer 1995), its potential for restricting child–adult interaction (Edwards and Maybin 1987; Edwards and Mercer 1987) and its potential for making explicit, though more often leaving implicit, the nature, purposes and principles of the learning to be undertaken (Donaldson 1978; Willes 1983; Edwards and Mercer 1987; Mercer 1995). Orchard (1996) found that in reception classes, teachers recognised the value of talking with children and considered it a priority. However, while the teachers themselves interacted non-stop with the children, from the children's point of view it was brief, teacher-led and restricted, as reflected in other studies of classroom discourse (Sylva *et al.* 1980; Tizard *et al.* 1983; Willes 1983). Similarly, Adams *et al.* (2004) noted that the introduction of the Foundation Stage Curriculum had done little to change what they describe as 'conceptually and emotionally "impoverished"' (Adams *et al.* 2004: 22) learning experiences for young children in reception classes, referring to the emphasis on narrowly defined literacy and numeracy activities.

The findings from the study in the South of England offer a finely grained analysis of the style of scaffolding taking place in the reception class which highlights some of the negative aspects for certain children. Given the discourse community children appear likely to join once at school, there is a need for further debate and investigation into how fostering co-construction in the preschool period may have a part to play in assisting such children to participate in interactive spaces of this kind in a manner that reduces the negative impact on their learning and learner identities.

During the study, a third approach to guidance was noted in the preschool in which a predetermined learning outcome existed (showing some similarities to scaffolding), but in which collaboration was emphasised, similar to 'proleptic instruction' (Forman *et al.* 1993). Proleptic instruction is characterised by communication in which the adult, or more capable peer, implicitly provides guidance or information or directs attention by stating something in a manner that appears to assume previous knowledge (though not yet held in reality). The child, or less capable peer, through resultant questioning, deduction, observation or partial participation makes the links and ultimately ends up sharing the knowledge or skill. Addison Stone argues that its strength lies in the way in which it highlights 'the creative or transformative effect of such discourse turns via the communicative tension introduced by the speaker' (Stone 1993: 174). The process can result in a redefining of the situation for the child to become more consistent with that of the adult. Indeed, Stone suggests that the way in which a shared knowledge perspective is assumed is conducive to mutual trust and intimacy and to the child adopting the adult's position as his or her own (Stone 1993: 174).

The third approach to guidance noted at preschool allowed for close adult guidance towards the learning goal, but fostered a range of participatory positions by the children, encouraging both risk-taking in making contributions and legitimate peripheral participation (Lave and Wenger 1991), contributing to more positive learner identities. This approach is illustrated below with an episode that also involved counting with 4-year-old children and that took place in preschool the day before the school episode related above.

Proleptic guidance at preschool – children allowed a range of positive learner positions

The supervisor worked with Stuart, Ann and Emma at a table on which mathematics resources were laid out. The resources comprised A4 cards, each with a numeral up to 10 and a picture of a dog in a particular colour, sets of plastic 'puppies' in three sizes and several colours to match the cards, and several round, shallow, plastic containers in the same colours. The activity began at 9.51 a.m. as the supervisor invited the small group to help her. 'Who's going to come and sort out these puppies for me?' She set the scene for the activity to be a collaborative task to which each person could contribute. 'We're sorting out all the colours. D'you want to do the red ones, Ann? You choose all the grey ones, yeah?' The activity, at the supervisor's suggestion, shifted to a counting activity. 'What about doing some numbers? Shall we start at . . .?' She picked out the card with the number 1 on it and showed it to Ann. 'D'you know what number that is, Ann? . . . Shall we put one green puppy on there, shall we? You find one green puppy then and put it there.'

Her tone of voice was light and friendly and her expression smiling. They continued in a similar manner, with the supervisor supporting the children's efforts and sharing the task between them (Figure 11.8). For example, by 9.55 a.m. they had reached the number 6. The supervisor showed the card to Ann and smiled. 'What number's that then, Ann?' Ann just smiled. 'D'you know that one?' As she gazed at Ann, the supervisor screwed up one eye while smiling, as if indicating that she could see that it was difficult for Ann. Ann gave a slight shake of her head, so the supervisor immediately turned to Stuart, still half smiling, and asked, 'Stuart know that one?'

The supervisor's facial expression, warm tone of voice, timing and her choice of words, such as 'we', framed the activity as a joint task in which each child contributed as much as she or he was able without tacit criticism or judgement for being unable to perform a specific part of the task. It avoided individual assessment or pressure to perform. Indeed, Emma, who was a year younger than Stuart and Ann, remained a largely silent though attentive observer of the counting part of the activity, becoming involved only when the supervisor included her in the colour-sorting at the beginning and the size-sorting task at the end. The guidance was none the less challenging and at times included elements of instruction. When Ann and Stuart jointly placed puppies on card four, accidentally placing five puppies, the supervisor urged them to check. 'Count them up, count them up.' They

Figure 11.8 Counting puppies (Preschool: 8 January 2003).

both counted them and Stuart put his hand to his mouth in mock horror as Ann gazed at the supervisor, making an unheard comment to which the supervisor replied, 'Yeah, you've got too many, haven't you? What d'you need to do? Yeah, that's right, take one away.' She noticed Stuart's mistake in attempting to count a set of puppies. His finger moved faster than his words as he touched each one and so ended up with the wrong figure: 'As you're counting, Stuart, keep your finger on it as you count it. Shall we just check? Shall we count them up?' This was followed by the supervisor counting with Stuart (Figure 11.9), demonstrating and guiding his finger to match the pace of his words.

Later, as the children reached card nine, Stuart placed six puppies on it. The supervisor urged them to check. 'We need nine, don't we? We've got six. How many more? We need nine, so we need . . .?' Stuart placed another puppy on the card, and the supervisor and Stuart counted them together, the supervisor again correcting and supporting Stuart's counting technique. 'Seven. Is that it? No? What do we need?' This challenging and supporting continued until the correct amount was placed on each card. The success of the task was attributed to the whole of the small group. 'Well done! So we've done them all, haven't we?'

Given that schoolteachers in England frequently work to predetermined learning objectives specified in government documents, there is the potential for such an approach to be of use in school settings and to offer the possibility for guidance which fosters more positive learner identities for all children. Evidence from this study suggests that the prolepsis which Stone describes was present in many of the exchanges at preschool, but that it was conveyed through not only the choice of words, which implied that 'we' could do things together, but particularly through

Figure 11.9 Supporting counting.

the tone of voice, facial expressions, pacing, gaze and the relationships implicit in those, which suggested a moving towards something alongside the adult, rather than the adult assessing individual competence and compliance.

Proleptic instruction also suggests instruction that takes place in anticipation of competence. Thus,

> a learner may be encouraged to participate in an activity which as yet they cannot perform alone. This assumption or anticipation of competence in a social context supports the individual's efforts and encourages the learner to make sense of the situation in a powerful way . . . Thus the child is led to infer a new perspective, one that is the joint product of the child's own initial perspective and that of the adult.
>
> (Daniels 2001: 113–114)

Such an approach to guiding allows for partial or full participation by the child and challenge from the adult, but with the opportunity for the child's learner identity to develop in a more positive light.

Conclusion

This chapter has shown that adults used different guidance strategies in different settings. They were more likely to use co-construction in the preschool setting that prioritised care and socialisation. However, scaffolding learning for children was the routine form of interaction in the school reception class, which prioritised specific educational objectives, allowing little opportunity for co-construction. The findings highlighted the differential impact of this form of scaffolding on individual children's learner identities. The alternative approach to guidance noted in the data, proleptic guidance, offered a way of providing guidance towards predetermined learning outcomes, but in a more collaborative environment, giving children the opportunity to adopt a range of positive learner identities.

Evidence from this and the Georgeson study suggests that the discourse styles of the settings were related to the settings' structures, aims and the 'arenas' (Kirshner and Whitson 1997) within which they operated. The papers raise several issues. They raise the question of the role played by the different styles of interaction in preparing children for later schooling and whether children used to co-constructing discourse environments may be at a disadvantage when faced with the school style of scaffolding. Evidence in Payler (2005) suggested that children from co-constructive backgrounds were able to negotiate the controlled discourse of the reception classroom in a more positive manner.

The findings raise questions about whether schooled discourse can potentially learn from the more co-constructive forms of discourse found in effective early years settings (Siraj-Blatchford *et al.* 2003). The findings suggest that Jordan's model of early years discourse may need to be extended beyond that of co-construction and scaffolding to encompass proleptic guidance. Future research using systemic functional linguistics and multi-modal analysis could assist in revealing the simple but important features of 'ordinary' discourse which appear to play an influential role in inducting children into pedagogic exchange. They could also shed light on how children might use co-construction to negotiate more intersubjectivity in school, and on the distinctive features of and implications for learning of proleptic instruction.

The findings from both papers also have implications for practice. They offer early years professionals the opportunity to reflect on their settings' organisational styles, pedagogic emphases and guidance strategies. In particular, they invite reflection on:

- How the ethos and organisation of their settings may be influencing children's meaning-making.
- The guidance strategies the adults routinely use and why.
- Whether/how their guidance strategies are influenced by the ethos of the setting and the implications of this for their own practice.
- Whether their guidance strategies differ for different (groups of) children and how they align to expectations and perceptions of 'ability'.
- The impact of their guidance strategies upon children's possible participation and developing learner identities.

Awareness of a more extensive range of guidance and discourse strategies and their impacts may assist early years professionals to select and use those most appropriate to different contexts.

Acknowledgement

Thanks to my father, William Harding, for the outline tracings of video stills.

References

Adams, S., Alexander, E., Drummond, M.J. and Moyles, J. (2004) *Inside the Foundation Stage: Recreating the Reception Year*. London: Association of Teachers and Lecturers.

Anning, A. (2003) Pathways to the graphicacy club: the crossroad of home and preschool. *Journal of Early Childhood Literacy*, 3(1): 5–35.

Argyle, M. (1988) *Bodily Communication* (2nd edn). London: Routledge.

Bernstein, B. (1996) *Pedagogy, Symbolic Control and Identity: Theory, Research, Critique*. London: Taylor & Francis.

Bourne, J. and Jewitt, C. (2003) Orchestrating debate: a multimodal approach to the study of the teaching of higher order literacy skills. *Reading, Literacy and Language Journal*, UKLA (July): 64–72.

Bruner, J. (1985) Vygotsky: a historical and conceptual perspective. In J.V. Wertsch (ed.) *Culture, Communication and Cognition: Vygotskian Perspectives*, pp. 21–34. Cambridge: Cambridge University Press.

Burgoon, J.K. (1994) Nonverbal signals. In M.L. Knapp and G.R. Miller (eds) *Handbook of Interpersonal Communication* (2nd edn). Thousand Oaks, CA: Sage.

Daniels, H. (2001) *Vygotsky and Pedagogy*. London: RoutledgeFalmer.

David, T. and Goouch, K. (2001) Early literacy teaching: the 'third way'. *Education 3 to 13* (June): 20–24. UK: Primary School Research and Development Group.

Donaldson, M. (1978) *Children's Minds*. London: Fontana Press.

Edwards, D. and Maybin, J. (1987) *Communication and Education: The Development of Understanding in the Classroom*. Milton Keynes: Open University Press.

Edwards, D. and Mercer, N. (1987) *Common Knowledge: The Development of Understanding in the Classroom* (2nd edn). London: Methuen.

Flewitt, R. (2003) Is Every Child's Voice Heard? Longitudinal Case Studies of 3-year-old Children's Communicative Strategies at Home and in a Preschool Playgroup. Unpublished Ph.D. thesis, University of Southampton.

Forman, E.A., Minick, N. and Stone, C.A. (eds) (1993) *Contexts for Learning: Sociocultural Dynamics in Children's Development*. Oxford: Oxford University Press.

Jordan, B. (2004) Scaffolding learning and co-constructing understandings. In A. Anning, J. Cullen and M. Fleer (eds) *Early Childhood Education: Society and Culture*, pp. 31–42. London: Sage.

Kirshner, D. and Whitson, J.A. (eds) (1997) *Situated Cognition: Social, Semiotic, and Psychological Perspectives*. Manwah, NJ: Lawrence Erlbaum Associates.

Knapp, M.L., Miller, G.R. and Fudge, K. (1994) Background and current trends in the study of interpersonal communication. In M.L. Knapp and G.R. Miller (eds) *Handbook of Interpersonal Communication* (pp. 3–22) (2nd edn). Thousand Oaks, CA: Sage.

Kress, G. (1997) *Before Writing: Rethinking the Paths to Literacy*. London: Routledge.

Kress, G. and Van Leeuwen, T. (2001) *Multimodal Discourse: The Modes and Media of Contemporary Communication*. London: Arnold.

Kress, G., Jewitt, C., Bourne, J., Franks, A., Hardcastle, J., Jones, K. and Reid, E. (2004) *English in Urban Classrooms: A Multimodal Perspective on Teaching and Learning*. London: RoutledgeFalmer.

Lancaster, L. (2001) Staring at the page: the functions of gaze in a young child's interpretation of symbolic forms. *Journal of Early Childhood Literacy*, 1(2): 131–152.

Lave, J. and Wenger, E. (1991) *Situated Learning: Legitimate Peripheral Participation*. Cambridge: Cambridge University Press.

Matoesian, G.M. and Coldren, J.R. (2002) Language and bodily conduct in focus group evaluations of legal policy. *Discourse and Society*, 13(4): 469–493.

Mercer, N. (1995) *The Guided Construction of Knowledge – Talk Amongst Teachers and Learners*. Clevedon: Multilingual Matters.

Newman, D., Griffin, P. and Cole, M. (1989) *The Construction Zone*. Cambridge: Cambridge University Press.

Orchard, J. (1996) A study of time utilisation in the reception class with particular reference to teacher–pupil interaction. *Early Child Development and Care*, 115(1): 125–139.

Pahl, K. (2002) Ephemera, mess and miscellaneous piles: texts and practices in families. *Journal of Early Childhood Literacy*, 2(2): 145–166.

Payler, J.K. (2005). Exploring Foundations: Sociocultural Influences on the Learning Processes of Four Year Old Children in a Preschool and Reception Class. Unpublished Ph.D. thesis, University of Southampton.

Rogoff, B. (1990) *Apprenticeship in Thinking*. Oxford: Oxford University Press.

Rogoff, B. and Lave, J. (eds) (1984) *Everyday Cognition: Its Development in Social Context*. Cambridge, MA: Harvard University Press.

Schaffer, H.R. (1996) Joint involvement episodes as context for development. In H. Daniels (ed.) *An Introduction to Vygotsky* (pp. 251–280). London: Routledge.

Sharpe, T. (2006). 'Unpacking' scaffolding: identifying discourse and multimodal strategies that support learning. *Language and Education*, 20(3): 211–231.

Sinclair, J. and Coulthard, M. (1975) *Towards an Analysis of Discourse: The English Used by Teachers and Pupils*. Oxford: Oxford University Press.

Siraj-Blatchford, I., Sylva, K., Taggart, B., Sammons, P., Melhuish, E. and Elliot, K. (2003) The Effective Provision of Preschool Education (EPPE) Project: Technical Paper 10, *Intensive Case Studies of Practice across the Foundation Stage*. London: Institute of Education.

Stone, C. (1993) What is missing in the metaphor of scaffolding? In E.A. Forman, N. Minnick and C.A. Stone (eds) *Contexts for Learning: Sociocultural Dynamics in Children's Development* (pp. 169–183). Oxford: Oxford University Press.

Sylva, K., Roy, D. and Painter, M. (1980) *Childwatching at Playgroup and Nursery School*. Oxford: Blackwell.

Thornton, S. (1995) *Children Solving Problems*. Cambridge, MA: Harvard University Press.

Tizard, B., Hughes, M., Carmichael, H. and Pinkerton, G. (1983) Language and social class: is verbal deprivation a myth? *Journal of Child Psychology and Psychiatry*, 24(4): 533–542.

Vygotsky, L. (1986) *Thought and Language* (revised and edited by A. Kozulin). Cambridge, MA: MIT Press.

Vygotsky, L. (1994) *The Vygotsky Reader*. Oxford: Blackwell.

Wang, X., Bernas, R. and Eberhard, P. (2001) Effects of teachers' verbal and non-verbal scaffolding on everyday classroom performances of students with Down Syndrome. *International Journal of Early Years Education*, 9(1): 71–80.

Wells, G. and Nicholls, J. (1985) *Language and Learning: An Interactional Perspective*. Lewes: Falmer Press.

Willes, M. (1983) *Children into Pupils*. London: Routledge & Kegan Paul.

Wood, D. (1988) *How Children Think and Learn*. Oxford: Blackwell.

Wood, D., Bruner, J. and Ross, G. (1976) The role of tutoring in problem-solving. *Journal of Child Psychology and Psychiatry*, 17: 89–100.

12 Forging and fostering relationships in play

Whose zone is it anyway?

Kathy Goouch

In this chapter, the principles and practice of teachers are considered in the context of high levels of curriculum and pedagogical prescription currently evident in the education system in England. In some early years contexts children quickly learn to comply and to forgo or compromise their urges, desires, passions or dreams in favour of completing teacher-led activities designed to propel them through a national programme of learning. This report of work in progress considers why some teachers are able instead to give status to play, to intuitively respond to children in storying play contexts, to co-construct play narratives, and to place the intentions of the children at the forefront of the play context rather than the nationally prescribed objectives and preconceived outcomes.

In this study of exceptional early years professionals, the influences and intentions of such teachers are identified and examined and their intuitive behaviour deconstructed. Through conversation they describe who they believe they are and how they view their professional roles, uncovering as they do so the respect they hold for children and childhood. In their nursery classrooms, instead of 'allowing' play or relegating it to corners of time and space, play is central, and is led, directed and orchestrated by the children. The adults support and maintain play rather than hijacking or redefining the purposes or the action. As the stories of the teachers begin to unfold, the subtlety of their practice is demonstrated and their skills, commitment and professionalism become clearly evident.

Introduction

> Language and the word are almost everything in life.
> The word is a drama.

> (Bakhtin 1986)

In many early years classroom settings it is possible to witness how teachers claim the play discourse, leading, directing, redirecting, approving or rejecting children's utterances as they attempt to identify and work, in a Vygotskian sense, within children's 'zone of proximal development' (Vygotsky 1978: 85). This may take children's performances towards pre-ordained curricula outcomes and 'allowing' play, while accounting for it in nationally recognised terms enables teachers to be creatively compliant (Lambirth and Goouch 2006). However, this approach also appropriates or hijacks children's play intentions and sends direct messages to them in relation to choice, freedom, control and dominance. In such circumstances, Wertsch asks the 'Bakhtinian' question 'Who is doing the talking?' and challenges the privileging of some texts and some speech genres over others (Wertsch 1991). There are echoes of Bernstein here and, as play, by some definitions, has now been legitimised (DfES 2007), it is possible to see that some teachers, without understanding the depth and complexity of the play, may use the opportunity to capitalise on the way children 'exteriorise' themselves through play, offering opportunities for 'surveillance' and screening (Bernstein 1997: 60). Play and the outcomes of play can then simply be reinterpreted and reshaped according to the prevailing requirements of the system and the explicit intentions of the teacher rather than to serve the intentionality of the child. Neutral positions though are also impossible and equally, as Bakhtin claims, 'there can be no such thing as an absolutely neutral utterance'; teachers and other adults involved directly in children's learning are, by their adulthood, at least involved in implicitly culturally related transmissions. Bakhtin further explores this idea that utterances or speech acts are not isolated or 'indifferent' to each other:

> Our speech, that is all our utterances (including creative works) is filled with others' words, varying degrees of otherness or varying degrees of 'our-own-ness' varying degrees of awareness and attachment.
>
> (Bakhtin 1986: 59)

This idea of mirroring and 'consensual dialogue' (Carter 2004: 67) must be viewed alongside issues of power relationships and the fact that children are pretrained in knowing the cultural space that is 'school' or 'nursery' and the expectations of them once they arrive. However, it is also true that although the context and the situation may not be voluntary for young children, moments of dialogue may be; young children invariably give permission for intimacy in dialogic exchanges with adults, most often teachers. The outcomes however remain the same, that 'any utterance is a link in a very complex organised chain of other utterances' (Bakhtin 1986: 69) and therefore the enormously significant role of adults sharing time with children at play ultimately becomes visible in children's words and their made worlds.

It is also possible to find an alternative practice. There are teachers who respectfully join with children in play, engage in intimate conversations and are themselves responsive to children's directions, language and intentions without appropriating the play for their own purposes. This kind of organic pedagogy, developing out of the moment, may be described as 'intuitive' (Atkinson and Claxton 2000). This chapter will report on the progress of a study which explores some elements of the identities and activities of teachers who engage in serious and complex play interactions and narrative co-constructions with young children, operating only within the 'zones' that children themselves describe.

The context

This study is being undertaken in a highly charged political context with professional identity being reconceptualised in relation to performativity, levels of professional accountability and new professional cultures (Ball 2004; Olssen *et al.* 2004). There are also growing concerns and a developing bank of anecdotal and research evidence that some teachers are engaged in 'strategic compliance' (Lacey, in Woods and Jeffrey 2004: 236), finding ways to retain integrity in curriculum corners rather than completely compromising either children's opportunities or their own place in a results and target-driven system.

Currently there also seems to be an 'interdiscipline' battle between psychologists, some of whom claim that, for example, the teaching of reading is straightforward if teachers simply deliver the code to children at the earliest possible opportunity and certainly before the age of 5, as recommended by *The Independent Review of Early Reading* (Rose 2006), and educators and educationalists who claim that *how* this occurs is as important as *that* it occurs. It is fascinating to see how, in this age of neuroscience and increasing technological support for understanding how we develop, think and learn, there remains a naive view that 'instruction' is synonymous with 'teaching' and that children therefore learn when 'taught' in a straightforward causal way. Understanding and conceptualising pedagogy has never been more important or more widely challenged than it is now. There exist such narrow views and systems of accountability for practice that simple causal connections appear attractive; that is, teachers teach and so learners learn; with the implication that if children are unable to learn in this way they, or indeed their teachers, are in some way deficient.

In the early years of education, however, there appears still to be an opportunity to account for children's learning through a pedagogy steeped in play and led by children, and to create classroom cultures that allow children to spend time learning before they encounter classrooms bounded by a culture of performance, driven by testing and results. In *The Early Years Foundation Stage* framework (DfES 2007), while there is clearly evidence of new influence from central government in the form of *The Independent Review of Early Reading* (Rose 2006), there remains a robust commitment to sound principles of early education, particularly in relation to the connectedness of children's development and learning, the acknowledgement that children learn at their own pace, the importance of enabling children to develop a positive sense of self and the central idea that learning generally occurs in social contexts. There are still, however, conflicting views being represented and the discourse in relation to play remains a challenge. In this latest policy document there are repeated references to 'planned, purposeful play' (DfES 2007: 11, 2.5) and *The Independent Review of Early Reading* refers to 'instructive learning play environments' (Rose 2006: 105). This contradictory use of terminology, the conflation of 'instructive' and 'planned' with play, appears to emanate from the difficulties we have in deciding what we (that is, a democratically elected government and their civil servants) want from and for children, childhood and schooling. The recent, and frequently cited, DfES-funded *Effective Provision of Pre-school Education* study (EPPE, Sylva *et al*. 2004) and the subsequent *Researching Effective Pedagogy in the Early Years* (REPEY, Siraj Blatchford *et al*. 2002) concluded first that 'good quality provision' can help to limit the effects of social disadvantage and then, most significantly:

> The provision of exploratory play environments (eg sand/water play) will only be 'effective' if the materials/apparatus are chosen carefully to provide cognitive challenge within the zone of proximal development *and* positive outcomes for the activity are either modelled, demonstrated, explained or otherwise identified in the children's experiences and actions, and encouraged.
>
> (Siraj-Blatchford and Sylva 2004: 727)

Although this statement is then qualified slightly, it remains the case that such predetermined outcomes, the intentions of teachers following a curriculum, extolling behaviours and language that are preconceived to be 'appropriate', are all intended to precede or potentially overpower the intentionality of the child. It seems that teachers are caught in the dichotomy of either planning to allow play in unregulated, and therefore, by association, unimportant corners of the classroom and the curriculum classroom (an example of this may be 'golden time') or allowing play as long as it fulfils, or can be shaped towards, pre-ordained curricula intentions, 'the zone' described above. Teachers whose practice cannot be easily characterised in this way are rare but are still to be found. The two teachers discussed in this chapter have not been chosen randomly, but have instead been identified as intuitive teachers who engage in serious and complex play interactions and narrative co-constructions with young children.

Methodology

Any attempt to understand play discourse is naturally challenged by the need to understand those involved, their motives, their influences, their intentions and, perhaps, their identities. While it would clearly be of interest to consider these separately in relation to policy-makers, politicians and parents, the purpose of this study is simply to look closely only at two teachers of young children, (3 and 4 year olds), and to try collaboratively with them to understand their practice from the inside out, the teachers themselves, as well as from the outside in, the evidence from observed practice.

Data have been collected from structured interviews, semi-structured meetings, less formal conversations, video material and field notes. Some aspects of the life histories of these teachers and the range of political, policy, institutional, cultural and cross-national influences on the teachers' identities are being examined, at a time when teachers' roles are being increasingly seen as technical in nature and skills-based in content and reduced to curriculum delivery rather than 'an engagement with other minds' (Pring 2004: 68) or 'an act of love' (Freire 1967: 38).

The teachers in this study, rather than allowing themselves to become technicians, are engaged in 'teaching as a personal activity' (Nias 1989). In his consideration of professional values and ethics, Carr claims that teachers need a combination of technical skills, in which he includes communication, management and organisation, with skills of evaluation to provide a context of 'professional judgement' (Carr 2000: 111). Making sense of this idea of professional judgement in early years education will contribute to the development of a theory of practice, not for proscriptive purposes but for the more important reason of exemplification to form a hypothesis about intuitive teachers and teaching, and about the nature of 'human encounters' (McLean 1991).

Rather than focus on all activities in early years settings in which teachers engage with children, the interactions of interest for this study have been confined to 'storying' events.

Storying events

A child (or children) are serving their own intentions in play and constructing stories, narrations, to inform and support that play.

A teacher (in this study, a title conferred on all adults intentionally concerned with children's learning) provides resources/props, observes, listens and interacts with storying children in order to offer care and support to the child and/or to confirm, consolidate, inform, extend the development or learning opportunity. The interaction may take the form of physical presence, gesturing or oral interjections.

'Storying' happens when children create narratives, without instruction, coercion or conventional use of pencil and paper, and for their own purposes. Within such events, children make visible, re-create, what is in their mind's eye, interweaving significant people, and often create complex intertextual narratives. Some teachers join in, play, engage in intimate conversations and are responsive to children through such storying events. Storying spaces are of particular interest because the personal investments of the child and of the teacher separately become visible. Bernstein's notions of invisible pedagogies and his theory of teacher responses to child spontaneity in play can be associated with the ways in which teachers attempt to co-construct stories with children in play as they may be using them either implicitly or explicitly to 'socialise, acculturate and educate' (Kiesling and Paulston 2005: 13).

In effect it is essential to consider this work in three distinct but overlapping parts; the first identifying and underlining the assumption that storying events are significant in early years education, the second examining the 'essence' of storying teachers and the third attempting to establish the nature of storying relationships, although these will only be considered in part in this chapter. In order to understand all of these elements it is important to interrogate the actions, interactions, processes and the people involved in storying. While it has been argued that 'teacher belief and action are bound together in complex ways' (McLean 1991:7), work on this study has required the participants to deconstruct action and account for it in terms of their beliefs. The teachers in this study have been asked to narrate their experiences, explore a reflexive self-awareness and to share in the analysis. Human behaviour is complex in its performance, and outsider interpretation is fraught with difficulty and susceptible to prejudice and bias. In an attempt to counter this, three-way conversations took place, also enabling the teacher/ researcher role to be expanded. In this way, and in trusting relationships, it became possible to uncover and articulate the teachers' depth of understanding of themselves and their professional role. This kind of collaborative interpretive analysis has now become central to this work.

Images and conversations: the data

For the purpose of structuring the first interview, categories derived from the work of Day *et al.* (2006) were adapted slightly and applied:

1 Self-image: Who do I think I am? How would you describe yourself in your professional role?
2 Self-esteem: How do you evaluate yourself as a teacher?
3 Motivation: Why are you so committed to your job?
4 Task perception: How do you describe your job, to yourself and to others?
5 Future perspective: What are your future expectations of your job?

Both participants offered full and thoughtful responses to each of the prompts. The following headings were useful at an initial stage to group together some of the key responses; for example:

• *Relationships*: Particular emphasis was placed on relationships with parents and families, 'We're all in this together', 'We're all learning together; getting parents to feel they're part of the process; I value what they've done and are doing'. In both interviews, relationships at all levels was the most consistent theme: 'I would describe myself as someone who thinks that relationships are the most important thing, with parents and children – without them you have nothing'; 'As I've grown in understanding about parenting and parents, I realise that only by understanding and responding to parents, supporting them, will I have any lasting impact on the child'.

- *Pedagogy*: Both listed aspects as they defined their job and both lists included listening, observing, talking and joining in play: 'Children are amazing. They're amazed at what seems ordinary. It's awe and wonder with little children', 'Knowledge is a small part, I've just got more confident that that's not the most important part of my role', 'It's for them to come to me, not for me to decide what's important to them, you've got to let them take you', 'I don't want to know what's going to happen before the children, some of the best things happen when I just give it a go'.
- *Professional reflections*: The teachers evaluated themselves highly in their work: 'I can see what I do at work – feedback from parents, teachers and children – is positive', 'My practice is good, I work at it, I know where it needs to improve', 'Sometimes I stop and look around and they're all involved; someone else can look around and think that's easy but it's not'.

Of course, talk about professional life may not correspond with the realities of practice and in this study methods included gathering field notes from observation and jointly viewing video material that the participants had created, as well as these semi-structured interviews. Such mixed methods were supporting the idea of collecting a mosaic of research material that the teachers could review and discuss during the process of analysis.

First observation

The first observation created the first surprise of the study. Although both teachers were known to me, through contact on other research projects and work with students as well as previous visits to both settings, for the purposes of this research, closer observations and analyses were required. During the process of analysing the data and reviewing the observations, I realised that, actually, the practice of the teachers was considerably different, though I had assumed, most recently from the interview data, that they would be working in similar, if not the same ways. There were of course similarities:

- Both demonstrate absolute respect for children.
- Both demonstrate absolute respect for play, play stories and play contexts.
- In both practices, the power of their relationships with the children is evident.
- In both practices, knowledge of the children is implicit in talk and actions.
- Both teachers appear to be intuitive in their responses and their practice generally.
- There was evidence of complete trust in the teachers by the children.
- There was no apparent predetermined 'direction' to the play.

The differences were significant.

- J initiates, models, participates, multi-voices, is a player.
- M is an 'addressee', leaves respectful spaces, observes more than plays.

J's talk is often a narration of the action of play:

> Hello is that your baby? She wants some toast, she whispered in my ear
> 'Have you got any strawberry jam?
> There is some toast but no strawberry jam to put on it.
> The dinosaurs might like to eat the toast.
> Do you know I think you've had burglars in your house! It's in a terrible mess.
> Look at S's house – she's got a lot of tidying up to do.
> Yummy, yummy, mmm, beans and sausages.
> Where's the knife gone – that's a spoon?
> Can you believe it? They've left all this food on the floor.
> Look Bs going to make food for her baby.

Rogoff describes this as the way in which 'middle-class adults often search for common reference points, translating the adult understanding of the situation into a form that is within children's grasp' (Rogoff 1990: 72). Unconsciously, Teacher J is initially, herself, constructing understandings of the moment, shaping them to make them intelligible to children and overlaying them on to the children's actions, thereby implicitly shaping their view of the world, drawing them into her assumptions of shared understanding.

Teacher M is often a silent observer/player, appearing useful to the children for carrying or helping to construct but often a lesser player rather than a lead. The notion of 'addressivity' is important in this context of play dialogues. Carter uses Bakhtin's work to explain this idea:

> *Addressivity* [underlines] the importance of an addressee, a listener who can also have a creative role to play in a dialogue, even if sometimes only a silent, non-verbal one.
>
> (Carter 2004: 68)

M's verbal contributions are often barely audible and complement rather than narrate action. For example, M made only 17 utterances in the 20-minute observed play period and they were all similarly unobtrusive:

> I think Sam might be blasting off here.
> Tell me what its going to be Billy?
> Is it part of the rocket?

She asked questions without always having the expectation of them necessarily being answered and always placing the children in the role of expert. Rogoff's claim (1990: 18) that in middle-class homes 'social interaction and children's activities are not designed explicitly for the future edification of the children' seems also to apply to Teacher M's practice. Rogoff (ibid.) continues:

> most of children's lives involve interactions and social arrangements that are organized to accomplish the task of the moment and may carry tacit lessons

for alert children, without being explicitly or intentionally focused on communication or instruction.

When discussing these behaviours with the teachers, they commented that 'You best guess their intentions and purposes', 'Observing, listening and making sense of what you see', 'influencing but not imposing'. They talked about how these pedagogical decisions were made and about influences that shaped their practice: 'Everything I do now comes from me, at the core, and experiences, courses, children and colleagues', 'significant others', 'Subconsciously, these influences get caught, like a filter, some things stick', 'It's about being professional'. There seems to be a sense in this conversation that the teachers are describing a 'melding' of who they believe they are with what they have experienced and how they view their professional roles; all intrinsically concerned with teacher identity.

Research conversations

There are, at this stage of the study, no concrete findings: only more questions and developing themes to consider with the teachers. While the question of 'What do the teachers believe they are doing?' has in many different ways already been discussed, this needs to be further pursued to cause them to articulate their core professional aims. Related to this is the second question of 'Why do they do the things they do? What do they hope to achieve for themselves and/or for the children? What is their ultimate aim or short-term objectives?' Further elucidation is also required in relation to the question of 'What is informing them?' and discussion of these issues in relation to their knowledge of public policy and their intuitive practice. Both teachers claim to be 'reluctant shapers' and yet there is subtle evidence that, as in all adult–child interactions, whether implicit or not, as Rogoff claims, whether by design or not, tacit lessons may be learned by the children. And so the questions 'In what knowing ways are they shaping the children?' and 'Is there any sense in which they feel they are manipulating the play?' both need to be asked at this stage of the study. While the teachers were surprised that there could be any doubt about cultural transmissions (we discussed their simple insistence on 'please' and 'thank you', taking turns and similar standard and often embedded cultural practices), they were equally robust that their intentions were not to mould children's behaviours. The examples used were viewed as being intrinsically important and not in question. Equally, questioning the tidiness of the playhouse appeared to be spontaneously delivered, not particularly retained as significant, nor considered to be especially worthy of deconstruction, connecting in part to Bernstein's notion of invisible pedagogy (Bernstein 1997).

Themes of awareness and detachment, addressivity, consensual collaboration, multi-voicing, seeking mutuality and leading or being led, all continue to be evident in conversations, observations and analysis. However, a developing, and now rather central challenge in the research conversations in the second stage of this study has been consistently to ask the teachers 'Who do you think you are?' in order to enable some deconstruction of both role and identity and the relationship between the two. This question, 'Who do you think you are?' has a dual function: while its first is literally to require some personal definition of identity with the stress on the question word 'who', the second purpose is to challenge the teachers' sense of autonomy and authority with the stress on the second half of the question. This test of any sense of professional authority is in answer to the kind of challenge made by Durkheim (1956) of the functional and societal requirements of education and therefore the accountability of public servants who work in the field. Those teachers who are currently employing a central and fundamental 'relational' approach to their pedagogical choices are not working within the current, political imperative to frame teaching as a technical act. Such teachers, in answer to the question asked earlier by Wertsch, are doing their own talking and furthermore allowing children to do *their* talking; thus allowing a democratic process to evolve in the early years of education. They have, however, both a moral and an economic duty to be accountable for such practice and this needs to be achieved, although perhaps in ways other than through creative compliance or spurious national testing arrangements.

'No one's got a clue how things should be'

Significantly, both participants in this study were very knowledgeable about current policies directly impacting on their practice as well as the broader political platform in relation to early years education now in evidence. However, their responses in relation to questions focusing on the purposes of education centred completely on children as individuals in their care rather than relating to the bigger policy picture:

Q: What do you think early education is for?
A: It's helping them to enjoy now, not preparing them . . .
   . . . helping them find things they might like to explore; didn't explore as confidently as they might; take more risks . . .
   . . . it's about helping children to be who they are; explore their strengths.
   . . . being with them to make sense, discovering what's going on.
   . . . being comfortable with who they are.
   . . . creating a place where they can develop decent human relationships.
   . . . helping children to have more control over their own lives.

In these extracts from the conversation, it is possible to see the ethical grounds on which the two teachers are basing their practice. This kind of ethical knowledge has been described as '*the* specialised knowledge base of teaching expertise' (Campbell 2003: 138, italics in original), which mirrors closely one participant's view reported earlier that 'Knowledge is a small part, not the most important part, of my role'.

   In many of our conversations the term 'genuine' was used, as in, for example, 'I'm genuinely interested in why and how children are doing the things they do'.

This level of authenticity – of honesty – in their role as teacher has shone through, for example, 'If you want to get to the children, build up real relationships, it's no good being the teacher'. Of course, children can 'sense when teachers genuinely care about them; they can sniff out hypocrisy in a flash; and they are alert to differences between the supercilious and the authentic' (Campbell 2003: 23), and young children invariably act upon their knowledge – either trusting their teacher or not. In fact, I have vivid memories of my own daughter's dilemma when, aged 5, she described her teacher as 'only smiling with her teeth' – perhaps an intuitive response to insincerity. Rogoff describes children as 'tuned to pick up the interpretation and viewpoint of others' (Rogoff 1990: 73) and often active in seeking intersubjectivity. In this study the participants frequently spoke, in Rogoff's terms, of 'inserting their interaction into the ongoing activity' and 'bridging understanding' (1990: 79). Although Rogoff is describing research with infants, the same is easily applied to the work of these teachers with three and four year olds:

> . . . You best guess their intentions and purposes.
> . . . Observing, listening and making sense of what you see.
> . . . What's important to me is you see what the child's intention is – you feed into it.
> . . . I let it go where its going.
> . . . You can do it by leading, modelling.
> . . . Show them another way to play.
> . . . You have an alertness to likelihoods.
> . . . You respond to how she makes sense of things.

This kind of 'joint participation' is very evident in the teachers' work with the children as they became co-players rather than instructors; guides rather than leaders.

Conclusions

Very strong policy imperatives have been emanating from central government to effect change in early years education in England. The political rhetoric of the moment is in need of careful examination as it seems to be offering teachers of young children conflicting messages, sometimes misappropriating the discourse of the research field but generally urging forward a standards agenda, irrespective of children's circumstances, their family or cultural context, their economic background or their early experiences. In his maiden speech, the Secretary of State for Children, Schools and Families claimed that his new department is the *Every Child Matters* Department and described a choice between taking account of 'standards' and taking into account the 'whole view of the child' as futile and 'old-fashioned'. He declared the need to 'break down the false divide between policies to support achievement and policies to support well-being' (13 July 2007). However, in a powerful critique of the 'instrumentalization of the expressive' Hartley (2006: 61) presents an argument to demonstrate how the creative or expressive arts are now being commodified to satisfy corporate, commercial and other newly perceived 'performative purposes'. Affective education then becomes of worth only if it satisfies the needs of the economic state and the 'knowledge economy'. Hartley concludes that 'creativity and emotional literacy are being "attached" to an educational practice which remains decidedly performance-driven, standardized and monitored' (2006: 69). Within this argument, political rhetoric – and the Secretary of State's apparently new concerns with a holistic view of education – has new meaning.

In reality, however, the only systems of accountability currently being addressed in schools in England are controlled very carefully by the Office for Standards in Education (OfSTED, which also monitors nursery provision) and the Teacher Development Agency and the publication of League Tables. At every level, 'the discourse of current and recent reforms couches all initiatives in terms of human capital and ensures that only government voices are heard' (Hall 2004: 1), thus diminishing or rendering invalid or weak any attempt to value children's achievements and their teachers' performances in alternate ways. Teachers who only attend to the discourse of 'official science' (Wertsch 1991: 137) and become 'restricted professionals' (Hall 2004: 48) are in danger of becoming highly successful in identifying zones into which government agencies require children to move and develop. Focusing professional engagement and children's valuable time on a somewhat blinkered approach to education and learning will always be at the expense of other pedagogical choices. As Young (2006: 20) argues, 'where education is increasingly directed to political and economic goals and justified by them . . . this instrumentalism necessarily reduces the space and autonomy for the work of specialist professionals'.

There seem, however, to be some small glimpses of hope for respect to be given to the zones of development that children themselves are motivated towards and consequently keen to reach. The teachers in this study appear to be spending their valuable time with children capitalising on opportunities to support and guide the creative, problem-solving, world-making, energetic and curious risk-takers whom young children invariably are.

References

Atkinson, T. and Claxton, C. (2000) *The Intuitive Practitioner, On the Value of Not Always Knowing What One is Doing*. Buckingham: Open University Press.

Bakhtin, M.M. (1981) *The Dialogic Imagination*. Austin, TX: University of Texas Press.

Bakhtin, M.M. (1986) *Speech Genres and Other Late Essays*, trans. Vera McGee, ed. Caryl Emerson and Michael Holquist. Austin, TX: University of Texas Press.

Ball, S.J. (2004) *The RoutledgeFalmer Reader in Sociology of Education*. London: RoutledgeFalmer.

Balls, E. (2007) The Every Child Matters Department. Speech by Ed Balls, Secretary of State for Children, Schools and Families, 18 July, Business Design Centre, Islington.

Bernstein, B. (1975) *Class, Codes and Control: Toward a Theory of Educational Transmission* (2nd edn). London: Routledge & Kegan Paul.

Bernstein, B. (1997) Class and pedagogies: visible and invisible. In A.H. Halsey, H. Lauder,

P. Brown and A.S. Wells (eds) *Education, Culture, Economy and Society*. Oxford: Oxford University Press.

Campbell, E. (2003) *The Ethical Teacher*. Maidenhead: Open University Press.

Carr, D. (2000) *Professionalism and Ethics in Teaching*. London: RoutledgeFalmer.

Carter, R. (2004) *Language and Creativity, The Art of Common Talk*. London: Routledge.

Day, C., Kington, A., Gordon, S. and Sammons, P. (2006) The personal and professional selves of teachers: stable and unstable identities. *British Educational Research Journal*, 32(4): 601–616.

Department for Education and Skills (DfES) (2007) *The Early Years Foundation Stage*. London: DfES.

Durkheim, E. (1956) *Education and Society*. New York: The Free Press.

Freire, P. (1967) *Education: The Practice of Freedom*. London: Writers and Readers Publishing Cooperative.

Hall, K. (2004) *Literacy and Schooling, Towards Renewal in Primary Education Policy*. Aldershot: Ashgate.

Hartley, D. (2006) The instrumentalization of the expressive in education. In A. Moore (ed.) *Schooling, Society and Curriculum*. London: Routledge.

Kiesling, S.F. and Paulston, C.B. (2005) *Intercultural Discourse and Communication*. Oxford: Blackwell.

Lambirth, A. and Goouch, K. (2006) Islands of independence. *Literacy, Reading and Language*. 40(3): 146–152.

McLean, S.V. (1991) *The Human Encounter: Teachers and Children Living Together in Preschools*. London: Falmer.

Nias, J. (1989) *Primary Teachers Talking: A Study of Teaching as Work*. London: Routledge.

Olssen, M., Codd, J. and O'Neill, A.M. (2004) *Education Policy, Globalisation, Citizenship and Democracy*. London: Sage.

Pring, R. (2004) *Philosophy of Education*. London: Continuum.

Rogoff, B. (1990) *Apprenticeship in Thinking, Cognitive Development in Social Context*. Oxford: Oxford University Press.

Rose, J. (2006) *The Independent Review of the Teaching of Early Reading*. London: DfES.

Siraj-Blatchford, I. and Sylva, K. (2004) Researching pedagogy in English pre-schools. *British Educational Research Journal*, 30(5): 713–730.

Siraj-Blatchford, I., Sylva, K., Muttock, S., Gilden, R. and Bell, D. (2002) *Researching Effective Pedagogy in the Early Years*, London: DfES, Research Report 356.

Sylva, K., Melhuish, E., Sammons, P., Siraj-Blatchford, I. and Taggart, B. (2004) *The Effective Provision of Pre-school Education* (EPPE). London: DfES Research Report.

Vygotsky, L. (1978 translation) *Mind In Society, The Development of Higher Psychological Processes*. Cambridge, MA: Harvard University Press.

Wertsch, J.V. (1991) *Voices of the Mind*. Cambridge, MA: Harvard University Press.

Woods, P. and Jeffrey, B. (2004) The reconstruction of primary teachers' identities. In S.J. Ball (ed.) *Sociology of Education*. London: RoutledgeFalmer.

Part III

Adult–adult relationships for professional development

Introduction

> The learner has experiences and knowledge that become the lenses through which new knowledge, information and experience are filtered and understood to identify relationships between them and construct new ideas that have personal meaning and inform their actions.
>
> (Chapter 1)

Professional development through a variety of professional interactions has to be a key area in considering relational pedagogy. Teachers learn from and through their learners and, provided they have the skills, passion, confidence and knowledge to reflect on their own learning, it is possible to secure a high-quality learning experience for all involved in pedagogical relationships. Quality learning experiences also require sensitivity, intuition and confidentiality in interactions with learners, parents and other professionals, and demand team-based decision-making and the practical resolution of differences of opinion. In adult–adult relationships there are also issues of credibility, trust, clarity of interactions, resilience, respect, successful collaboration and emotional competence to consider as well as personal and professional growth and development. These are just some of the themes which readers will find embedded in the final five chapters of this book.

Analysing, evaluating and making changes to everyday practice can be an extremely complex and a potentially threatening venture for many practitioners, particularly those who work in multidisciplinary teams where understanding of other viewpoints might be superficial. Yet the processes of relational pedagogy demand that current practice is scrutinised, examined and interpreted in ways that may not be 'comfortable' to the participants (see Moyles and Adams 2001). As Margonis (1999) explains, some educational relationships proceed smoothly as if the learner and teacher are already comfortable with one another's attitudes, ways of acting and ways of speaking. This is what we should be aiming for in relational pedagogy terms whether the 'learners' are two professionals, practitioners and parents or teachers and children. This fostering and forging of relationships (in this context at the professional level) and ways of working with children, families and colleagues was a key element throughout the original ARU conference. Gold (2005) assures us that relationships are seen as always in motion, always subject to variation and in need of repeated assessment: in adult–adult relationships this is certainly the case, as 'knowing' may well occur at deeper and deeper levels as professional and personal relationships develop. Being secure in professional relationships means being secure in oneself and having a clear understanding of one's own identity and self-knowledge. One's own role also functions in itself as the basis for interactions with others. Support from other people to extend and enhance this understanding can come from such systems as mentoring and other participative ventures (Moyles *et al.* 1999).

This final section commences with Chapter 13, written by Kim Insley and Sylvia Lucas, who explore the collaborative relationships between teachers and teaching assistants working together. They suggest that the current UK focus on adult–child relationships (embodied in the *Every Child Matters* agenda, DfES 2003) must now also shift to the professional development of adults working together. They feel that early childhood practitioners must take account of their own relationships to enable them to ensure that children are able to establish secure relationships. Insley and Lucas assert that little attention has been paid to understanding schools in the light of the psychology of organisations or applying group relations theory to staff teams and feel that the opposite is often true, where funding and time for supporting schools in this deeper self-reflective work is non-existent.

In Chapter 14, Florence Dinneen offers a slightly different perspective in presenting her research on relationship training for Educare students training to work with babies. Quoting Arnett's (1989) study, she reports that caregivers who have completed a four-year university-based programme in early childhood studies unsurprisingly rate higher in skill and competence in their work compared with those who have had less training. In her own preliminary research, her findings to date suggest that there is a direct correlation between relational pedagogy, sensitivity of carers and the developmental potential of young children, and that focused training of students empowers the recipients to become confident and professional *educarers*.

Ruby Oates, Andrew Sanders and colleagues (Chapter 15) present a very adult-to-adult perspective in discussing the development of relationships behind the processes of a multidisciplinary team reframing a BA Early Childhood Studies degree at an English university. In the chapter, the group articulate different and emerging team views, putting the process of potential change in context and offering key background thinking, practical challenges and issues so that others may learn from their experiences. In relational pedagogy terms, Oates and her colleagues consider that reclaiming relational pedagogy is currently about aiming to enrich their interactions in a context one step removed from the student/child encounter. The very diversity of experience in the team means that they have started to appreciate rather than suppress differences and also begun to move away from mechanistic and uniform delivery of the degree course into the far less certain, yet infinitely more exciting and groundbreaking arena of relational pedagogy.

We move to Iceland in Chapter 16 to learn about cooperation between play-schools and families and the challenges being faced in building relationships between homes and schools. Johanna Einarsdottir and Bryndis Gardarsdottir report on research they have conducted regarding playschool teachers' attitudes towards parents. They point out that the idea of parents as equal and active partners is new to Icelandic playschool teachers and parents. They conclude that cooperation with parents concerning their children's education and welfare and their involvement in decision-making is an important aspect of quality early childhood programmes. However, Icelandic playschool teachers have an urgent need to reflect on and evaluate this important part of their work and to try to find ways and methods to communicate with all parents to enhance the children's education.

Our final chapter takes us back to the UK and research conducted by Kate Fowler, Alison Robins and their colleagues on the essential role of mentors in early childhood settings. The contributors feel that successful mentoring should be set within an action–reflection cycle for both mentor and mentee and must be based on several key principles of relational pedagogy (i.e. confidentiality, credibility and clarity), and that mentoring should, and does, engender trust between those involved. These interactions and relationships are thought to impact positively on early childhood practitioners themselves and also ultimately on the children. Above all, the writers suggest that critical skills of reflection are crucial to all workers in the field of early childhood, as the importance of insight and under-standing will shape and form not only their immediate practice but potentially the lives of children in education and care and their families.

References

Arnett, J. (1989) Caregivers in daycare centers: does training matter? *Journal of Applied Developmental Psychology*, 10: 541–552.

Department for Education and Skills (DfES) (2003) *Every Child Matters* (Green Paper). London: HMSO.

Gold, L. (2005) An introduction to relational pedagogy: relationships at the heart of learning. Paper presented at the Third International Conference on New Directions in Humanities. Cambridge, 2–5 August.

Margonis, F. (1999) *Relational Pedagogy Without Foundations: Reconstructing the Work of Paulo Freire*. Philosophy of Education Society. Available online at http://www.ed.uiuc.edu/EPS?PES-Yearbook/1999/margonis.asp (accessed 6 May 2007).

Moyles, J. and Adams, S. (2001) *StEPs: Statements of Entitlement to Play*. Maidenhead: Open University Press.

Moyles, J., Suschitzky, W. and Chapman, L. (1999) *Teaching Fledglings to Fly . . .? Mentoring in the Primary School*. London: Association of Teachers and Lecturers.

13 Making the most of the relationship between two adults to impact on early childhood pedagogy

Raising standards and narrowing attainment

Kim Insley and Sylvia Lucas

It is recognised that a relationship of trust between child and adult is crucial to the success of many intervention programmes in raising standards of attainment. Where this is extended to a group of children supported by two adults working as a team within a secure relationship of trust, the benefits for the child and the school are further enhanced.

Many programmes use one-to-one interventions; others group children together. Nurture groups exploit the collaborative relationship between the two adults establishing a knowledge base which includes trust, intuition, attachment theory and the dynamics of relationships. Educating teachers and assistants together develops this understanding. This has implications for early childhood pedagogy in particular within emotional competence, interpersonal relationships and resilience. Reflection on strategies such as conflict resolution, extended conversation opportunities, sharing commitment and trust results in the recognition that these need to be modelled, impacting upon children's attainment through enabling them to establish attachment.

Early childhood practitioners must take account of their own relationships to enable children to establish secure relationships through assimilation. The outcomes of *Every Child Matters* (DfES 2003) imply the need for good relationships to enable children to be healthy; stay safe; and enjoy and achieve. Through established relationships children will make a positive contribution and so achieve economic well-being.

Introduction

In this paper we have chosen to use cameos to describe the practice we are considering so that we can illustrate our critical analysis and ideas behind the research. We start with such a cameo to set the scene:

Cameo 1

Janet, the class teacher, is discussing with the whole class the wonder of the large patchwork quilt she has laid on the floor. She is sharing with the children the beauty of the patterns that happen in the columns and rows. There are 100 squares and the children have cards with numbers on and are placing them on the quilt in the regular pattern of a 100 square. Janet works with her teaching assistant, Claire; another child has an individual support assistant, Jo. Janet and Claire often exchange glances and while Janet is leading the lesson, Claire helps to 'enclose' the children on the floor around the quilt. Jo talks quietly to the child she is supporting; they talk about the 'nine' column. The lesson continues and Claire and Janet share a smile when another child exclaims with delight about the patterns he is seeing: 'Each column has the same numbers but each row has them too but they're different' – both Janet and Claire know he has reached some understanding about tens and units. They will discuss this and record it later, but for now, Janet moves the children to group activities, looking for patterns in different arrangements of 100 number squares.

We could go on, but the description of this Year 1 classroom is chosen because it reflects an aspect of children's learning that is not often explored. We maintain that relationships between adults are as important in enabling children's access to the curriculum as the adult–child relationships. In exploring this statement, we draw on our experiences as teachers, senior managers and partners in educating teachers, teaching assistants and others.

Relationships of trust

Erikson (1950) used the term 'basic trust' to describe the good effects of a child's early care. Bowlby's attachment theory (1952, 1953, 1969) arose from observing children's behaviours when left alone in hospital. As practitioners we are very aware of children who find it difficult to leave parents or carers and settle into school. It is clear that children need to be able to trust and form relationships if they are to settle and learn.

There have been two (or more) adults working in early years settings for much longer than in other aspects of education and care, partly as a recognition that settling children into the school environment needs more than one person, although the knowledge and skills involved in this work have never been clearly defined. In raising standards, the English government, through the Department for Education and Skills (DfES) and the Training and Development Agency for schools (TDA), has recognised that 'every member of staff matters' (Tabberer 2005: 1). Tabberer has suggested that the days of the hero teacher of *Dead Poets Society* fame is no longer the model recognised. The DfES focus is on children

(*Every Child Matters*, DfES 2003) and the importance of the child–adult relationship. Little has been researched within education of the adult–adult relationships. To continue the improvement in standards, we suggest the focus must now shift to the professional development of adults working together.

Adult interventions

There are many interventions to support children's learning. Jo, in Cameo 1, occupies a role recognised by many teachers – the individual support assistant (ISA), although it may include working within a group (and so be supporting others too) where the child is assigned. This deployment of the ISA may lead to the child becoming dependent and may not always be an effective and efficient use of scarce special educational needs (SEN) resources.

Other children may be supported through programmes such as the Early Literacy Support (ELS) and Additional Literacy Support (ALS) of the *National Literacy Strategy* (DfES 2001a) or Reading Recovery (Burroughs-Lange 2006). There are also therapeutic provisions which target children's emotional states; for example, The Place to Be (Batmanghelidjh 2006), and strategies such as circle time (Mosley 2005) which enable children to learn about appropriate social and moral responses. We recognise that all these interventions are helpful and increasingly popular but the emphasis is primarily on the adult–child relationship.

Others who may be working in the classroom include the teaching assistant (TA) such as Claire and learning mentors (LMs). Good practice (Frederickson and Cline 2002) suggests that it is important for the teaching team (the practitioners) to plan, discuss and develop policies together so that all have input into the provision for children. This may have issues for workload: time factors are often cited as the reason why the practice does not always occur although the recent Workforce Reform in schools has established planning, preparation and assessment (PPA) time for teachers. Increasingly TAs 'deliver' teachers' plans in order to release them for PPA time (discussion on the quality assurance of this will not be explored further in this chapter). All these strategies and interventions rely on one adult only.

A nurturing provision

Our argument is that standards are raised when two adults working together establish a knowledge base which includes trust, intuition, attachment theory and the dynamics of relationships. Effective team work is more than knowledge and understanding of the curriculum to be taught. We draw on nurture group practice and observation from over 35 years' experience of working with nurture group teachers and assistants both in schools and in Continuing Professional Development (CPD) at the Institute of Education, University of London. Since their beginning in England in the early 1970s, nurture group teachers and TAs, known as primary helpers in the early days and later classroom assistants, have attended in-service training together. The CPD that we now offer has built on that experience and recognition of the value of the practice; the four-day university courses – Understanding the Theory and Practice of Nurture Groups – are particularly planned so that the nurture group staff team, teachers and classroom assistants are able to learn together.

Nowadays we also find that these teams are frequently accompanied by their headteachers, learning support mentors, educational psychologists and local authority officers, as the relational aspects are more clearly understood and appreciated. These extended teams have proved to be a particularly effective way of disseminating good practice across local authority areas and support practice within individual and clusters of schools. As well as sharing in the learning of theory and practice, support and help is given to the developing relationship between the adults. In our growing recognition of the crucial importance of this relational aspect of the work we are often disappointed to see the adult–adult relationship undervalued. In particular, when resources are stretched, it is often the second member of staff who is the casualty of the first cutback (and this threat is at all levels: school, local authority and higher education institution). This does not necessarily apply to the LSA role, even though it may be a less effective resource.

Children having 'ownership' of learning

It has become increasingly important in the teaching environment to enable children to have 'ownership' of their learning. It follows practice in the early years classroom, where although Piaget may have suggested that the young child is 'egocentric', this egocentricity is an essential step towards developing auton-omy. Alexander (1995: 31) used the phrase 'the teacher as intervening non-interventionist' to describe the dilemma teachers may have between allowing children their freedom and challenging their learning. The debate regarding the teaching of subjects out of which developed the English National Curriculum (Education Reform Act 1988), and which has continued to inform the *National Strategies* (DfEE 1999; DfES 2001a) and *Curriculum Guidance for the Foundation Stage* (CGFS, QCA/DfES 2001), has determined the content of the curriculum but not the process, the 'how' of teaching. We suggest that a pedagogic 'knowledge base' for practitioners should include affective aspects of pedagogy, dynamics of relationships and understanding of child development and attachment theory.

Relationships enable interchangeable roles. We can observe this in cameos 1 and 3 between the class teachers (Janet and Suzanne) and the teaching assistants (Jo and Doreen). In Cameo 1 the role described is a familiar one, but importantly Jo's focus with one child is enabled because Janet is managing the whole group. In Cameo 3 these roles are reversed, with Doreen managing the whole group enabling Suzanne to focus on Ravi. A more subtle role of the teaching assistant is often not as clearly defined as the Janet–Jo role. Janet and Claire are working as one with Janet at this time taking the lead. Claire is modelling for the children how they should respond: she is teaching the children how to be pupils. TAs often sit on the floor, join in, put their hands up, nod to a child/affirm for the child that they can answer or respond. Crucially, in good practice, these roles can be reversed with the TA leading and the teacher modelling, showing respect, listening to the TA and so on.

In Cameo 2, however, there is evidence that children can learn appropriate behaviour (sitting and waiting for permission) but apply it inappropriately; whether deliberately or not is part of a different discussion.

Cameo 2

In the nursery two adults are discussing a student teacher's learning. They are mentors in teacher education; the student teacher is working in Year 4. One aspect of his teaching is his over-control of the classroom. Following the advice of his class teacher he has agreed rules with the class such as 'We put our hands up if we want something' and 'We stay in our seats'. Observation of this student teacher had suggested that children were not working or focused on task as a result of these rules. One child was observed with his hand up (and down) for 20 minutes and all he wanted was a pencil. During the discussion two nursery children appeared. 'We've had a bit of an accident', they said. 'We spilt some water in the kitchen, but we've used the mop to clean it up.'

It is interesting to note that while the Year 4 child would not get out of his seat to find a pencil, the nursery children were confident in their ability to control the situation and, unlike the Year 4 child, they took responsibility and 'modelled back'. Teachers of older children further demonstrate the interchange of roles and responsibilities when they deliberately choose a child to report on his or her learning to the rest of the class, usually because that learning demonstrates the achievement of learning objectives. At the same time the class teacher models respect for the child, listening and approving by use of body language. Other children may be called upon to evaluate the work, but first they must respect the child.

Standards of attainment

In 1998 legislation was introduced to ensure that target-setting occurred in the core subjects. The guidance offered (DfES 2001b) points to the connection between pupils' emotional and behavioural development and improved standards. The importance of children having 'ownership' or a 'central role in their own learning' (Moyles 2001) is emphasised (criteria 2, 11, 12 and 14: DfES 2001b) when considering their social, emotional and behavioural development (EBD). The criteria and other writing (e.g. Moyles 2001) imply that relationships are important between children and children/adults, but there is no consideration of the adult/adult relationship except in the process of deciding on behaviour targets: 'School management and staff decide on agreed action' (DfES 2001b: 4). The holistic approach of nurture groups that includes the presence of and relationship between the two adults as an essential element of good practice has been recognised as contributing positively to raising educational attainment as well as behaviour (Wood and Caulier-Grice 2006).

Contextualising relationships

It has been the practice from the beginning of nurture groups in the early 1970s to have two adults, a teacher and an assistant, working together with a group of up to 12 children. These children are unable to meet the usual expectations of the classroom and are vulnerable to exclusion as a result of social, emotional and behavioural difficulties. They will generally be at 'school action plus' on the school's special needs register. Although these children also frequently have some degree of learning difficulty, they are often excluded from much of the curriculum and even at some stage may be excluded from the school. In addition, they may be a cause of disruption to the learning of other children.

The underlying principles of nurture group work drew on theories of early childhood development and attachment (Bowlby 1952, 1969; Bretherton 1992; Erikson 1950; Winnicott 1964, 1971). The establishment of relationships is the priority: two-person relationships, child–adult, and later triangular relationships, child–adult–adult. The adults' own relationship with one another is crucial (Winnicott 1971: 179–182). As already discussed, the practice of having additional adults in the classroom is increasingly common, but there is little clear understanding outside of nurture work of the importance and value of having two adults working together (Cline 2003), or of what constitutes an effective partnership (Fredrickson and Cline 2002). Thomas (cited in Fredrickson and Cline 2002) makes seven recommendations for effective teamwork. These seek to clarify the roles and communication needed but they are not necessarily seen as integral to pedagogy. We believe that by making this relationship explicit the pedagogy is enhanced.

In nurture work, the collaborative relationship between the two adults, which may appear to be similar to that found in other good early years settings, is deliberately exploited for clear pedagogical reasons. The six nurture group principles (Lucas *et al.* 2006) set out some of the features necessary to ensure an authentic nurture group provision which is essentially an early years pedagogy but at a pre-nursery developmental level. The relationships are modelled on those of the primary caregiver with a very young child, baby or toddler, in the 'good enough' home but modified to meet the physical and intellectual needs of somewhat older children, usually primary age but increasingly KS3 or 4. Thus the adults will respond intuitively to the child's need for attention whatever the chronological age in the developmentally appropriate way (for example, a temper tantrum) by holding or offering a distraction rather than by attempting an oral response which usually has the effect of exacerbating the situation. Verbalising the incident, talking it through so as to enable the child to understand and achieve a more age-appropriate response comes later when calm is restored. The presence of two adults allows this to happen, one focusing on the relationship with the distressed child while the other continues with the management and teaching of the rest of the group. The organisation of the group is flexible enough to allow for this level of give and take and exchange of roles as well as the different levels of response, either more or less cognitive or affective depending on the needs of the moment. Nurture practitioners observe that the other children in the group are also helped by this practice; they are reassured that the potentially distressing situation is under control and their trust and confidence in the adults increase. They are taught how to move away from the incident and to continue with their own work or activity under the watchful presence of the second adult.

Communication between the adults is crucial, verbally but also non-verbally through eye contact, gesture, facial expression and tone of voice, modelling the communication between two or more adults in either the traditional family grouping or a contemporary social family grouping. This includes single parent families where children enjoy a range of relationships through the socially extended family. They refer constantly to one another, checking out their responses to each situation. This presupposes empathy and deep understanding which, while it might be described as intuitive, relies also on a knowledge and level of awareness of the other that allows for a rapid reading of their body language and responds to it. Through this communication, the adults will agree as to who should intervene, who will take the lead at any one time. While this will be decided in principle in the short-term planning, the need to act quickly in a volatile situation cannot rely solely on pre-planning.

The capacity for good oral communication is a prerequisite. Communication and language are inextricably linked and intrinsic to the development of attachment and trust (Schaffer 1990). Caregivers express their interest and concern both orally and emotionally, using a form of language understood across all cultures. In the context of the adult–child relationship this is a crucial feature of the earliest levels of learning: the adults keep up a running commentary about what is happening, they verbalise thoughts and feelings, they encourage recall of earlier events and anticipate those yet to come, they share stories of everyday events, pass on the history of the group establishing a sense of individual as well as group identity. They are able to enter into extended conversations with children in a way that is not possible in the normal early years classroom (Holmes 1995) with the obvious benefits to children's personal, social and emotional development as well as language. They may also gently draw into their exchanges children who have language and communication difficulties rather than them responding directly in a one-to-one conversation: children may spend some days, weeks or even longer listening and observing before making a first tentative response. However, they are not passive but are taking in a great deal from quietly watching and listening.

In addition, the two adults working together can do more than this as they become a model of positive interaction, very likely the only experience of its kind for many vulnerable children; they are able to model empathy, sharing understanding, resolving conflicts and, very importantly, sharing pleasure, enjoyment and humour.

Knowledge base

It is our belief that the knowledge base that early years practitioners have must be expanded to include attachment theory and its wider application to the adult–adult relationship. Aspects of the work of psychoanalysts and developmental psychologists relevant to education had been included in some teacher training courses in the 1950s and 1960s (University of Durham 1956–1958) and the developments in education through the 1960 and 1970s continued to be informed by theories of child development current at the time (e.g. Piaget, Donaldson, Bruner and, later, Vygotsky (Liverpool Institute of Higher Education: Notre Dame College 1975–1979)). Theories of early child development, early language development and attachment underpin nurture work. Initially, nurture practitioners were encouraged to relate intuitively to one another and to the children using the model of the mother or primary caregiver with the young baby or toddler. Inevitably, for the teachers concerned, this was informed by previous experience and education, usually from initial teacher training (ITT). In nurture work, these theories were always considered through the prism of the mother–child relationship in the belief that while not all adults can experience parenthood all have experienced childhood. All adults therefore have the capacity within them to relate to children in a developmentally appropriate way (Boxall 2002). In Cameo 3, Doreen (the TA) is managing the whole class during a creative activities afternoon while Suzanne is working with one child.

Cameo 3

Suzanne is playing on the carpet alongside Ravi. She is showing him the plastic bricks and both are building with them. Ravi picks one up and puts it on his head. It slips off on to the floor; he looks at Suzanne and grins. Suzanne abandons trying to build with the bricks and puts a number of them on Ravi's head. They fall off and both laugh. The game continues and Ravi shows the first signs of interaction with someone else – of building a relationship – but one that reflects a baby of 9 months playing with his mother, not a 5-year-old.

This breakthrough has occurred for a number of reasons: Suzanne and Doreen are able to exchange roles due to the nature of their relationship; Suzanne abandons the building game; Ravi recognises that in this situation he is free to behave at his developmental level; Suzanne follows, and her knowledge of child development and intuition enable her to respond to Ravi at the age he presents in his behaviour (9 months).

The evidence of research (Cooper *et al.* 1998; Insley 2006) and evaluation (Bennathan and Boxall 2000; Lucas *et al.* 2006) demonstrates the effectiveness of the intuitive approach. In a 'nurturing school' (Lucas 1999), the principles of nurture groups are disseminated across a school. The ability to form relationships relies heavily on intuition but to speak of intuition is potentially controversial, especially today when we are encouraged to rely on facts and analysis. Webster's dictionary defines intuition as 'immediate apprehension or cognition': immediate here being contrasted with 'mediated', that is, the use of formal methods of analysis and proof. Bruner (1977) considers the concept and suggests that it is well-informed and knowledgeable practitioners who use intuition simply because they have a good knowledge base. Furlong (2000) suggests that teaching has become so technical that in responding to the 'professional crisis' (Furlong 2000: 18), intuition is a vital response. Bruner goes on to suggest that intuitive practitioners consider the whole problem rather than trying to analyse the small steps, and in doing so they seem to come upon an answer rather than work it out. The focus on learning objectives and analysis of learning, the 'mediated' apprehension or cognition may mean that intuition is undervalued. We believe that intuitive thinking is an important consideration in professional development, which is not opposed to theory but complements it. In supporting Ravi, Suzanne demonstrates this.

Language and communication

Understanding that the development of language and communication is an intrinsic feature of social interaction and emotional development is crucial (Wilkinson 1971; Trevarthen 1977; Schaffer 1990). Young children need to internalise this process (as described earlier) so that they develop an understanding of the reciprocity involved in the language and behaviour of normal everyday relationships with both adults and other children. Jaffey (1990) has studied the development of communication and language of children in nurture groups and concluded that through experiencing the earliest stages of interaction within a reciprocal relationship children learn about dialogue and are helped to express feelings, needs and wishes. This provides the foundation for future learning. There is currently serious concern (OfSTED 2007) about the standards for 3- to 5-year-olds in communication, language and literacy that has grave implications for future attainment in all areas of learning. Our experience suggests that the emphasis on the relational aspects of nurture work can contribute to raising attainment in this area of learning and, subsequently, in children's learning overall.

Attachment theory

Understanding of attachment theory has influenced practice in children's healthcare but has had little effect on education where the emphasis has until recently been on the cognitive rather than the social and emotional aspects of learning. Children who might be described as being insecurely attached (Ainsworth *et al.* 1971) will find it difficult fully to access the curriculum. It is our assertion that by enabling them to make constructive relationships, and revisiting and filling the gaps in their early experiences, they will make rapid progress in learning. That this is possible is supported by the findings of neuroscience (Greenfield 1999; Gerhardt 2004).

Pedagogy

At a recent Social Market Foundation and End Child Poverty event (8 November 2006) the Rt. Hon. Beverley Hughes, the then Minister of State for Children, Families and Young People in England, spoke of the need to help children and young people to stay in education; the need for an emphasis on 'soft skills' as well as academic attainment. She described these skills as those which encourage the development of resilience – problem-solving, initiative and interpersonal skills – crucial for all children but especially those who are disadvantaged and most at risk. Feinstein (2006) described these as 'non-cognitive' skills and stressed their importance for education over the next ten years. All the speakers recognised the crucial importance of relationships: between adults and politicians, teachers, health and social workers and parents – as well as child–adult.

Many of the practices described in this chapter reflect these aspects. We acknowledge elsewhere the importance of the processes of planning and assessment (Lucas *et al.* 2006) and practitioners' understanding of children's development in language, emotional competence and learning behaviour. Part of the practitioners' pedagogical knowledge base will include understanding of the range of possible responses a child might make and modelling of successful, secure and mature relationships which include conflict resolution and compromise.

Conclusion: the way forward

Currently much of education policy and funding in England is being directed towards the early years. Evaluations of Sure Start are beginning to show evidence of gains for some children. However, research is also showing that these gains are not necessarily sustained once a child starts school: there is a tendency to 'fade out' (Wood and Caulier-Grice 2006). Children who have the need and are given the opportunity to adjust to school demands through placement in a nurture group are seen to be less liable to 'fade out' and go on to flourish in a normal school setting (ibid.).

We would suggest that an important factor in this flourishing is the continued recognition from preschool to school of the importance of the relational dimension of schooling. With this increased understanding and conviction we believe that a deeper understanding of attachment theory and its implications for pedagogy would better support decision-making at all levels of the education system. For instance, little attention has been paid to understanding schools in the light of the psychology of organisations or applying group relations theory to staff teams. Indeed, the opposite is often true, and the funding and time for supporting schools in this deeper self-reflective work is non-existent. The psychological health of school staff members as evident in good, healthy relationships is taken for granted.

Like good physical health, good mental health is assumed until it lets us down. Too often, it is only when we are feeling unwell that we comment or take action. If we are to raise children's attainment still further, we must understand the importance of healthy adult/adult relationships and how they are a fundamental component of pedagogy. *Every Child Matters* (DfES 2003) identifies five outcomes for children; as Tabberer (2005) suggests, these should also apply to the adult workforce: 'Every member of staff matters.'

References

Ainsworth, M.D.S. *et al.* (1971) Individual differences in strange situations behaviour of one year olds. In H.R. Schaffer (ed.) *The Origins of Human Social Relations.* London: Academic Press.

Alexander, R. (1995) *Versions of Primary Education.* London: Routledge.

Batmanghelidjh, C. (2006) *Shattered Lives: Children Who Live with Courage and Dignity.* London: Jessica Kingsley.

Bennathan, M. and Bexell, M. (2000) *Effective Intervention in Primary School – Nurture Groups.* London: David Fulton.

Bowlby, J. (1952) *Maternal Care and Mental Health.* World Health Organisation, London: HMSO.

Bowlby, J. (1969) *Attachment and Loss.* Vol. 1: *Attachment.* London: Hogarth Press.

Bowlby, J. and Fry, M. (1953; 2nd edn 1965) *Child Care and the Growth of Love.* London: Pelican.

Boxall, M. (2002) *Nurture Groups in School: Principles and Practice.* London: Paul Chapman.

Bretherton, I. (1992) The origins of Attachment Theory: John Bowlby and Mary Ainsworth. *Developmental Psychology,* 28: 759–775.

Bruner, J. (1977) *The Process Of Education.* Cambridge, MA: Harvard University Press.

Burroughs-Lange S.G. (2006) *Evaluation of Reading Recovery in London Schools: Every Child a Reader 2005–2006.* London: Institute of Education, University of London.

Cline, T. (2003) Nurture Groups in a Changing World (keynote talk at First Nurture Group Network AGM). St Alban's Centre, London, 11 October.

Cooper, P., Arnold, R. and Boyd, E. (1998) *The Nature and Distribution of Nurture Groups in England and Wales.* Cambridge: University of Cambridge, School of Education.

Department for Education and Employment (DfEE) (1999) *The National Numeracy Strategy.* London: DfEE.

Department for Education and Skills (DfES) (2001a) *The National Literacy Strategy.* London: DfES.

DfES (2001b) *Supporting School Improvement: Emotional and Behavioural Development.* London: QCA.

DfES (2003) *Every Child Matters.* London: DfES.

Erikson, E.H. (1950) *Childhood and Society.* New York: Norton.

Feinstein, L. (2006) Raising the educational attainment of poor children (speech to Social Market Foundation and End Child Poverty event). London, 8 November.

Frederickson, N. and Cline, T. (2002) *Special Educational Needs, Inclusion and Diversity – A Textbook.* Maidenhead: Open University Press.

Furlong, J. (2000) Intuition and the crisis in teacher professionalism. In T. Atkinson and G. Claxton (eds) *The Intuitive Practitioner on the Value of not Always Knowing What one is Doing.* Maidenhead: Open University Press.

Gerhardt, S. (2004) *Why Love Matters: How Affection Shapes a Baby's Brain.* Hove and New York: Brunner-Routledge.

Greenfield, S. (1999) Learning and the Brain: A Public Enquiry. The Lifelong Learning Foundation and The Royal Institution (Seminar) Royal Institution, London, 23 October.

Holmes, E (1995) Educational intervention for young children who have experienced fragmented care. In T. Trowell and M. Bower (eds) *The Emotional Needs of Young Children and their Families*. London: Routledge.

Hughes, B. (2006) Raising the educational attainment of poor children (keynote speech to Social Market Foundation and End Child Poverty event). London, 8 November.

Insley, K. (2006) *Nurture Group Provision at Ballikinrain: Report and Evaluation*. London: Institute of Education, University of London.

Jaffey, D. (1990) An Evaluation of the Work of Nurture Groups: An Analysis of Teacher and Child Verbal Interaction in the Nurture Group and Mainstream Classroom. M.Sc. thesis, Tavistock Clinic.

Lucas, S. (1999) The nurturing school: the impact of nurture group principles and practice on the whole school. *Emotional and Behavioural Difficulties*, 4(3): 14–19.

Lucas, S., Insley, K. and Buckland, G. (2006) *Nurture Group Principles and Curriculum Guidelines: Helping Children to Achieve*. London: Nurture Group Network.

Mosley, J. (2005) *Circle Time for Young Children*. London: Routledge.

Moyles, J. (2001) Just for fun? The child as active learner and meaning maker. In J. Collins, K. Insley and J. Soler (eds) *Developing Pedagogy: Researching Practice*. London: Paul Chapman in association with the Open University.

Office for Standards in Education (OfSTED) (2007) *The Foundation Stage: A Survey of 144 Settings*. London: OfSTED. Accessed online at: http://www.ofsted.gov.uk/assets/Internet_Content/Shared_Content/Files/2007/mar/fsin144sttngs.pdf (accessed 16 January 2007).

Qualifications and Curriculum Authority (QCA)/DfES (2001) *Curriculum Guidance for the Foundation Stage*. London: QCA/DfES.

Schaffer, H. (1990) *Making Decisions About Children: Psychological Questions and Answers*. London: Blackwell.

Tabberer, R. (2005) News Release, 1 September. Accessed online at: http://www.tda.gov.uk/about/mediarelations/2005/20050901.aspx (accessed 19 January 2007).

Teacher Development Agency (2007) *Draft Revised Standards Framework for Teachers in England*. London: TDA.

Trevarthen, C. (1977) A descriptive analysis of infant communicative behaviour. In H.R. Schaffer (ed.) *Studies in Mother–Child Interaction*. New York: Academic Press.

Wilkinson, A. (1971) *The Foundations of Language: Talking and Reading in Young Children*. London: Oxford University Press.

Winnicott, D.W. (1964) *The Child, the Family and the Outside World*. Harmondsworth: Penguin.

Winnicott, D.W. (1971) *Playing and Reality*. London: Routledge.

Wood, C. and Caulier-Grice, J. (2006) *Fade or Flourish: How Primary Schools can Build on Children's Early Progress*. London: Social Market Foundation.

14 Does relationship training for caregivers enhance young children's learning and language?

Florence Dinneen

In Phase 1 of this study, 12 students at Mary Immaculate College were randomly selected out of a class of 60 in the spring of 2007 to have the sensitivity of their interactions with toddlers measured through the use of Arnett's (1989) Caregiver Interaction Scale (CIS). Running records were used with 12 other students in order to capture the occurrence and development of joint involvement episodes (JIEs) in their interactions with babies. Simultaneously, the existence of correlates was probed between the sensitivity of the students as measured on the CIS and their ability to promote relational pedagogy using a variety of other research methodologies. (Phase 2 of this study will take place with the same students in similar settings in the autumn of 2008.) This chapter, prepared at the completion of Phase 1, details the aim and objective of the study and outlines the research methodology. The findings for Phase 1 support the hypothesis that relationship training does matter. The research aim was threefold: to examine the correlation between relational pedagogy and the sensitivity of the student-carers; to document the emerging ability of students to promote and enhance language and total development; and to provide clear insights into supportive methodologies for the training of educarers.

Introduction

The evidence is overwhelming: training for caregiving *does* matter (Arnett 1989; Dunn 1993; Burchinal *et al*. 1996; Dinneen 2002a). The realisation of its importance spans almost two decades and, as a research topic, it is still attracting attention (Cain *et al*. 2007) as having a significant role in the holistic development of young children. The type of training indicated here is that of the professional development of educarers. Studying early childhood to degree level is common practice in the twenty-first century in many developed countries globally, and Ireland is no exception. While the intake on all programmes universally is predominately female, in spite of EU and national targets in Ireland to attract more males into the profession (National Children's Strategy 2000), the recognition that high levels of qualifications are a prerequisite for the delivery of a quality service is beyond dispute (McCartney 1984; Moss and Pence 1994; *Cost, Quality and Child Outcomes in Child Care Centers, Public Report* 1995).

One such degree programme in early childhood care and education (ECCE) is the focus of the research outlined in this paper. This is a four-year degree with an average annual intake of 60 students. The graduates will be known as *educarers*. The current first-year students (2006–2007), as a group, consented to take part in the study which makes direct links between the training they receive prior to embarking on a two-week placement period in the first and third years of their study and how they perform on placement. On both occasions they are located in baby and toddler rooms. The study, therefore, is longitudinal and the objective is to document the developmental changes in the student's attitudes and practice in facilitating the learning and development of very young children over the period. In summary, this study links training with the provision of quality programmes for children from birth to 3 years of age. The objective therefore may be summarised as follows:

> To devise and implement strategies within training programmes for educarers so that they can promote relational pedagogy in a natural and spontaneous way in their professional practice.

Quality programmes and research issues

Many of the studies on children in non-parental care show that the care received by them does *not* promote cognitive, social and physical development (Cryer *et al*. 1988; Whitebook *et al*. 1989; Galinsky *et al*. 1994). Conversely, other studies show that good-quality educare makes a considerable difference to developmental outcomes as has been demonstrated many times through programmes with children deemed to be 'at-risk' (Schweinhart and Weikart 1980; Lazar *et al*. 1982; Carnegie Corporation of New York 1994). In a comprehensive study of centre-based child-care in four states in America, the findings revealed the startling statistic that only one in 12 infant and toddler rooms were providing developmentally appropriate care (*Cost, Quality, and Child Outcomes in Child Care Centers, Public Report* 1995).

Quality programmes and relationship training

A positive developmental outcome for young children in non-parental caregiving environments hinges to a large extent on the quality of staff training. Arnett (1989: 551) focused on one aspect of quality (i.e. training) in a monumental study that posed the question *Does training matter?* He concluded that:

> regulations requiring even a modest level of training for caregivers in day-care centers [*sic*] could have important and salutary effects on their job performance and on the quality of day-care environments.

Arnett devised and used what has come to be known as the Caregiver Interaction Scale (used also in the present study) to test the effectiveness of caregiving, based on the competency and skill of carers as a result of having different levels of specialised training. Caregivers who had completed a four-year university-based programme in early childhood studies, unsurprisingly, rated higher in skill and competence in their work compared with those who had less training. He concluded that training in the area of child development and communication (especially behaviour management) should form the core content of all courses, however brief.

The ability of non-parental caregivers to interact properly with young children in a developmentally appropriate manner is a highly specialised and skilful task, as is evident in the current literature regarding joint involvement episodes (JIEs, Schaffer 1992). This focus on JIEs as providing a context for development highlights the training of the carer as a crucial factor in facilitating holistic development (Bruner 1995; Smith 1996; Zanolli *et al.* 1997; Dinneen 2002b). Schaffer (1992), for example, places the development of cognition firmly within a social context and affirms, along with many others, that cognitive development is closely allied to socio-emotional development in line with Vygotsky's thinking. He sees such episodes as being of:

> a primarily formative nature, i.e. those in which the adult is actively involved in extending the child's behavioural repertoire by helping it to master some new problem and thus progress to a higher level of competence in coping with environmental demands. It is these we shall refer to as Joint Involvement Episodes, meaning any encounter between two individuals in which the participants pay joint attention to, and jointly act upon, some external topic.
>
> (Schaffer 1992: 101)

Quality programmes and communication

Non-verbal communication is as powerful as verbal communication. Smiling in childcare settings, according to research, received affectionate child responses earlier than affectionate words or even affectionate contact (Zanolli *et al.* 1997). Howes (1983) found, in her study of toddlers in childcare settings, that caregivers were affectionate only 15 to 18 per cent percent of the time. Twardosz *et al.* (1987) found that, while all types of affection occur mostly in unstructured settings, affectionate touch occurs more frequently than smiling and affectionate words. Perhaps the most important findings for non-parental daycare settings are those demonstrating that adults within these settings initiate affection more often than children and that these initiations are low (Honig and Wittmer 1985; Twardosz *et al.* 1987). Other studies have demonstrated that affectionate words are powerful motivators for learning (Larsen 1975). Bruner's (1983) theoretical work, *Child's Talk*, traces the beginnings of language as a communicative tool by highlighting joint attention as the underlying mechanism for creating mother-and-child 'formats' of interaction. He also identifies language as a necessary component of playful activities that are 'the delight of human immaturity' (ibid.: 45). In so doing, the *peek-a-boo* variety gets special mention for its universal appeal throughout many cultures. McCartney's (1984) study probed the correlation between high levels of caregiver speech and language development in daycare, and concluded that, where verbal interaction with caregivers is high, the resulting communicative competence among children increases. McCartney sums it up by saying: 'the children respond to a verbally stimulating environment' (ibid.: 258).

Contemporary knowledge around the importance of early language enrichment (Pan *et al.* 2005) emphasises once again the importance of the primary caregivers' educational level, children's early exposure to nouns and relational language input, shared book-reading, narratives, explanations, participation in extended discourse and warm, accepting relationships. Once again we can say categorically that 'Training does matter!'

Research methodology

Background information

The learning focus of each placement is thematic. The theme for Phase 1 was 'How to promote language and development through building meaningful relationships with young children'.

Organisation of Phase 1 of the study

Training

Students were given six hours of focused training, spanning a three-week period, covering the following topics:

1   How to communicate with babies and toddlers – an introduction to the possibilities, expectations and limitations linked with the complexity and fluidity of development at individual levels.
2   How to promote joint involvement episodes (JIEs).
3   How to share books, poems, songs and rhymes with young babies and toddlers.

Supervision of students on placement

Each ECCE student receives a minimum of three visits lasting one hour from a dedicated supervisor. The consultant supervisor also monitors the students while on placement conducting a mixture of random and requested calls and in this way assists with the standardisation of the supervision process. It was the consultant supervisor who directed the research in the current study and took direct responsibility for the training sessions for students and supervisors. Supervisors, who are lecturers in early childhood care and education or qualified teachers, underwent a two-hour training period prior to embarking on placement supervision.

Selection of the research subjects – ethics

The class as a whole gave their permission to the consultant supervisor to document visits in such a way that the theme of the placement could be clearly identified and researched. In addition, seven of the students gave permission to be videoed while on placement for the sole purpose of analysing their interactions with their peers at tutor-led tutorials following the placement period. This latter development necessitated gaining permission, not only from the setting and the staff but, more importantly, from the parents of the children. Ethical issues concerning research of this nature were discussed with the educational institution involved and given clearance based on the necessary permissions being received.

Instruments used

The main instruments used were:

1   The Caregiver Interaction Scale (Arnett 1989);
2   Running records;
3   Student reports (questionnaires).

In addition, documented reflections gleaned from students working in small tutorial groups were used along with student timed narrative observations. Finally, the standard method of assessing student performance helped with the triangulation process which assisted validation of the research act (Denzin 1970).

1   *The Caregiver Interaction Scale* (CIS, Arnett 1989): Twelve students located in toddler rooms had their sensitivity measured according to this scale which was subsequently analysed using the SPSS analysis system. Each student was observed for a period of 30 minutes prior to the marking up of the characteristics of their sensitivity in action. This scale has 26 caregiver characteristic statements and is organised into four subscales: (a) positive; (b) punitive; (c) firm/permissive; (d) detachment. In this phase of the study, one statement relating to the students' ability around the problem-solving technique of behaviour management was not used due to the limited training time available. An inter-rater reliability of .93 was established for the whole scale by two observers prior to its use in the field. (Any score above .75 may be considered adequate reliability.)

2   *Running records*: Another 12 students located in baby rooms were observed for a set period of ten minutes by the sole researcher on the study to examine their interactions with babies in order to determine what efforts they were making to promote and extend the children's language. The focus in particular was to see if students could identify opportunities to promote joint involvement episodes (Dinneen 2002b). Once identified, the next stage was to determine if the students could sustain and develop them. In preparation for this placement, students were made aware that the definition for a JIE was: 'any

encounter between two individuals in which the participants pay attention to, and jointly act upon some external topic' (Schaffer 1992: 101).

They were also made aware that *two* adult inputs were necessary in both child and adult-led encounters before it would qualify as a JIE for the purpose of this study and that each encounter should culminate in the reciprocal sharing of attention (Dinneen 2002b). A video demonstration using a baby-like doll took place at the commencement of the training and the footage was repeated at intervals to assist the students' familiarisation with JIEs.

3 *Student reports (questionnaires)*: [Note: This marks the participation of the whole class in the research act]. For ease of analysis, the questionnaire was organised into three themes: (a) the tutorials; (b) The needs of babies and toddlers (selective); (c) my personal placement supervisor. Again, the analysis was carried out using the SPSS package. A total of 47 students returned the questionnaire (78.3 per cent response rate).

Additional information-gathering instruments used

- *Documented student reflection (small group work – whole class)*: Following the practical experience of placement, the students formed small focus groups to reflect on various aspects of their work.
- *Student-timed narrative observations – whole class*: The purpose here was twofold: (a) To promote the use of observation techniques in daily practice; (b) To identify the incidence, promotion and progression of JIEs in the relationships between *other* adults and children in the centres.
- *Standard method of placement assessment – whole class*: By incorporating this standard method of assessment for placements into the research act it was hoped to draw correlations between the results of the various instruments used.

Findings and analysis

The findings are displayed and discussed in a manner that integrates the threefold aim of the research; that is:

- To examine the correlation between relational pedagogy and the sensitivity of the student carers;
- To document the emerging ability of students to promote and enhance language and total development;
- To provide clear insights into supportive methodologies for the training of educarers.

Analysis of student caregivers' sensitivity

The results from the analysis of the CIS give us some indication of how sensitive these student carers were in their interactions with toddlers (18 to 36 months). Table 14.1 demonstrates a wide variation between the positive characteristics of the study group ranging from 3.8 to 1.9.

Table 14.1 Analysis of Caregiver Interaction Scale (CIS)

Student	Positive	Punitive	Permissive	Detached
Student A	3.8	1	2.8	1
Student B	2.1	1	2.5	1.5
Student C	3.1	1	3	1
Student D	3.4	1	2.8	1
Student E	3	1.1	3	1
Student F	1.9	1.3	2.8	1.8
Student G	2.6	1.1	2.8	1
Student H	2.8	1	2.8	1
Student I	3.2	1	3	1
Student J	2.9	1	3	1
Student K	2.3	1	2.5	2.5
Student L	3	1	2.8	1

Key to the above scale: A score of 1 indicates that it is not at all characteristic, 2 indicates that it is somewhat, 3 indicates that it is quite a bit and 4 indicates that it is very much characteristic.

Note: For the purpose of comparison, a significant difference at the 5 per cent level is equal to 0.2 on any item on the above scale.

Source: Arnett (1989).

The term 'punitive' for the subscale of the same name may best be understood when the words *critical, threatening, authoritian* and *harsh* are invoked. It was through the authoritian interpretation that three students erred. The term *permissive* was taken to mean firm rather than the affordance of liberty without limits: therefore, all students fall within an acceptable range. The term *detached* is self-explanatory and the results indicate that two students are significantly removed from the acceptable range while one student is between 'somewhat' and 'quite a bit' detached.

But, how did the study group as a whole rate in terms of sensitivity? Figure 14.1 provides the cumulative result (see p. 176). It is clear from Table 14.1 that there is a direct correlation between low scores on the positive subscale and high scores on the detached subscale. Therefore, to effect any improvement, students must focus on warm interactions, learn how to listen to children, and how to encourage their efforts. Figure 14.1 is best understood in light of the individual analysis provided by Table 14.1 which demonstrates the effect three very poor scores in the positive and detached subscales can have on the overall result.

Student–caregivers' interaction in joint involvement episodes

In relation to babies, the results from the running records which were carried out on a further 12 students interacting with babies (3 to 18 months) tell their own story. In a set ten-minute period during the consultant supervisor's visit, each of the 12 students was observed for their ability to promote, sustain and develop JIEs (Table 14.2). Missed opportunities for relational interactions were also noted along with their contexts. The fact that all of the students except for one demonstrated

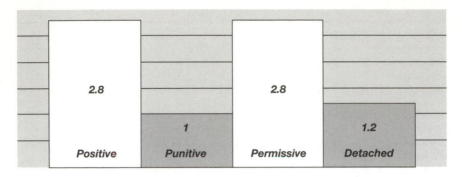

1 = Not at all   2 = Somewhat   3 = Quite a bit   4 = Very much

Figure 14.1 CIS caregiver characteristics.

an ability to commence a JIE-type interaction based on their prior training was encouraging. It was also encouraging that 50 per cent of them demonstrated this ability at a high to very high level. Only one-third of the students, however, managed to sustain the interaction culminating in episodes of joint involvement – two of these at a very high level. Rich contexts for the promotion of JIEs were also documented and correspond with known contexts throughout the literature (Smith 1999; Dinneen 2002b). Students' lack of awareness in progressing babies' vocalisations through repetition of the sounds was particularly evident, as was the inability to scan the entire group of children for relational opportunities (one child unattended for a long period) and this by a student who demonstrated high and medium ability in promoting and sustaining JIEs respectively.

Can JIEs be overdone? Goldschmeid and Jackson (1994) seem to think that this is a distinct possibility when they warn against over-encroachment on babies' time to reflect and concentrate when they are visibly absorbed in sensorial learning. The example they give is through the use of the treasure basket where supervision rather than involvement by the adult is strongly recommended. Interestingly, the video footage taken of one student during the ten-minute running record clearly demonstrates the student's inability to read the signs of tiredness in a 6-month-old baby where the student gave precedence to the promotion of JIEs instead of a suitable response to the baby's need for much less stimulation.

In order to analyse the attitude of students towards the task of promoting learning and development in others we must look to the students themselves. Student reports or questionnaire analyses give us some insights. The questionnaire was organised into three themes as follows: (1) the tutorials; (2) the needs of babies and toddlers (selective); (3) my personal placement supervisor, and will be dealt with in this order through the mode of graphic analysis and discussion.

Table 14.2 Analysis of running records for student–caregivers' interaction in JIE

Running record analysis

Student	Demonstrated ability to promote a JIE type interaction (commence) ***	Demonstrated ability to sustain a JIE type interaction ***	Resulting JIEs	Observed context missed
Student M	Low	Low	0	Peek-a-boo opportunity
Student N	Medium	Low	0	One-to-one language opportunities
Student O	Medium	Low	0	Repeating vocalisations with babies
Student P	High	Low	0	Showing empathy
Student Q	Very high	Very high	4	None
Student R	High	Medium	2	One child unattended for a long period
Student S	Medium	Low	0	Through repeating babbling
Student T	High	Low	0	Through poor positioning of student with non-mobile children
Student U	Very high	Very high	5	None
Student V	High	Low	0	Feeding routines
Student W	Medium	Low	0	Feeding routines
Student X	Medium	Medium	1	None
Total JIEs			**12**	

Key: *** Low = None: Medium = 1–2: High = 3–4: Very high = 4-5

Preparation for effective communication through tutorials (theme 1)

This theme contained 11 statements to elicit the views of the students on how well the tutorials prepared them to communicate effectively with babies and toddlers both with and without such supports as toys, books, poems, songs and rhymes, and used a five-point scale moving from '*Strongly agree*' to '*Strongly disagree*' with a '*No opinion*' option in the middle. While an average of two students out of 47 offered '*No opinion*' to some of the questions, the overall consensus of those who did offer an opinion is outlined in Figure 14.2.

The tutorials

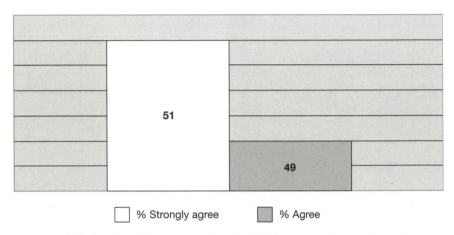

% Strongly agree   % Agree

Figure 14.2 Student-caregivers' preparation for effective communication through tutorials.

Child development and communication skills: key elements of training courses (theme 2)

This part of the questionnaire was devised when the study was well underway in an effort to gauge the areas of weakness and to inform future training needs. Since Arnett (1989) had concluded that child development and communication skills (especially behaviour management) should form the key elements of all training courses in the first year, the selective elements of theme 2 dealt almost exclusively with communication-related topics, as Table 14.3 demonstrates. Clearly these results demonstrate a high level of confusion regarding the correct judgement for three of the statements in particular (2, 3 and 4). In addition, the high levels of '*No opinion*' for three out of the five statements indicate uncertainty in relation to child development and behaviour issues in particular, and overall should direct future training linked with experiential learning on placement.

Table 14.3 Child development and communication skills: key elements of training courses

	Statement	Cumulative agreement	No opinion	Cumulative disagreement
1	Babies and toddlers need time on their own.	61.7	8.5	29.8
2	Babies and toddlers need adult company at all times.	40.4	12.8	46.8
3	Toddlers should be taught obedience.	50.0	32.6	17.4
4	Toddlers should be sanctioned for antisocial behaviour.	34.0	19.1	46.8
5	Freedom is important for babies and toddlers.	89.4	2.1	8.6

Note: A variance of up to 1 per cent may occur due to the rounding-off process for cumulative results.

Relationship between student caregiver and supervisor (theme 3)

Relationship-building between supervisor and student was at the core of the statements in this theme. These statements were linked with quality guidance, accretion of learning and confidence-building. Figure 14.3 graphically illustrates the results from the 47 respondents. While 93.1 per cent of the students either strongly agreed or agreed with the statements, an average of three students offered '*No opinion*' on three of the four statements and an average of two students disagreed with three of the statements. On average, one student disagreed with the aspects of adequate guidance and confidence-building. Finally, the analysis of the qualitative questionnaire statement – 'There was a mismatch between the advice given at tutorials and lectures and that given by my supervisor on the ground' – yielded the results given in Table 14.4.

My personal placement supervisor

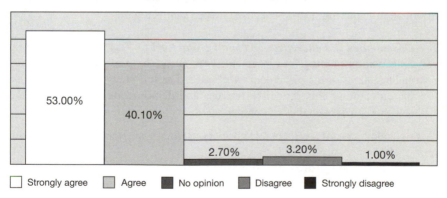

Figure 14.3 Relationship between student caregiver and supervisor.

Table 14.4 Mismatch of advice given in lectures, tutorials and by supervisors

Respondents (n 47)	Verdict
26	'No mismatch'
10	'Yes, there was a mismatch'
11	Did *not* comment

The ten respondents above who affirmed that there was a mismatch regarding the two sets of advice given may further illuminate the way forward towards devising the most supportive methodologies for the training of educarers. It must be stated, however, that not all of the supervisors attended the two-hour training session. Here are some selected student 'mismatch' comments (paraphrased):

'Supervisor was critical that I did not mingle with all of the children even though I was trying to establish JIEs with individuals.' (Questionnaire 19)

'Supervisors expect students to take control – tutorial advice was to comply with the wishes of the setting.' (Questionnaire 15)

'The advice given at tutorials was to communicate at all times with the children but the supervisor advocated giving the children time for reflection.' (Questionnaire 13)

'The supervisor expected the student to handle behaviour management issues. Student felt ill-prepared for this.' (Questionnaire 12)

It is evident from some of the above comments that a degree of inexperience in terms of discretionary ability comes to the fore. Other comments undoubtedly indicated that, while the word *mismatch* took their attention, they failed to specify the nature of the mismatch (Questionnaire 14).

How can we integrate the threefold aim of the research further? The additional information-gathering instruments used helped in this regard.

1   *Documented student reflection (small group work)* – Task A called for group reflection on training for placement. Task B sought to identify the positives and negatives of the placement experience. The following points summarise the outcome of this reflective process and demonstrate a maturity in the students' professional development:

   • Training on JIEs was found to be very useful for relationship-building with children;
   • Video training (demonstration) was considered very beneficial;
   • Video filming of students on placement is highly recommended, coupled with peer reviewing of the footage at tutorials;
   • Supervisors were generally considered very good;

- Consultant role is essential as an added support and for standardisation purposes;
- Students were critical of the short preparation period prior to placement;
- There was a critical of lack of preparation on aspects of behaviour management and special educational issues;
- Students demonstrated an awareness of controversial practice witnessed in some placement settings.

2 ***Student-timed narrative observations*** – 55 of these were submitted for analysis and were considered a vital part of the training process since observation informs practice at all times. In relation to the promotion of JIEs, Table 14.5 helps to place the work on JIEs covered in this study in context with similar work carried out in 2002 (Dinneen 2002a). Table 14.5 clearly demonstrates that the training offered to students in the present study has enabled them to establish the JIE format of interaction and to identify this type of communication in others. It also helps to confirm that relationship training does matter!

3 ***Standard method of placement assessment by a variety of supervisors*** – This helped with the triangulation process in confirming validity through the correlation of results between methods. High-scoring students on the CIS (relational sensitivity focus) and on the promotion of JIEs were also deemed by a variety of placement supervisors to merit scores on the placement module that ranged from a low honours grade right up to the first class honours mark. The lower scoring students on the research instruments likewise scored lower overall.

Table 14.5 Training enabling interaction and communication

Observer category	Study	JIEs	Babies/carers	Observation time involved
55 first year students	Present	15	55 babies/55 adult carers minimum	9 hours
Consultant supervisor	Present	12	12 babies minimum – 12 students maximum	2 hours
Doctoral research student	Dinneen (2002a)	28	18 babies maximum with 18 adult carers minimum	6 hours

Conclusion

In conclusion, it is evident at this stage that this is a worthwhile study. It has yielded rich qualitative data with a quantitative dimension. The main conclusions are as follows:

1   There is a direct correlation between relational pedagogy, sensitivity of carers and the developmental potential of young children.
2   Focused training empowers the recipient to become a confident and professional educarer.
3   The 'talk-and-chalk' days are over: innovative ways, supported by the technological era and research, have much to offer humanistic teaching methodologies.
4   Coordinated training for placement supervisors can radically reduce the incidence of 'mismatch' of information/advice given to students and assist with the development of a confident and professional workforce.
5   The consultant supervisor plays a key role in integrating the various strands that are pertinent to the training of educarers.

Finally, it must also be acknowledged that, since Phase 1 of this study focused almost exclusively on the theme 'How to promote language and development through building meaningful relationships with young children' in its research orientation, and since preparation time prior to students embarking on the placement experience was limited to three weeks, many aspects of child development, in the holistic sense, did not receive the attention they deserved. However, the decision to focus the training almost exclusively on relationship-building and language development is not regretted: in fact, the results emphasise the importance of focused training sessions within a broadly based curriculum. Phase 2 of the study which commences in autumn 2008 will focus on the emergence of fully rounded professional educarers. Watch this space!

References

Arnett, J. (1989) Caregivers in day-care centers: does training matter? *Journal of Applied Developmental Psychology*, 10: 541–552.

Bruner, J. (1983) *Child's Talk: Learning to Use Language*. Oxford: Oxford University Press.

Bruner, J. (1995) From joint attention to the meeting of minds: an introduction. In C. Moore and P. Dunham (eds) *Joint Attention: Its Origins in Development*. New York: Teachers College Press.

Burchinal, M.R., Roberts, J.E., Nabors, L.A. and Bryant, D.M. (1996) Quality of centre child care and infant cognitive and language development. *Child Development*, 67: 606–620.

Cain, D., Rudd, L. and Saxon, T. (2007) Effects of professional development training on joint attention engagement in low-quality childcare centers. *Early Child Development and Care*, 177(2): 159–185.

Carnegie Corporation of New York (1994) Carnegie Task Force on Meeting the Needs of Young Children, *Starting Points: Meeting the Needs of our Youngest Children*. New York: Report of the Carnegie Task Force.

Cost, Quality and Child Outcomes in Child Care Centers, Public Report (1995) (2nd edn). Denver, CO: University of Colorado, Department of Economics.

Cryer, D., Clifford, R.M. and Harms, T. (1988) *Day Care Compliance and Evaluation*

Project: Final Report. Chapel Hill, NC: University of North Carolina at Chapel Hill, Frank Porter Graham Child Development Centre.

Denzin, N.K. (1970) *The Research Act in Sociology: A Theoretical Introduction to Sociological Methods*. London: The Butterworth Group.

Dinneen, F.E. (2002a) *The Concept of Educare in Public Day-care Facilities in Ireland and in the Irish Psyche at the Start of the Third Millennium*. Unpublished Doctoral thesis, Cork: University College.

Dinneen, F.E. (2002b) Joint involvement episodes with babies: lessons from research for the new millennium. In M. Horgan and F. Douglas (eds) *Lessons for the 21st Century: Research, Reflection, Renewal*. OMEP Ireland. Proceedings of the Conference held in the DIT Aungier Street, Dublin 2, 20 April, pp. 175–186.

Dunn, L. (1993) Proximal and distal features of day care quality and children's development. *Early Childhood Research Quarterly*, 8(2): 167–192.

Galinsky, E., Howes, C., Kontos, S. and Shinn, M. (1994) *The Study of Children in Family Child Care and Relative Care: Highlights of Findings*. New York: Families and Work Institute.

Goldschmeid, E. and Jackson, S. (1994) *People Under Three: Young Children in Day Care*. London: Routledge.

Honig, A. and Wittmer, D.S. (1985) Toddler bids and teacher responses. *Child Care Quarterly*, 14(1): 14–29.

Howes, C. (1983) Caregiver behaviour in centre and family day care. *Journal of Applied Developmental Psychology*, 4: 99–107.

Larsen, J.M. (1975) Effects of increased teacher support on young children's learning. *Child Development*, 46: 631–637.

Lazar, I., Darlington, R., Murray, H., Royce, J. and Snipper, A. (1982) Lasting effects of early education: a report from the Consortium for Longitudinal Studies. *Monographs of the Society for Research in Child Development*, 47.

McCartney, K. (1984) Effect of quality of day care environment on children's language development. *Developmental Psychology*, 20(2): 244–260.

Moss, P. and Pence, A. (eds) (1994) *Valuing Quality in Early Childhood Services*. London: Paul Chapman.

National Children's Strategy (2000) *Our Children – Their Lives*. Dublin: The Stationery Office.

Pan, B.A., Rowe, M.L., Singer, J.D. and Snow, C.E. (2005) Maternal correlates of growth in toddler vocabulary production in low-income families. *Child Development*, 76(4): 763–782.

Schaffer, H.R. (1992) Joint involvement episodes as context for development. In H. McGurk (ed.) *Childhood Social Development: Contemporary Perspectives*. Hove: Lawrence Erlbaum Associates.

Schweinhart, L.J. and Weikart, D.P. (1980) *Young Children Grow Up: The Effects of the Perry Pre-school Program on Youths Through Age 15*. Monographs of the High/Scope Educational Research Foundation, No. 7. Ypsilanti, MI: The High/Scope Press.

Smith, A.B. (1996) *The Quality of Childcare Centres for Infants in New Zealand*. Monograph No.4 of the New Zealand Association for Research in Education, State of the Art series.

Smith, A.B. (1999) Quality childcare and joint attention. *International Journal of Early Years Education*, 7(1): 85–98.

Twardosz, S., Botkin, D., Cunningham, J.L., Weddle, K., Sollie, D. and Shreve, C. (1987) Expression of affection in day care. *Child Study Journal*, 17(2): 133–151.

Whitebook, M., Howes, C. and Phillips, D. (1989) The National Child Care Staffing study: *Who Cares? Child Care Teachers and the Quality of Care in America*. Oakland, CA: Child Care Employee Project.

Zanolli, K., Saudargas, R. and Twardosz, S. (1997) The development of toddlers' responses to affectionate teacher behaviour. *Early Childhood Research Quarterly*, 12: 99–116.

15 Making a little difference for early childhood studies students

Ruby Oates and Andrew Sanders
with Christine Hey, Jon White, Val Wood
and Ellen Yates

Drawing on individual experiences and contributions, this chapter explores and makes visible a process of change. A necessary reframing of the BA Early Childhood Studies and personnel changes prompted discussions between team members: thus was born the notion of the quality encounter and its location, the 'little space' where a difference might be made. Quality, it is asserted, is fundamentally 'what children experience' in early years settings and a leading factor here is the nature of the relationships they enter into with adults there. This chapter documents our process towards redirecting students' attention to this area. It was originally written as a presentation concerning the reclaiming of relational pedagogy and an account of a journey together within this revalidation process.

In articulating different and emerging team views, this chapter puts the process in context and offers key background thinking, practical challenges and issues on the journey. One such challenge, for example, is the 'one-step-removed' point; by this, the realisation that the team cannot make a little difference themselves and rely on students who may become (or already be) practitioners in children's services to do so. There is a focus, therefore, on the *how*, in the context of higher education, of getting the message across. Students' confidence, depth and reflective skills are some areas that are highlighted for attention which inform the overall degree revalidation process and, with an introspective stance, an interim position is described on which the way forward can be loosely mapped.

Introduction

This chapter documents the process of the University of Derby's BA (Honours) Early Childhood Studies team in beginning to consider how we promote the values and practice of relational pedagogy with our students in their practice settings. Many of our learners are (and will be) in positions which enable them to influence what has emerged in our team as something we refer to as the 'quality encounter'.

This is briefly described as a forum for negotiated co-construction of meaning (Westcott and Littleton 2005) – relational pedagogy at its best!

This is an account of our initial journey together. First, we will introduce some key themes of the chapter. We will then expand on some notions and challenges. The difficulties will be described and questions posed which edge towards an interim group position and a platform for moving forward together. We consider the key themes and the concept of quality encounters.

Key themes

We are a new multidisciplinary team of six who have been working together for 18 months. Our backgrounds include nursing and midwifery, primary school-teaching, social and care work and management in nursery, primary, secondary, further and higher education. One member of the team continues to teach in a local school for part of the week. During the formation of the team we have been reviewing the BA (Honours) Early Childhood Studies programme modules in preparation for revalidation and, through this process, our differing ideas about pedagogy have emerged. So far we have agreed that our aim is to produce a revalidated programme that provides opportunities for our students to appreciate the complex nature of pedagogical relationships and to provide them with skills and insights into how to effectively and equitably relate with young children and their families. Our challenge is to embed these skills and values into an outcomes-based higher education curriculum.

Emerging concerns from the team members have been the differing interpretations of the term 'pedagogy' and how current teaching and learning in early years settings, we believe, over-emphasises the measuring of young children at the expense of providing opportunities for them to explore and make sense of their worlds. These concerns have led us to question how we prepare our students for the workplace, particularly in relation to the skills they require in order to facilitate children's learning and experiences. In so doing we have been exploring together the term 'relational pedagogy', taking into account competing perspectives from around the world.

We found two definitions of pedagogy useful. Readings' (1996: 158) definition of pedagogy as 'a relation, a network of obligations' that reinforces the rights of children, and Rinaldi's (1998) concept of pedagogy as the ability to listen and not to talk were particularly valued by the primary schoolteachers in the team. These definitions have also been reflected in the work of Moss and Petrie (2006: 143) who regard pedagogy as an attempt to address the whole child and not a child separated into parts as in psycho-therapeutical and medical models. The challenge of these definitions to the dominance of child developmental theories provided us with a lens through which to view children.

During these early days of meeting as a new team, grappling with unfamiliar concepts and attempting to make sense of them, we recognise that we are at different positions in our understanding of current debates and theoretical perspectives. The primary schoolteachers among us were unfamiliar with the terms and concepts used by postmodern writers such as MacNaughton (2005). Yet when they reflected on their work with young children, they recognised the contradictions and complexities noted by MacNaughton (2005: 22) in their everyday work.

We found that a useful way forward was to consider competing narratives on early childhood and explore our understanding of modern and postmodern ideas. Further exploration into dominant ways of thinking against what we called 'emerging narratives' proved useful; for example, children's linear development, on the one hand, alongside complex, multi-layered, unfinished development on the other; National Curriculum versus local cultural projects; formal quality and inspection alongside reflective, critical thinking practitioners.

Drawing on the work of MacNaughton (2005) assisted us in developing an emerging understanding of post-structuralist ideas relating to children and childhood:

> poststructuralists believe that our knowledge about childhood and about early childhood pedagogies is inherently and inevitably contradictory, rather than rational; and, consequently, that many different truths about the child and early childhood pedagogy are possible.
>
> (MacNaughton 2005: 22)

We are keen to provide opportunities to build within the degree programme the skills, key concepts, narratives and strategies that enable our students to work effectively with young children. Our challenge, as a newly developing team, is to embed within the programme an appropriate knowledge base alongside the development of students' self-confidence, critical thinking, creative, communication and reflective skills.

'Quality encounters'

For some months, we had been wrestling with what relational pedagogy actually is, and its relationship with the quality encounter. The 'quality encounter' dynamic is appraised as a 'focus on the moment-to-moment co-constructive processes through which meaning is negotiated, renegotiated and contested' (Westcott and Littleton 2005: 144). Relational pedagogy is an approach, therefore, which values this process.

The premise goes like this: what children experience of children's services is very much to do with the quality and messages contained within the interactions they have with adults (and their peers, big and small) in the setting (Mathers *et al.* 2007). We wish to draw students' attention towards the dynamics and content of this little space – that in-between communication zone. We would wish to emphasise that the quality of this encounter has a significant effect on what children experience; this we call a 'quality encounter'.

Reclaiming relational pedagogy is, currently, for us, about aiming to enrich that very interaction (little space). It is about making a 'little difference', influencing that space but, crucially, we are not in daily contact with children – we are one-step removed from the student/child encounter.

Challenges, dilemmas and opportunities

Given this position (of one-step removedness), there are particular challenges, dilemmas and opportunities, four of which we will mention here.

A fair proportion of students appear to need a range of reasonable certainties (Doyle 2006: 125) in which to locate their learning. Naturally, they ascribe a role to us within the expectations they bring as consumers. We know that, especially for the increasing numbers of students who are working practitioners, the daily pressures of work may be overwhelming. Thompson (2007) suggests that these pressures may be softening, but the reality and expectations of the early years foundation stage documentation nevertheless appears to inform these pressures.

We do therefore need to focus succinctly on quality encounters and how they can be influenced. Many of these take place every day and we remain positive about influencing this opportunity. We already believe that this is about a student's knowledge, skills and confidence as much as it is about the broader system, resources and organisation of services.

Opportunities to reclaim pedagogy in the quality encounter may well be greater within the early years sector than other possible age ranges. It is important that these opportunities are taken, not only because, arguably, what happens early on shapes dispositions for life but also an early years environment may offer a relatively flexible place and space to exercise innovative practice. Children's experiences in early years settings, we now know, can result in both positive and negative outcomes. Research over the past decade or so suggests that the quality of the early years' workforce is low and this impacts on the developmental opportunities of very young children (Abbott and Hevey 2001; Sylva *et al.* 2004; OECD 2006).

Sharing together in itself was a challenge given the demands on our time. During this process we came across an inherent problem: in attempting to reach a clear definition among us about what constitutes relational pedagogy, are we not just attempting to produce the final result, the certainty, the defined discourse, the very thing we are trying to move away from?

At this stage, we have a fluid and evolving concept, a sense of relational pedagogy being a way of thinking, a positive attitude towards the contexts in which there may well be chances to apply it confidently. Rinaldi (1998: 6) suggests:

> If we believe that children possess their own theories, interpretations, and questions, and they are co-protagonists in the knowledge building process, the most important verb in educational practice is no longer 'to talk', 'to explain' or 'to transmit' but 'to listen'.

Team views

This ability to listen has been paramount within our team. Listening to each others' views has made us aware of individual team members' positions and contributions. While it seems that each individual team member can only contribute some of her or his own personal experiences, some common thinking emerged. The following section outlines a number of perspectives from individual team members concerning the impact of the quality encounter and its application in our higher education sphere. These will inevitably both shape and reflect the key relational pedagogical values. The areas covered are: longer term impacts, learning and teaching with students, processes and timings, and our own current position with regard to relational pedagogy.

Longer term impact

If working in the 'little spaces' with children can promote values of thoughtfulness and sensitivity, then the potential breadth and spread of influence may be immeasurable. There are so many encounters that take place in early years, revealing so many opportunities. We are concerned here about affecting that quality encounter and allowing the participants (the students at the encounter) to respond to their unique contexts at the time and place, record the process and allow space to dissect and discuss it later (Rinaldi 2006).

Furthermore, quality encounters may need to have a neutral flavour; a co-constructing ethos in which neither participant claims dominance. Appropriate and confident application and attention to the little spaces implies a close focus which seems to be a prerequisite when working with children. Duckworth (2007: 23) indicates the danger that if areas are 'not recognised and responded to' then the opportunity to address disadvantage may be missed.

These quality encounters permit and lend confidence to an awareness that some children may not 'be ready' for a predetermined learning journey; as Duckworth points out, there are many factors involved. There is the perspective, quite alarmingly, of 'lost' children on the pathways of curriculum development. This is illuminated by the experiences of practitioners who recognise the tension between the politically driven curriculum and their own understanding of children's needs. As Yates (2007: 1) suggests:

> It becomes clear to me that many children arrive in settings with their own personal 'baggage', but there is an assumption that this can be disregarded and that we should 'soldier on' with the curriculum regardless. The curriculum assumes that children arrive willing, ready and able to learn, and clearly this is the case for some, but not all.

Rinaldi's (1998) sentiment links in here, of course, and these points demonstrate the urgency that needs to inform implementation of a learning and teaching strategy which embraces relational pedagogy.

We have, of course, to appreciate that this is about the overall student experience and it is thus a team process, so we now turn to look at the possible implications for implementation of the degree course.

Learning and teaching with students

This section considers initially basic questions and pedagogical style. First, it is important to offer a background and context, and to pose a number of questions and healthy uncertainties, which document the thinking so far. These are tinged with a special flavour which focuses on the one-step-removed issue. The issue needs to be 'located'; in that it sits between the tutor and the student and that the target sits between the student and the child. A fundamental question is therefore: What is the relationship between students and tutors in higher education and do we offer a quality encounter which would resonate with their early years practice? A second question relates to the dilemmas of presenting this thinking in a relatively structured educational framework: How can we address this contradiction especially in relation to the importance of scaffolding learning processes in higher education?

Crucially, there is a direct challenge as to whether we are really helping our students. This contradiction stems from an offer which, on the one hand, promotes a necessarily critical stance with associated reflective thinking skills and, on the other, the encouragement of skills and competences which students will need to apply in their practice. Perhaps the most important feature of these questions is the process of making them visible to both our team and to our students.

In exploring this relationship, there are features at two levels: those of delivery and institution but crucially the assertion that re-examining 'spaces' needs to be driven forward as a deliberate act. These focus on the 'lived space between teacher and learner, where new knowledge is constructed' (Bergum 2003: 124). The team therefore advocate that they must offer a passionate commitment, which includes an awareness and sensitivity of the potential uncertainty and novelty of the dynamics of changing this space. This informs the approach to changing the teacher–student relationship; one suggested as being supportive to the process and offering encouragement.

It is equally important that the change process at institutional level is allowed to evolve by ensuring that there are opportunities for ideas to be shared, which need to be recognised by organisations. Further, institutions need to understand and recognise the notion of risk and that this will take time away from more traditional areas of teaching. However, this is balanced by the possibility that learners will better develop their understanding of both knowledge and the role of the teacher in acquainting them with that knowledge (Race 2005). Both of the above offer an essentially practical approach to the actual change dynamic, highlighting the anticipated stresses and strains which need to be thoroughly explored to implement the processes which promote the quality encounter.

Processes and timings

A further team challenge is that we have to be more explicit in promoting reflective disciplines with our students as a way forward. We are aware that much is made of reflective practice in the training of early years workers and, being in agreement with Ebbeck (2003), we believe that reflection is more than a technical act and that early years practitioners have the potential to be agents of change in children's lives. To facilitate this we need to establish our own team processes and position before we can make that objective as clear as possible. The very diversity of experience in our team means that we have begun to appreciate rather than suppress our differences and also to begin to move away from mechanistic and uniform delivery into the far less certain, yet infinitely more exciting and groundbreaking arena of relational pedagogy.

Another, quite specific, perspective is one which analyses the nature of the student group and suggests that our students form an inverted structure. This means that unlike other higher education degree cohorts, ours tends to increase in size as students move through their studies. Year Three is bigger than Year One and the blend of senior practitioners in relation to full-time students increases in the final phase where around a quarter are entering from other sources, typically the foundation degree. Our challenges here are varied but it may be that an approach embracing the thinking behind relational pedagogy could support broader learning opportunities in Year One (of our three-year course) and enable these students, as they move towards the completion of their degree, to more fully embrace, appreciate and engage with the overall student experience. If we are able to explore these key notions during the first year of study we can lay the foundations for confident learners in the second year, the absorption of new group members and the inevitable changes they bring to the group dynamic. This indicates that we need, as a team, to approach and introduce this key underpinning idea as early as possible along with our considerations around the teacher/learner power dynamics so often assumed rather than directly addressed.

Our consequent 'position'

At this point, it is important to articulate our position which recognises and yet seeks to distance itself from what Dahlberg *et al.* (2003: 100) identify, which is:

> Both the discourses of child development and of quality adopt a de-contextualised approach, or, at best, attempt to bring 'context' in as an explanatory variable, divorcing the child and the institution from concrete experience, everyday life, the complexities of culture, the importance of situation.

We make no apology for the term 'quality encounter'; we realise that some sort of conformity and measure will not disappear overnight. As partners and agents in the change process, however, there remains a challenge to the flavour and balance of the criteria used to formally assess children's and professionals' performances. Clearly, there continues to be a belief that there is room, indeed little spaces, to offer and that a focus on how children make progress through these encounters (with the documentation, visibility and debate of that process – see Luff 2007) contributes to the spirit and intention of the more holistic objectives within the *Every Child Matters* agenda (DfES 2003).

Optimistically, an emerging focus on the 'ecology of children's lives' (Early Childhood Studies Network 2007: 1) begins to propel the child centre stage. We believe that this will form a key guiding factor in our forthcoming revalidation event later on this year. The tactics in the first instance are pragmatic; affecting those little spaces and, arguably, 'reclaiming by the back door'. This is, of course, always a (political) dilemma; does one confront the world head-on or chip away at the edges? It is important to want to make a little difference now and the process is affirmed through some of the emerging lessons and pointers outlined above.

First, it is agreed that this is, at the point of delivery, probably an individual quest whose shape and depth may include some common notions of being 'in-between the meaning making process' and containing dimensions of reflective review, practical, often creative activities and feelings, summarised as 'head, hands and heart' (Petrie *et al.* 2006: 22); a 'being with' totality.

Second, it is pivotal that 'one of the most important determinants of whether children receive appropriate and responsive education and care is the level of staff qualification . . . better qualified teachers provided better quality care in the "child/teacher closeness"' (University of North Carolina *et al.* 1999 in Alakeson 2004: 21). In this respect it is additionally acknowledged that 'personalised learning' for the early years may be creeping up the agenda; DfES Consultation (DfES 2006: para 3.2, emphasis added) suggests that:

> The learning and development requirements set out the standards that providers need to meet to support the development of babies and young children *without prescribing a uniform approach* to early learning and development. They are fully flexible in order to accommodate a range of early years' philosophies and to be responsive to the needs of individual children.

Thus there is room to work in the little spaces, to enhance the quality encounter.

Similarly, Burton and Bartlett (in Kassem *et al.* 2006: 53) state that 'the key determinant is the extent to which the teacher has a detailed knowledge of each learner's progress, strengths and challenges in a particular learning context'. This supports 'little thinking' and has lessons on the value, spirit and intention of 'being with'. Enhanced scope, responsibility and innovation are located, then, within the influence of the individual facilitator, features we seek to normalise and promote by overtly concentrating on students' confidence and inspiration. This could be about reclaiming enthusiastic professionalism to influence those little spaces.

Next, and obviously, we have to address the content and style of our teaching and learning processes. This is beginning to point towards emphasising individual reflective skills and discourse analysis; both of which make the process the subject of investigation. Importantly, this is not without base or purpose (or vagueness); clarity needs to consider that 'reflexivity should not replace "a view from now here" with a "dream of everywhere" but rather it should admit and explore the implications of the view from somewhere quite particular indeed' (Alldred and Burman 2005: 189) and encouraging confidence in the students as individuals and professionals. This can be illustrated by a recently debated example. It has been mentioned earlier that students ascribe a power position to tutors and the associated challenges of uncertainty. Advanced students do encounter a different world of expectations on entry into higher education. There are too many to explore here but student responsibility and ownership of learning processes might be two (Race 2005).

The point here is that it is of vital importance to offer a learning partnership and a framework where these issues are made visible and become the subject; enabling an equitable co-constructing space where occupants can contribute to this process. Individually, this is a key element for learners and students alike, but this may represent a focus on our little spaces and quality encounters. There are ways forward, of course, but the position is interim; a continuing challenge is to grapple with the practicalities of the knotty little problem: to repeat, we remain one step removed from the adult/child encounter. This means, crucially, that it has to be worked out as to *how* to put the relational pedagogy message across and it is believed that progress is being made and the destination may be becoming clearer. As we inch towards the idea that there must be some sort of narrative and experiential element (in our courses), we nevertheless recognise that this 'process' focus is tempered, for the time being, within modular curriculum requirements.

Boyd *et al.* (2006) express some ideas for classroom practice but it is the question of the values outlined in their paper that may perhaps offer a pointer and emphasis: it is social interactions that give the teacher opportunities to demonstrate caring, fairness and respect. Others are mentioned such as giving a voice, empathy, a trusting atmosphere and a dynamic teaching and learning relationship. It is these values and the manner in which we may promote them as messages within the quality encounter that offers us a way forward in our future partnerships with students.

Summary and conclusion

The position remains interim; some of the whats and whys have been recounted and issues made visible. Quality encounters are practically explored; definitions, challenges, depth and change potentials towards influencing what children experience in the little spaces have been considered. Some future directions towards addressing the one-step-removed dilemma are indicated, as is reflective learning in partnership with students, transparency, the importance of values, continuing discussion and appreciation of diversity. Our position appears paradoxically united and definite yet inherently fluid. It would be unfair to describe us as a group in turmoil; rather we are at rest with our differences and in agreement with our similarities.

We celebrate, then, and continue to examine and explore our 'little spaces' within the concept of relational pedagogy.

References

Abbott, L. and Hevey, D. (2001) Training to work in the early years: developing the climbing frame. In G. Pugh (ed.) *Contemporary Issues in the Early Years* (3rd edn). London: Paul Chapman.

Alakeson, V. (2004) *A 20/20 Vision for Early Years*. London: SMF/Daycare Trust.

Alldred, P. and Burman, E. (2005) Analysing children's accounts using discourse analysis. In S. Green and D. Hogan (eds) *Researching Children's Experiences*. London: Sage.

Bergum, V. (2003) Relational pedagogy. Embodiment, improvisation and interdependence. *Nursing Philosophy*, 4(2): 121–128.

Boyd, R., MacNeill, N. and Sullivan, G. (2006) Relational pedagogy: putting balance back into students learning. *Curriculum Leadership*, 4(13), 5 May. Available online at: http://cmslive.curriculum.edu.au/leader/default.asp?issueID=10277andid=13944 (accessed 29 January 2007).

Burton, D. and Bartlett, S. (2006) Shaping pedagogy from psychological ideas. In D. Kassem, E. Mufti and J. Robinson (eds) *Education Studies: Issues and Critical Perspectives*. Maidenhead: McGraw-Hill/Open University Press.

Dahlberg, G., Moss, P. and Pence, A. (2003) *Beyond Quality in Early Childhood Education and Care*. London: RoutledgeFalmer.

Department for Education and Skills (DfES) (2003) *Every Child Matters*. London: HMSO. Also available online at: http://www.everychildmatters.gov.uk/_files/F9E3F941DC8 D4580539EE4C743E9371D.pdf (accessed 12 January, 2007).

DfES Consultation (2006) Available online at: http://www.dfes.gov.uk/consultations/ conSection.cfm?consultationId=1447anddId=747andsId=4332andnumbering=1anditem Number=3 (accessed 13 January 2007).

Doyle, J. (2006) Postmodernism and the approach to writing in Irish primary education. *Journal of Early Childhood Literacy*, 6(2): 123–143.

Duckworth, K. (2007) On your marks. *Nursery World*, 107: 4058, 15 February.

Early Childhood Studies Network (2007) *Draft Benchmarking Document*. Available online at: http://www.gaa.ac.uk/academicinfrastructure/benchmark/statements/EarlyChildhood Studies07.pdf (accessed 16 April 2008).

Ebbeck, M. (2003) Global pre-school education: issues and progress. *International Journal of Early Childhood*, 34(2): 1–11.

Kassem, D., Mufti, E. and Robinson, J. (eds) (2006) *Education Studies: Issues and Critical Perspectives*. Maidenhead: McGraw-Hill/Open University Press.

Luff, P. (2007) Written observations or walks in the park? In J. Moyles (ed.) *Early Years Foundations: Meeting the Challenge*. Maidenhead: Open University Press.

MacNaughton, G. (2005) *Doing Foucault in Early Childhood Studies: Applying Post-structural ideas*. London: Routledge.

Mathers, S., Sylva, K., Joshi, H., Siraj-Blatchford, I., Melhuish, E., Sammons, P. and Taggart, B. (2007) Childcare in the Millennium Cohort Study DfES. Available online at: http://www.cls.ioe.ac.uk/text.asp?section=00010002000100140004 (accessed 20 July 2007).

Moss, P. and Petrie, P. (2006) *From Children's Spaces to Children's Services*. London: RoutledgeFalmer.

OECD (2006) *Starting Strong II Early Childhood Education and Care*. Available online at: http://www.oecd.org/document/63 (accessed 31 January 2007).

Petrie, P., Boddy, J., Cameron, C., Wigfall, V. and Simon, A. (2006) *Working with Children in Care*. Maidenhead: McGraw-Hill/Open University Press.

Race, P. (2005) *Making Learning Happen. A Guide for Post-compulsory Education.* London: Sage.

Readings, B. (1996) *The University in Ruins.* London: Harvard University Press.

Rinaldi, C. (1998) The thought that sustains educational action. *Rechild (Reggio Children Newsletter)* N2, April.

Rinaldi, C. (2006) *In Dialogue with Reggio Emilia.* Abingdon: Routledge.

Sylva, K., Melhuish, E., Sammons, P., Siraj-Blatchford, I. and Taggart, B. (2004) *The Effective Provision of Pre-school Education Project (EPPE).* London: Institute of Education University of London.

Thompson, R. (2007) EYPS framework sets out providers' responsibilities. *Nursery World*, 107: 4053, 11 January.

Westcott, H. and Littleton, K. (2005) Exploring meaning in interviews with children. In S. Greene and D. Hogan (eds) *Researching Children's Experience.* London: Sage.

Yates, E. (2007) Contribution to the conference paper at the Reclaiming Relational Pedagogy in Early Childhood Conference at Anglia Ruskin University, 19 to 21 April (unpublished).

16 Parental participation

Icelandic playschool teachers' views

Johanna Einarsdottir and
Bryndis Gardarsdottir

This chapter presents a study on Icelandic playschool teachers' views concerning cooperation between playschools and families, the types of parental participation and cooperation that occur within the playschools, the goals of parental cooperation, the methods used and the problems and barriers. Playschool teachers in approximately 72 per cent of Icelandic playschools answered a questionnaire that was sent to all playschools in Iceland. The responses were compared among different groups and by age of the children with whom the teachers were working. The results revealed that the teachers in general had positive attitudes towards parents and felt that the parents were interested in and wanted to support their children. The main barriers that prevented parental involvement were, in their view, parents' lack of time and lack of interest. Playschool directors' and the special educators' opinions and practices differed somewhat from the others. The special educators held most frequent individual parent conferences, and they found reciprocal information-giving about the child being important, more so than the other groups. They also reported more frequent problems in discussing deviations and parents' language difficulties. The playschool directors, on the other hand, were more concerned than the other groups that parents were satisfied with the playschool. They valued confidentiality and respect in interactions to be more important and that the parents should feel secure with their child there. They also mentioned more often than the other groups that they found it difficult to discuss neglect and abuse with the parents.

Introduction

In Iceland, the term *playschool* is used for early childhood programmes for children up to 6 years old, prior to the age of compulsory education. University-educated early childhood educators are called playschool teachers. According to a 1994 law, playschools are the first level of schooling in Iceland (Law on Playschools, No. 78/1994). Children can start playschool as early as 1 year old, but most children are enrolled when they are 2 or 3 years old. Early childhood programmes have grown rapidly in the past decades in accordance with the increase of women's participation in the workforce, and today most Icelandic parents work outside their homes. In 1984, 55 per cent of children aged 3 to 5 years attended playschool compared to only 10 per cent of 1 to 2-year-olds. Today approximately 30 per cent of 1-year-olds attend playschools, as do 90 per cent of 2-year olds and 94 per cent of children aged 3 to 5 years (Hagstofa Íslands 1997, 2006).

Local authorities supervise the building and operation of most playschools and bear the expenses involved. Parents' contributions cover approximately 30 per cent of the costs of operation, except for the oldest children for whom playschool is, in most municipalities, free of charge for four hours a day. The Ministry of Education formulates the educational policy for playschools and publishes the *Playschool National Curriculum Guidelines* (Menntamálaráðuneytið 1999).

This study focuses on the cooperation and relationship between Icelandic playschool teachers and parents.[1] Parent cooperation is a relatively new concept in Icelandic early childhood education. It was not until 1991 that cooperation with the home was mentioned in the laws (Law on Playschools, No. 48/1991), and in 1993 the importance of cooperation with parents was added to the *Educational Plan for Playschools* (Menntamálaráðuneytið 1993). According to current laws on playschool education, playschool directors should promote cooperation between the parents of the children attending the playschool and the playschool staff, with the welfare of the children as the guiding principle (Law on Playschools, No. 78/1994). The objectives of parental cooperation, according to the National Curriculum guidelines, are to:

1 provide parents with information on the playschool's activities;
2 provide parents with information on their child's development and the child's situation at the playschool;
3 gather information on the circumstances and educational views of parents;
4 encourage parental participation in playschool activities;
5 foster cooperation and exchange between the playschool and the home;
6 create a forum for exchanging views on children's education (Menntamálaráðuneytið 1999). Thus, cooperation and participation with parents are regarded as important components of the playschool's responsibility.

The aim of this study is to shed light on the views of Icelandic playschool teachers concerning cooperation between playschools and families, the types of parental participation and cooperation that occur within the playschools, the goals of parental cooperation, the methods used, problems and barriers, and the support parents are given within the playschool settings.

Teachers' beliefs

It is widely accepted that teachers' beliefs affect teaching and learning and shape their pedagogy. Price (1969) defines beliefs as what an individual holds to be true and sees them as guidelines to actions and practical decisions. Further he claims that a person can believe a proposition without realising it, and that there are unconscious or repressed beliefs.

Van Fleet (1979) builds on Herskovits' (1963) idea of cultural transmission and suggests that teachers acquire knowledge and beliefs about teaching through three different processes: enculturation, education and schooling. This means that teachers' sociocultural backgrounds affect their beliefs and interactions and how the process of parent and family involvement is constructed. The school culture and school's attitude towards parents and cooperation with them also influence teachers' practices and become the accepted standard (Souto-Manning and Swick 2006). Further, teachers' beliefs and actions cannot be understood without considering the social, cultural and historical contexts within and into which they grow (Kagitcibasi 1996; Kitayama and Markus 1999a; Rogoff 2003; Shweder *et al.* 1998). Bruner (1996) proposed that culture is central in shaping human life and the human mind. He used the term *folk psychology* for the underlying beliefs in a culture about human tendencies and how minds work. Along the same lines, Rogoff (2003) talks about how people follow cultural processes to organise their lives. She argues against treating individuals as entities separate from cultural processes, existing independently of their cultural communities. Further, she states that culture is not merely an entity that influences individuals. Instead, people contribute to the creation of cultural processes, while at the same time cultural processes contribute to the creation of people. Thus, teachers' beliefs about parent cooperation and involvement are heavily influenced by current and past contextual and cultural elements.

Home and school relations

Dencik (2006) implies that children today grow up in two worlds, in a 'double-socialization-situation'. Children today are more independent of their parents than before. They experience things away from their parents, things that the parents do not have experience of themselves because when they were growing up they lived different lives from their children. Dencik *et al.* (1988) introduce the concept of *sociotop* which represents a space in which the individual lives, a space characterised by unique conditions. For instance, the home where the child lives is one *sociotop*, and the school is another. They stress the importance of interaction between these two spaces. In order to understand children and their lives, it is necessary to study the two worlds of children and how these worlds connect (Dencik 2006; Dencik *et al.* 1988).

Bronfenbrenner's ecological model has been widely used by researchers to explain the interrelation between children's homes, schools and social conditions (Bronfenbrenner 1979, 1986; Connors and Epstein 1995). His framework recognises the multiple and interdependent influences of various contexts on children's development and emphasises that children's development is nested within the microsystem, mesosystem, exosystem and macrosystem. The microsystem consists of relations between the child and his or her immediate setting, of which he or she is a part. The mesosystem refers to the relation between the settings in which the child participates (e.g. how events at home can affect the child's progress in school and vice versa). The exosystem represents other settings that affect the child but do not contain the child. The macrosystem refers to patterns of cultural or societal beliefs that influence behaviour (e.g. ideas concerning the roles of school, teachers and parents).

Epstein has integrated and extended Bronfenbrenner's model and introduced a social-organisational perspective of overlapping spheres of influence for understanding and studying school and family relations (Epstein 1987). Similarly, Keyes (2002) built on Bronfenbrenner's model and social system perspective in developing her theoretical framework for the parent/teacher partnership. Pianta and Walsh (1996) developed a theoretical framework called the Contextual Systems Model which sees development as framed by culture and history. The model is helpful in understanding the relationship between child, family and schooling.

Benefits of parents' involvement

Research indicates that parents' involvement in their children's schooling has positive effects on children, parents and teachers. Parents who are involved in their child's schooling exhibit increased self-confidence in their parenting and more knowledge of child development (Baum and McMurray-Schwarz 2004; Eldridge 2001; Epstein 2001; Rennie 1996; Whalley 2006). Schools and teachers also benefit from parental involvement. Through parental cooperation, teachers gain a greater understanding of individual children's lives and their cultural backgrounds, and schools benefit from greater community support (Baum and McMurray-Schwarz 2004; Eldridge 2001).

Children are, however, those who benefit the most from parents' participation. Studies suggest that children whose parents work closely with the school do better overall, and have fewer discipline problems, better school attendance, higher graduation rates and greater enrolment rates in higher education (Casanova 1996; Eldridge 2001; Epstein 1996, 2001; Feuerstein 2000; Funkhouser, Gonzales and Moles 1998; Henderson and Berla 1994; Henderson and Mapp 2002; Moriarty 2002). Parental participation increases teachers' expectations for the child, which encourages the child and increases her or his academic achievement (Rennie 1996). Parents who work closely with the school also gain a better understanding of the school's expectations and how they can work with the teachers to support the children. Further, children whose parents participate and cooperate with the school get the message that schooling and education are important and valuable (Connors and Epstein 1995; Epstein and Dauber 1993).

Parents' participation in early childhood education

One of the hallmarks of quality early childhood programmes is seen by the degree to which they involve families. The frequency of parent–staff relationships is positively linked to the quality of education and care (Chazvini and Readdick 1994;

Olmsted and Montie 2001). A recent OECD report on early childhood education and care emphasises family involvement in early childhood services. Continuity of children's experiences across environments is greatly enhanced when parents and staff members exchange information regularly and adopt consistent approaches to socialisation, daily routines, child development and learning (OECD 2006). A developmental project at the Pen Green Centre in Corby (England) has focused on collaboration with children and families right from the start. The core of the project was dialogue between parents and professionals on children's learning and achievements and pedagogical practice. The results suggest that rich and challenging dialogue can develop when early years practitioners work collaboratively with children and families and when, given the opportunity, parents demonstrated a deeper and more extended interest about their children's learning and became equal and active partners.

Ghazvini and Readdick (1994) classified communication between parents and caregivers into *one-way communication*, such as notes posted on the entrance door; *two-way communication*, such as telephone conversations; and *three-way communication*, such as exchanges between parent, caregiver and speech therapist. Their research revealed that compared to parents, caregivers rated all forms of parent–caregiver communication as more frequently occurring and as more important than parents rated such exchanges.

Home–school communication in early childhood education has been found to be greatest during the drop-off and pick-up transition. Endsley and Minish (1991) studied communication between parents and staff in daycare centres during morning and afternoon transitions. Results revealed large differences between centres in the frequency and usefulness of these exchanges. Drop-off and pick-up meetings were often short and focused only on immediate concerns, although in other instances they were fruitful exchanges. Analysis by time of day suggested that caregivers were relatively more accessible during the morning transition, while parents were relatively more accessible during the afternoon transition. There was also more communication with parents of younger children than with parents of older daycare children.

Studies have revealed that teachers hold various misconceptions about parents' perceptions and behaviours. Knopf and Swick (2007) reviewed some of the stereotypes that teachers hold to be true and discussed how they influence parent and family involvement:

1   The first misconception they mention is that *parents do not care*. If parents for some reason do not participate or become involved in their child's school, teachers assume they do not care about the child's education. The reason, though, could be due to competing responsibilities, lack of resources or time constraints.

2   Another stereotype is that *parents do not have the time or motivation to be involved*. However, studies have found that when parents feel connected to the school they take the time to be involved, and when teachers involve parents in the planning of activities and events, their participation increases.

3   The third misconception is that *parents are not interested in leadership roles*. Research indicates conversely that if teachers see parents as capable leaders, they will become more involved.

Studies have also found that parents who were employed part-time or unemployed were more satisfied with their experiences of their child's early education programme than parents who were employed full-time. Married parents were also more satisfied with their teacher contact than non-married parents. These non-married parents are also generally less involved at the school site (Epstein 1995; Fantuzzo *et al.* 2006).

Literature also indicates that it is easier for teachers to be in contact with some parents than others. Given the many benefits to having meaningful relationships with all parents, Knopf and Swick (2007) have suggested the following strategies for early childhood educators:

1   Actively pursue meaningful relationships with all of the families in the classroom. The tendency to interact frequently says to parents that the teacher cares about them and wants their involvement in the programme.
2   Make sure that the initial contact with parents is positive and early. The first interaction with families sets the tone for the entire relationship. If the first interaction with a parent comes as a result of a problem, teachers are creating a negative perception in the minds of the parent.
3   Communicate with parents consistently through a variety of means. Interactions do not have to be every day, but should be often enough that parents get the sense that they are informed members of the classroom community. Personal, face-to-face communication is preferable, but if this opportunity does not present itself, letters, phone calls and e-mail will also help. Teachers should be active in adapting our plans to the complex schedules of the families we serve.
4   Share the small accomplishments and meaningful interactions that children have during the day. By that teachers tell the parents that they know their child and are focused on her or his individual development.
5   Learn individual parent needs and communicate how these needs are being met.
6   Listen to parents' concerns and respond to them. When parents come to the teacher with concerns they need to make sure the parents know that the teacher has listened to them. The best way to do that is to either remedy the situation that has caused the parents to become concerned or simply explain to them what was happening in the situation.
7   Ask parents to come in to school and assist when their help is really needed, while at the same maintaining an open-door policy where parents feel free to come in and visit with the children in the class.
8   Explicitly convey the message that parents are valued as their child's first and most influential teachers.

Icelandic schools have a scarce tradition of parental participation. In the past, the school was for teachers and children, but the home and the labour market were for parents. Although this is gradually changing, knowledge is limited about parental cooperation in Icelandic playschools today. This study will examine playschool teachers' views and methods of cooperation with parents in times when most Icelandic parents of playschool children work outside the home, and most children attend full-day playschool from the age of 2.

The following research questions guided the study:

1   What are the playschool teachers' beliefs and views on cooperation with parents?
2   What are the playschool teachers' aims on cooperation with parents?
3   What methods do the playschool teachers use in interacting with parents?
4   What does parent participation and cooperation involve?
5   What are the difficulties, concerns and barriers that playschool teachers see in cooperation with parents?

Method

Data were collected through a survey sent to playschool teachers in Iceland. A questionnaire developed in cooperation with the other researchers was sent by mail to all playschools in Iceland for the playschool teachers to answer.

The questionnaire started with questions on background information regarding the playschools and the participating playschool teachers. These were followed by questions on the playschool teachers' practices and their views and beliefs on cooperation and involvement of parents. The questions were mostly open-ended, but there were also questions where the participants could choose one of five options on a spectrum ranging from 'strongly agree' to 'strongly disagree'.

All playschool teachers working in Icelandic playschools were asked to participate in the study. In total, 900 lists were sent to 248 playschools. After obtaining permission for the study from the playschool authorities in each municipality, a letter explaining the study and its importance was sent to the playschool directors. They were asked to deliver the enclosed questionnaire, cover letter and postage-paid envelope (to use in returning the completed questionnaire) to the playschool teachers working in their playschools. Approximately five weeks after the questionnaires were mailed, a reminder letter was sent, and a few weeks later the researchers phoned those playschools that had not yet returned the questionnaires. For some of the playschools, several calls were made and e-mails sent.

The number of lists sent out (n = 900) is misleading since it was not known in advance how many playschool teachers were working in each playschool and therefore it is not used to calculate response rate from teachers. Of the 248 playschools that received questionnaires, 590 lists were eventually returned from 178 playschools. This means that playschool teachers in approximately 72 per cent of Icelandic playschools answered the questionnaire. The responses to the open-ended questions were grouped together and compared between different groups:

by positions (playschool teachers, headteachers, playschool directors, assistant directors and special educators) and by age of the children with whom the educators were working.

Results

The playschool teachers were asked about their views on cooperation between the playschools and families, the aims of parent cooperation, the methods used for interacting with parents, and the types of parental participation and cooperation that occur within the playschool.

Understanding and beliefs on cooperation with parents

The participants were asked open questions about how they understood parental involvement and participation in childcare. Their answers were sorted into the following five groups:

1 Reciprocal information-giving about the child.
2 Trust, confidentiality and respect in interactions.
3 Collaboration on the child's well-being and safety.
4 Introducing the playschool curriculum to parents.
5 Listening to the wishes and viewpoints of parents.

Figure 16.1 illustrates that *reciprocal information-giving about the child*, and *trust, confidentiality and respect in interactions* were most often mentioned as important areas of parental involvement and communication. When comparing views of different groups of educators, some differences became evident. Playschool

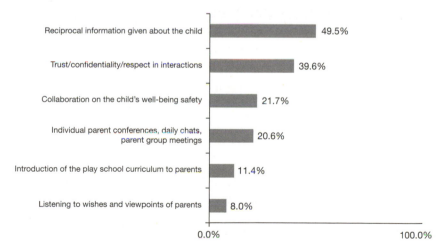

Figure 16.1 Understanding of parental involvement.*

Note: * Multiple response question. Sum greater than 100 per cent.

directors mentioned *listening to the wishes and viewpoints of parents*, and *trust, confidentiality and respect in interactions* more often than the other groups. The special educators, who work mainly with children with special needs, reported more often than the other groups that they found *reciprocal information-giving about the child* to be important, and playschool teachers emphasised *introducing the playschool curriculum to the parents* more than the others.

The playschool teachers agreed that parents in general were interested in their children's lives and education. When they were asked to indicate on a five-point scale if they found parents to be interested in their child's life in the playschool, almost all of them agreed to that. When they were asked if they found parents willing to support their child's learning, approximately 85 per cent agreed or strongly agreed to that (Figure 16.2).

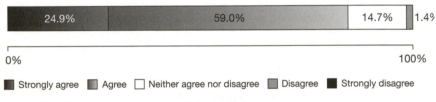

Figure 16.2 Parents want to support their child's learning.

When the playschool teachers, on the other hand, were asked if they found that the parents wanted to contribute to the playschool activities, the numbers were lower. Sixty-two per cent agreed or strongly agreed that the parents wanted to contribute, but 16 per cent did not agree (see Figure 16.3).

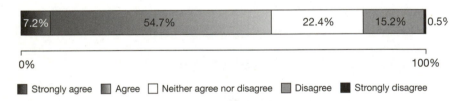

Figure 16.3 Parents want to contribute to the playschool activities.

Aims for cooperation with parents

The participants were openly asked about their aims for cooperation with parents. Out of their answers emerged five groups:

1   Unstrained interaction characterised by trust and confidentially.
2   Learning to know the individual child and his or her family in order to meet his or her needs.
3   Parents are satisfied with the playschool and feel secure with their child there.

4   Parents know about the curriculum of the playschool.
5   Parents are informed about the development/behaviour of their child.

The most frequent response, mentioned by 49 per cent of those who answered the question, was *unstrained interaction characterised by trust and confidentiality*. The second most mentioned aim was *learning to know the individual child and his or her family in order to meet his or her needs* (see Figure 16.4).

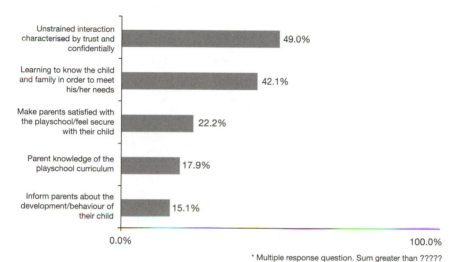

* Multiple response question. Sum greater than ?????

Figure 16.4 Aims for cooperation with parents.*

Note: Multiple response question.

Looking at the answers by positions in the playschool, special educators mentioned *learning to know the individual child and his or her family in order to meet his or her needs* more often than the other groups. Playschool directors mentioned *unstrained interaction characterised by trust and confidentiality* more often than the other educators, as well as *parents are satisfied with the playschool and feel secure with their child there* (Figure 16.5).

When responses from educators working with the youngest children (1–3) were compared with the responses from educators working with the older playschool children (3–5), there were also some differences. Those who worked with younger children valued unstrained interaction characterised by trust and confidentiality most. But those who worked with the older children found learning to know the individual child and his or her family in order to meet his or her needs to be more important. Those who worked with the youngest children also said more frequently that they want the parents to be satisfied with the playschool and to feel secure with their child there. Those who worked with the oldest children on the other hand responded more frequently that they wanted the parents to know about the curriculum and be informed about the development and behaviour of their child.

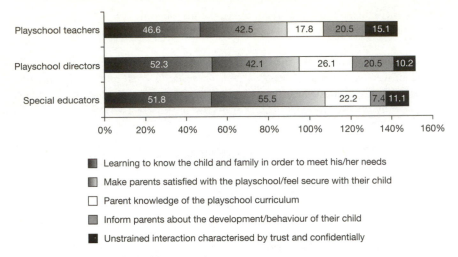

Figure 16.5 Cooperation with parents.*

Note: Multiple response question. Sum greater than 100 per cent.

The participants' responses to an open-ended question on why they promoted cooperation with parents were categorised into three groups:

1   To ensure the welfare and security of the child.
2   Everyone feels better if the relationship is good.
3   I will be able to meet the needs of an individual child better if I know about his or her home context.

Most participants, or 61 per cent of those who answered the question, responded that their reason for cooperation with parents was *to ensure the welfare and security of the child* (Figure 16.6). When answers were categorised by positions, it became evident that special educators stood out, mentioning most often that the reason they

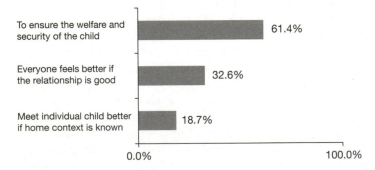

Figure 16.6 Reason for cooperation with parents.*

Note: Multiple response question. Sum greater than 100 per cent.

cooperated with the parents was *to ensure the welfare and the security of the child*, and they mentioned least often that the reason they cooperated was that *everyone feels better if the relationship is good*.

Methods of parent cooperation

When the early childhood educators were asked in an open question to describe the methods they used for involving parents, their responses were categorised into eight groups:

1   Daily chats.
2   Individual parent conferences.
3   General information/introduction to the playschool.
4   Parent group meetings.
5   Telling parents about their child.
6   Being positive and respecting the parents' views.
7   Introductory meeting in the beginning.
8   Emphasising the importance of parent cooperation.

The most frequently mentioned categories were *daily chats* and *individual parent conferences* (Figure 16.7). When different groups were compared, playschool teachers and headteachers were the educators who most often mentioned daily chats, and the special educators most often reported holding individual parent

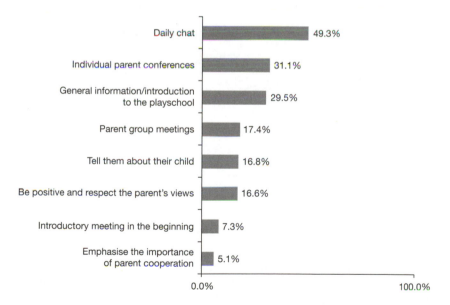

Figure 16.7 Methods of parental involvement.*

Note: Multiple response question. Sum greater than 100 per cent.

conferences and talking to the parents about their child. Playschool teachers working with the older children more often reported that they held individual parent conferences and gave general information about the playschool. Playschool teachers working with the younger children, on the other hand, more often reported that they talked to the parents about their child and respected the parents' views.

Types of parent cooperation

The playschool teachers were asked in an open question to describe how parents are visible in the playschool. The answers were grouped into the following six categories:

1 Attending events in the playschool.
2 Active parent organisation.
3 Expressing their views on the curriculum.
4 Attending meetings.
5 Participating in the school day.
6 Participating in field trips.

As Figure 16.8 illustrates, the most frequent answer was that parents attended events in the playschool which 64 per cent of the participant mentioned. Over one-third of the playschool teachers mentioned that there was an active parent organisation in the playschool.

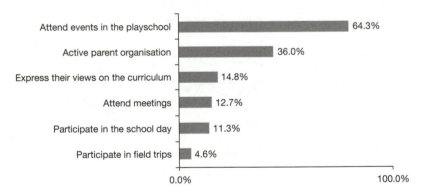

Figure 16.8 How do parents participate?*

Note: Multiple response question. Sum greater than 100 per cent.

When the participants were asked if they discussed child-rearing and issues concerning the child with parents, almost all of them reported that they did. When they were asked to mark on a scale if they saw it more often as their responsibility to advise parents on parenting, approximately 74 per cent of them either agreed or strongly agreed (Figure 16.9). Playschool teachers working with the younger

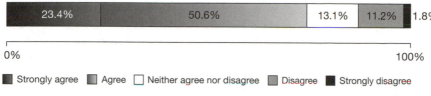

Figure 16.9 The playschool is responsible for advising parents on parenting.

children particularly saw this as their responsibility. Playschool directors and headteachers saw this more often as the role of the playschool than the other groups.

When the playschool teachers were asked in an open question what were the most common topics that they discussed with parents, their answers were grouped into eight categories:

1   How the child is doing.
2   Routine and the playschool day.
3   Learning and development.
4   The child's accommodation.
5   The child's behaviour.
6   Amusing events.
7   Daily hours and rates.
8   Child-rearing.

The most common responses were about how the child was feeling and doing in playschool, or approximately 49 per cent of the responses. The second most common were discussions about the playschool day and the child's learning and development. The least common discussions were concerning child-rearing and practical matters about rates (Figure 16.10).

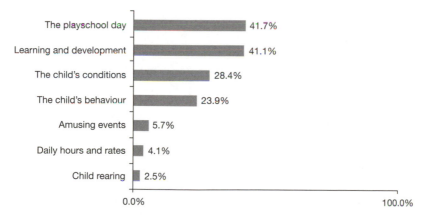

Figure 16.10 The most common topics discussed with parents.*

Note: Multiple response question. Sum greater than 100 per cent.

When the playschool teachers were asked if they talked more often about issues that could be classified as care or if they discussed more often children's learning, most of them reported that they discussed it equally often (approximately 58 per cent). However, more respondents answered that they discussed care rather than learning. Approximately 27 per cent said that they emphasised care more often in their conversations with parents, while approximately 14 per cent said that they emphasised learning more often (Figure 16.11).

Figure 16.11 Discussions concerning learning and care.

Playschool teachers working with the younger children more often reported that they discussed care with the parents than those working with the older children did (42.7 per cent), but only 22.9 per cent of those working with the older children reported that they discussed care more often. They, on the other hand, said they discussed learning more often (16.5 per cent), compared to only 8.2 per cent of those working with the younger children. Special educators stood out in this respect, 44.4 per cent of them reporting that they discussed learning more often.

Difficulties, concerns and barriers to cooperation with parents

When the participants were asked what they found most difficult to deal with while cooperating with parents, their responses were grouped into six categories:

1   Handling closed, uninterested parents.
2   Discussing difficult matters.
3   Discussing deviations.
4   Parents denying the child's problem.
5   Parents who were unhappy with the playschool curriculum.
6   Cases of neglect and abuse (see Figure 16.12).

It is notable how many educators mentioned that they found it difficult to deal with closed, uninterested parents (37.4 per cent) (Figure 16.12).

The responses of educators holding different positions when they were asked what they found most difficult in cooperation with parents showed different results. The playschool teachers most often talked about *closed, uninterested parents* and problems in *discussing difficult matters*. The special educators, on the other hand, reported difficulties in *discussing deviations* more often than the other groups. Playschool directors mentioned more often *neglect and abuse* as difficult matters to discuss.

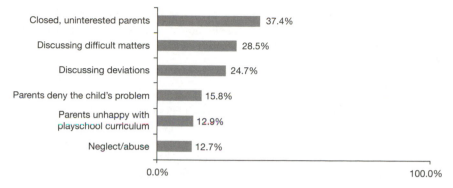

Figure 16.12 Difficulties in cooperation with parents.*

Note: Multiple response question. Sum greater than 100 per cent.

The results show that playschool teachers who taught older children (ages 3–5) more often reported difficulties with closed and uninterested parents and difficulties in discussing child's deviations. The playschool teachers who worked with the younger group (ages 1–3), on the other hand, reported more problems in discussing difficult matters with parents and when parents were not happy with the playschool.

The participants were asked about barriers that prevented parental involvement and participation. Figure 16.13 shows that the most frequent barriers mentioned were parents' lack of time and parents' lack of interest. Least frequent answers were parents' language difficulties and parents' social problems. When the results were compared according to the age groups the educators taught, it is interesting to note that those who worked with the older children more often mentioned lack of time on the side of the parents, and those who worked with the younger children mentioned lack of interest. The special educators more often mentioned parents' language difficulties, and the playschool directors mentioned parents' social problems most often.

The study focuses on Icelandic playschool teachers' views on cooperation and relationships with parents. The results revealed that the teachers in general had positive attitudes towards parents and felt that the parents were interested in and

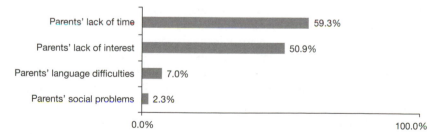

Figure 16.13 Barriers to parental involvement and participation.*

Note: Multiple response question. Sum greater than 100 per cent.

wanted to support their children. When the participants were asked about the main barriers that prevented parental involvement, they mentioned parents' lack of time and parents' lack of interest.

Discussion

When the views of different early childhood educators were compared it became evident that the playschool directors' and the special educators' opinions and practices differed somewhat from the others, which is in accordance with the line of their work. The special educators held most frequent individual parent conferences, and they found reciprocal information-giving about the child to be important, more so than the other groups. They also discussed learning more often with parents than the other groups. Further, they reported more often difficulties in discussing deviations and parents' language difficulties. The playschool directors, on the other hand, were more concerned than the other groups that parents were satisfied with the playschool. They valued confidentiality and respect in interactions to be more important and that the parent felt secure with their child there. They also mentioned more often than the other groups that they found it difficult to discuss neglect and abuse with the parents. Clearly as leaders it is their responsibility to discuss this issue with these parents, whereas the playschool teachers would discuss it with their superiors.

When the views of playschool teachers working with different age groups were compared, it became evident that those who worked with the younger children emphasised communication on an individual basis and caregiving more often than those working with the older children who emphasised learning more often. Whalley (2006) and others have pointed out that parents are most keen to know about their children's development, learning and well-being when the children have just started nursery. Therefore, it is crucial to establish a good foundation for further cooperation in the beginning when the children are starting playschool.

Conclusion

Teachers' beliefs about their work are influenced by current and past contextual cultural elements (Bruner 1996; Kagitcibasi 1996; Kitayama and Markus 1999b; Rogoff 1993; Shweder *et al.* 1998). Parent participation does not have a long tradition in the Icelandic school system and has not been a prominent part of early childhood teacher education. These are influential contexts currently shaping how the participating playschool teachers think about and construct family involvement and cooperation. The methods the teachers use in communicating with parents are congruent with the recommendations of the National Curriculum guidelines, although the emphasis seems to be more on providing the parents with information rather than getting information from the parents and exchanging views on children's education. Whalley (2006) has suggested that parents should be viewed as equal and active partners engaged in the process of education. Unless practitioners truly value the contribution made by parents, parents will continue to assume a less powerful role. This is an important message for Icelandic playschool teachers, but according to the results of this study it is not clear what responsibilities and roles the playschool teachers see parents playing.

As in other studies on family cooperation in early childhood (Endsley and Minish 1991), parent–teacher communication occurred most frequently through daily chat. According to the Endsley and Minish study (1991), parents are more available when they pick up their children, but teachers are more accessible during drop-off. This is also the situation in Icelandic playschools today. Playschool teachers are often not available for parents in the afternoon, and since most Icelandic parents work full-time they are rushing to work when they drop their children off in the morning, but often have the time and opportunity to chat when they pick up their children in the afternoon. As Knopf and Swick (2007) have pointed out, early childhood educators need to find ways to communicate to parents through a variety of means and adapt to the parents' schedules. The results of this study indicate that Icelandic playschool teachers find that most parents are interested in their children and want to support their child's learning. They also find most parents easy to communicate with, but have problems reaching out to others. Icelandic playschool teachers need to find ways to involve all parents. According to the long time experience of the Pen Green Centre it has to be the early childhood educators' initiative to reach out and involve parents, not the other way around. Parents need to become familiar with the ideology and have opportunities to discuss and learn about the curriculum in order to become equal partners in the education of their children (Whalley 2006). Thus, Icelandic playschool teachers have to find ways to present, discuss, and make their work more visible for parents and others to understand. The issue of family involvement has not been discussed to a great extent among Icelandic early childhood professionals. The idea of parents as equal and active partners is new to Icelandic playschool teachers and parents. Cooperation with parents concerning their children's education and welfare and their involvement in decision-making is an important aspect of quality early childhood programmes. Therefore it is significant that Icelandic playschool teachers reflect and evaluate this important part of their work and try to find ways and methods to communicate with all parents and be ready for them during times of their preference.

Note

1   The study is a part of a cross-cultural parental participation project, which involves professionals from Estonia, Finland, Iceland, Lithuania, Norway and Portugal.

References

Baum, A.C. and McMurray-Schwarz, P. (2004) Preservice teachers' beliefs about family involvement: implications for teacher education. *Early Childhood Education Journal*, 23(1): 57–61.

Bronfenbrenner, U. (1979) *The Ecology of Human Development*. Cambridge, MA: Harvard University Press.

Bronfenbrenner, U. (1986) Ecology of the family as a context for human development: research perspectives. *Developmental Psychology*, 22: 723–742.

Bruner, J. (1996) *The Culture of Education*. Cambridge, MA: Harvard University Press.

Casanova, U. (1996) Parent involvement: a call for prudence. *Educational Researcher*, 25(8): 30–32.

Chazvini, A.S. and Readdick, C.A. (1994) Parent–caregiver communication and quality of care in diverse child care settings. *Early Childhood Research Quarterly*, 9: 207–222.

Connors, L.J. and Epstein, J.L. (1995) Parent and school partnerships. In M. Bornstein (ed.) *Handbook of Parenting: Applied and Practical Parenting*. Mahaw, NJ: Lawrence Erlbaum.

Dencik, L. (2006) Parent–child relationships in early childhood in contemporary welfare societies. Paper presented at the European Early Childhood Education Research Association, Reykjavik, August.

Dencik, L., Bäckström, C. and Larsson, E. (1988) *Barnens två världar [The child's two worlds]*. Falköping, Sweden: Gummerssons Tryckeri.

Eldridge, D. (2001) Parent involvement: it's worth the effort. *Young Children*, 56(2): 65–69.

Endsley, R. and Minish, P.A. (1991) Parent–staff communication in daycare centers during morning and afternoon transitions. *Early Childhood Research Quarterly*, 6: 119–135.

Epstein, J.L. (1987) Toward a theory of family–school connections: teacher practices and parent involvement. In K. Hurrelmann, F. Kaufmann and F. Losel (eds) *Social Intervention: Potential and Constraints*. New York: deGruyter, pp. 121–137.

Epstein, J.L. (1995) School, family, community partnerships: caring for the children we share. *Phi Delta Kappan*, 76: 701–712.

Epstein, J.L. (1996) Advances in family, community, and school partnerships. *New Schools, New Communities*, 12(3): 5–13.

Epstein, J.L. (2001) *School, Family, and Community Partnerships: Preparing Educators and Improving Schools*. Boulder, CO: Westview Press.

Epstein, J.L. and Dauber, S.L. (1993) Parents' attitudes and practices of involvement in inner-city elementary and middle schools. In N.F. Chavkin (ed.) *Families and Schools in a Pluralistic Society* (pp. 53–72). Albany, NY: State University of New York Press.

Fantuzzo, J., Perry, M.A. and Childs, S. (2006) Parent satisfaction with educational experiences scale: a multivariate examination of parent satisfaction with early childhood education programs. *Early Childhood Research Quarterly*, 21: 142–152.

Feuerstein, A. (2000) School characteristics and parent involvement: influences on participation in children's schools. *The Journal of Educational Research*, 94(1): 29–41.

Funkhouser, J.E., Gonzales, M.R. and Moles, O.C. (1998) *Family Involvement in Children's Education: Successful Local Approaches*. Washington, DC: US Government Printing Office.

Ghazvini, A.S. and Readdick, C.A. (1994) Parent–caregiver communication and quality of care in diverse child care settings. *Early Childhood Research Quarterly*, 9: 207–222.

Hagstofa Íslands (1997) *Landshagir: Statistical Yearbook of Iceland*. Reykjavík: Hagstofa Íslands.

Hagstofa Íslands (2006) Available online at: http://www.hagstofa.is/ (accessed 26 July 2006).

Henderson, A.T. and Berla, N. (1994) *A New Generation of Evidence: The Family is Critical for Student Achievement*. Washington, DC: National Committee for Citizens in Education.

Henderson, A.T. and Mapp, K.L. (2002) *A New Wave of Evidence: The Impact of School, Family and Community Connections on Student Achievement*. Austin, TX: National Center for Family and Community Connections with Schools.

Herskovits, M. (1963) *Cultural Anthropology*. New York: Alfred Knopf.

Kagitcibasi, C. (1996) *Family and Human Development Across Cultures: A View from the Other Side*. Hillsdale, NJ: Lawrence Erlbaum.

Keyes, C.R. (2002) A way of thinking about parent/teacher partnerships for teachers. *International Journal of Early Years Education*, 10(3): 177–191.

Kitayama, S. and Markus, H.R. (1999a) The pursuit of happiness and the realization of sympathy: cultural patterns of self, social relations, and well-being. In E. Diener and E. Suh (eds) *Subjective Well-being Across Cultures* (pp. 113–161). Cambridge, MA: MIT Press.

Kitayama, S. and Markus, H.R. (1999b) The pursuit of happiness and the realization of sympathy: cultural patterns of self, social relations, and well-being. In E. Diener and E. Suh (eds) *Subjective Well-being Across Cultures*. Cambridge, MA: MIT Press.

Knopf, H.T. and Swick, K.J. (2007) How parents feel about their child's teacher/school: implications for early childhood professionals. *Early Childhood Education Journal*, 34(4): 291–296.

Law on Playschools No. 78/1994. Available online at: http://www.althingi.is/lagas/nuna/1994078.html (accessed 10 July 2007).

Law on Playschools No. 48/1991. Available online at: http://www.althingi.is/altext/stjt/1991.048.html (accessed 10 July 2007).

Menntamálaráðuneytið (1993) *Uppeldisáætlun fyrir leikskóla [Educational plan for playschools]*. Reykjavík: Menntamálaráðuneytið.

Menntamálaráðuneytið (1999) *Playschool National Curriculum Guidelines*. Reykjavík: Menntamálaráðuneytið.

Moriarty, V. (2002) Early years professionals and parents: challenging the dominant discourse? In V. Nivala and E. Hujala (eds) *Leadership in Early Childhood Education: Cross Cultural Perspectives* (pp. 127–136). Oulu: Oulun Ylippisto.

OECD (2006) *Starting Strong II: Early Childhood Education and Care*. Paris: OECD.

Olmsted, P.P. and Montie, J. (2001) *Early Childhood Settings in 15 Countries: What are Their Structural Characteristics?* Ypsilanti, MI: High/Scope Educational Research Foundation.

Pianta, R.C. and Walsh, D.J. (1996) *High-risk Children in Schools, Constructing Sustaining Relationships*. New York: Routledge.

Price, H.H. (1969) *Belief*. London: Allen & Urwin.

Rennie, J. (1996) Working with parents. In G. Pugh (ed.) *Contemporary Issues in the Early Years: Working Collaboratively for Children*. London: Paul Chapman.

Rogoff, B. (1993) Children's guided participation and participatory appropriation in sociocultural activity. In R.H. Wozniak and K.W. Fischer (eds) *Development in Context: Acting and Thinking in Specific Environments*. Hillsdale, NJ: Lawrence Erlbaum.

Rogoff, B. (2003) *The Cultural Nature of Human Development*. New York: Oxford University Press.

Shweder, R.A., Goodnov, J., Jatano, G., LeVine, R., Markus, H. and Miller, P. (1998) The cultural psychology of development: one mind, many mentalities. In W. Damon (ed.) *Handbook of Child Psychology* (Vol. 1, pp. 865–937) New York: Wiley.

Souto-Manning, M. and Swick, K.J. (2006) Teachers' beliefs about parent and family involvement: rethinking our family involvement paradigm. *Early Childhood Education Journal*, 34(2): 187–193.

Van Fleet, A. (1979) Learning to teach: the cultural transmission analogy. *Journal of Thought*, 14: 281–290.
Whalley, M. (2006) *Involving Parents in their Children's Learning*. London: Sage.

17 Fostering identity and relationships

The essential role of mentors in early childhood[1]

Kate Fowler and Alison Robins, with Sue Callan and Eryl Copp

Mentoring in early childhood settings should be a dynamic system of advice and support in the context of ongoing professional training and development which makes sense of reflective thinking and reflective practice. Successful mentoring is set within an action–reflection cycle and is based on the key principles of confidentiality, credibility and clarity, and ultimately engenders trust between those involved. 'Reflective' practitioners are supported by 'reflective' mentors.

As the pursuit of quality within a multidisciplinary early childhood workforce is paramount to practitioners and high on the political agenda, in this chapter we consider the dynamics of mentoring roles in managing increased complexity and in responding to change. Areas of particular significance include: reflective thinking; relationships; strategies for successful collaboration; personal and professional growth; policy influences; and the impact of effective mentoring on early childhood practitioners and children.

Introduction: the role of the mentor

Few practitioners[2] within the sector will deny that the past 15 years or more have transformed the status of early childhood services in the United Kingdom. Within this context the role of the mentor has increased in both importance and complexity, especially as work-based training is an established element of vocational qualifications as well as academic programmes across further and higher education. Wilkin (1992) suggests that the role of the mentor should be related to specific frameworks, such as training or qualification requirements. This approach provides a principle that may be broadly applied to early childhood contexts if we accept that the framework within which both mentor and practitioner operate is determined by the 'curriculum' for the child and the vision of the professional practitioner within it.

Within the context of the workplace setting, the early childhood mentor will help practitioners find answers to challenging situations, assist with strategies for action in the job role, promote both nurture and challenge within the boundaries of the relationship with the practitioner and encourage sustained motivation in the workplace (Zachary 2000). Qualities that facilitate the mentor role and mentor/ practitioner relationship may include enthusiasm, inspiration, problem-solving, knowledge and competence in subject skills and practices, good interpersonal skills, an ability to resolve or diffuse conflict and skills of reflection. While Clutterbuck (2004) challenges a definitive list of qualities/competencies on the basis that it is difficult to define the role being measured, his list of 'ten mentor competencies' (Clutterbuck 2000) reflects similar ideas. Pegg (2000) notes that such qualities provide mentors with credibility for the role. Underpinning these qualities is the fact that mentors will be/have been successful practitioners in their own right and be recognised as 'street-wise' in this respect in order to encourage evaluation and reflection in the practitioner. This particular mix of qualities will also enable the mentor to bring realistic expectations and a sense of proportion to a role which is complex and challenging.

The early childhood mentor will inevitably strive to combine these qualities with a mix of approaches and strategies within a philosophy of mentoring and train- ing that fits with the theoretical traditions of the sector. Many practitioners will recognise the concept of 'scaffolding' within pedagogy for children's learning and development. Indeed, Vygotsky (1978), Bandura (1977) and Bruner (1996) all suggest that learning is a social process governed by social interactions within the social context where 'human learning presupposes a specific social nature' (Vygotsky 1978: 88). This concept is as pertinent to adult learning as it is to child- ren's, especially in the context of mentoring in early childhood. In the mentoring process with early childhood practitioners we are making the shift from pedagogy to andragogy (adult learning principles) and, as Knowles *et al.* (1998) suggest, this works best when adapted to suit the needs of individual learners in individualised practice contexts.

Building on this earlier premise, the way in which the mentor role is conducted in practice will set the tone for the experience and outcomes for the practitioner. Mentoring serves practitioners in that it encourages, empowers and enhances a continuing commitment to experiential learning at the heart of work-based practice and offers the possibility of change. The guidance offered by the mentor is carried out in the spirit of mutual respect, where power is shared as far as the situation allows, and there is an expectation of two-way learning. Bronfenbrenner (1979: 60) determines in his research into 'interpersonal structures' that learning and development are enhanced when a person is 'in activity with someone with whom that person has developed a strong and enduring attachment'. Moyles *et al.* (1999: 170) further suggest that 'the idiosyncratic nature of practices . . . reflects the very individuality of those being mentored and those mentoring and the special relationships likely to be formed'. Both mentor and practitioner are stimulated in their thinking through the mentoring process so that aspects of practice are examined with depth and clarity.

The mentor helps the whole relationship and process by:

- assisting the transmission of knowledge and skills;
- guiding the induction and nurturing of practitioners;
- linking theoretical models and philosophical approaches to practice;
- reflecting standards and understanding of quality issues;
- promoting shared good practice and professional values;
- presenting solutions to professional challenges;
- enabling the exercise of professional judgement;
- focusing on the capability and potential of the practitioner;
- enhancing the development of individuals and organisations;
- drawing on and developing the research base for the sector.

(Callan 2006: 10–11)

In short, the early childhood mentor will operate within an appropriately staged framework of facilitating the development of the practitioner. This developmental framework will take account of needs, but also operate on the basis of professional expectations to which all partners to the training of the practitioner agree.

The general principles noted above stress the importance of clarity in defining the mentor role and, whatever the context, an early agreement and understanding about roles, responsibilities and expectations of the members of the partnership is crucial to any criteria for 'success'. Confidentiality is paramount to professionalism and is an underpinning requirement for successful mentoring in that it promotes trusting relationships – a prerequisite for honest, constructive evaluation and self-assessment in supported reflective practice.

There may be certain expectations of the mentor including professional competency, a current knowledge base, ability to respond to needs and manage the process, availability of time for preparation, observation and feedback, maintenance of confidentiality and a belief in the potential of the practitioner. Conversely there may also be expectations of the practitioner and these would include realistic expectations of the mentor, acceptance of their own responsibilities for the process, a willingness to action plan or set the direction for self-assessment, a willingness to be challenged, behaving appropriately towards 'third parties' and the keeping of confidentiality.

Time given at the beginning of the process to thinking about the conduct of the relationship and, equally important, at its end, will hopefully avoid the difficulties presented when, for example, a practitioner might be overly dependent on the mentor, or confidentiality principles are not clearly understood.

Fostering and forging relationships

Successful mentoring is based on the key ethical principles of:

- confidentiality;
- credibility;
- clarity of role,

all of which engender trust between those involved. The mentor is really 'the one in the middle' and may be visiting or working within the setting. An external mentor may have to strive harder to achieve the key ethical principles than the internal mentor who already has the advantage of familiarity.

Confidentiality is paramount to mentoring taking place within an ethical framework of good practice. It is also one of the most complex areas in terms of the fine line that the mentor treads in maintaining the 'mentoring relationship' set up with the practitioner within the setting and adherence to their own professional mandate. In order to avoid ambiguity and misunderstanding, ground rules for confidentiality must be owned by all parties, explicit from the outset and renegotiated if necessary. Mentors must also be prepared to acknowledge their own thoughts and attitudes towards confidentiality and be certain, especially if they are visiting/external mentors, that they can identify the point at which confidentiality is superseded by the need to share information with others.

The *credibility* of the mentor as a professional principle enhances confidentiality and is essential to the ability to mediate between various parties involved in the mentoring relationship in order to effectively support learning and reflective practice. The qualities the mentor demonstrates to establish credibility with a more senior practitioner would be those that emphasise professionalism weighted by experience, qualifications and success as a practitioner.

In order to achieve and maintain credibility the mentor must pay heed to:

- the perceptions of the practitioner, senior practitioners and others as to the role and professional status of the mentor;
- effective strategies for engaging with the practitioner;
- the need for credibility to be established as an important aspect of the mentor's role in supporting, offering advice and sharing knowledge.

Clarity of role is also identified as an essential component of a mentoring relationship and relates closely to both confidentiality and credibility. The mentors should negotiate collaboratively aspects of the mentoring relationship with senior practitioners in order to achieve clarity of role. For visiting mentors who are not only 'in the middle' of workplace relationships but may also be outsiders, this presents a particular challenge – senior practitioners need to be a part of the process if the practitioner is to derive maximum benefit. The mentor who is able to develop and work within this collaborative model will be highly effective in negotiating the key issues identified earlier – confidentiality, credibility and clarity – and well placed to deal appropriately with the challenges posed by being in the middle of a web of complex personal and professional interactions.

Once the mentoring relationship is established there are several critical issues that may influence mentoring in practice. These include:

- workforce developments and policy – at national, local and setting level – specifically qualification and training requirements;
- workplace culture, relationships – hierarchies, ethos, morale and team dynamics;

- gender balance of the workforce – the influence on mentoring style;
- personal issues – the self-concept of the practitioner and feedback that promotes reflective practice;
- the senior practitioner – attitudes and action;
- confidence and performance in the role;
- motivation of the mentor and practitioner.

The mentor in the midst of such influences will utilise various approaches when negotiating a way forward. Hamilton (1993) identifies three behaviours when the mentor may be acting as a:

- *Coach* – as a directive means of support, offering instruction or demonstration when needed and setting goals.
- *Counsellor* – encouraging and supporting, giving clarity and discussing options.
- *Role model* – a source of information and a standard by which practitioners can evaluate their own performance.

These behaviours when applied to the mentoring role will inevitably overlap and will help set the tone for different interactions with the practitioner, as well as influencing the overall style of mentoring in terms of the more directive approach which involves coaching or guiding and the non-directive or developmental approach of counselling and sharing of information. The effective mentor will be prepared to adopt all of the behaviours at different points in the relationship. Some of these behaviours will emerge as a result of the purpose of the mentoring role (as defined by the mentoring relationship) and, for the same reason, others may *not* be helpful because of the particular context. The role of the mentor is *not* to solve problems for the practitioner, but to provide a framework of approaches within which to facilitate self-management.

Inexperienced mentors should be aware that there is inevitably a blurring of personal and professional roles when mentoring as a 'professional friend'. This more personally based relationship can affect the clarity of mentoring relationship previously examined in terms of establishing professional boundaries. However, it is the 'friendship' element that enables the practitioner to gain empowerment. Positive feelings and responses can be generated by the close relationship that exists. Gardiner (2003) points out that, while formal mentoring cannot replace the informal systems that are part of everyday work relationships, mentors and practitioners will benefit if a 'professional friendship' can be established within the mentoring relationship because this promotes the self-esteem of the practitioner. While aspiring to this type of style, mentors should be wary of pitfalls. Initially very nurturing, there is a danger that the closeness of the friendship can have an adverse effect as the practitioner develops as a professional – relating to issues of separation and termination of the mentoring relationship.

The familiarity of the role of professional friend brings its own challenges. It is therefore important that clear boundaries are agreed from the outset. The depth of trust and mutual respect on which the 'friendship' is established can be compromised if one of the parties loses confidence in the other. The mentor as professional friend must be prepared to manage the situation and not let over-familiarity undermine the relationship. The influence of a senior practitioner within the setting may be used to mediate in order to bring the relationship back on track or to facilitate renegotiation of the mentoring relationship. A key strategy for all mentors will therefore be to establish a positive relationship with the senior practitioner. If difficulties do arise in the mentoring relationship some form of 'troubleshooting' may be necessary. Once the mentor has considered and identified which critical influences are contributing to difficult situations experienced in the mentoring process, the following key points for 'troubleshooting' may be used to identify ways of moving forward:

- Keep in mind the purpose of the mentoring relationship – review the mentoring relationship and any personal professional development plan.
- Review goals – they will no doubt change as the practitioner begins to develop professionally.
- Encourage self-management – adjust the balance of power to enable the relationship to continue as appropriate.
- Support through feedback which builds on success – confidence maintains motivation.
- Assist in evaluation – it may be appropriate to amend the mentoring relationship.

(Callan and Copp 2006: 29)

By bearing these issues in mind the mentor should be able to intervene appropriately to address complex situations (Parsloe and Wray 2000). The process involved is cyclical and should ideally include the senior practitioner in order to consolidate the collaborative approach described. In all cases the aim is to maintain the professional relationship through an evolving mentoring relationship.

All mentors are encouraged to remember:

- that good teamwork requires all individuals to recognise and value others;
- to establish and maintain communication with other colleagues;
- to be positively assertive and confident in themselves in order to instil confidence in others;
- to always demonstrate good practice and professionalism.

The important message is that the mentor is genuinely 'the one in the middle' (Callan and Copp 2006: 21), not simply between the practitioner and senior practitioner, but in among a range of critical interrelated personal and professional issues which together influence relationships in settings. The mentor ultimately draws the whole thing together and holds the key to a successful experience for everyone involved. The success of this will be facilitated by the development of 'reflective' practitioners supported by 'reflective' mentors.

Continuing personal and professional development and links to quality

The provision of quality within settings is related to the willingness of practitioners to be open to challenge and to take ownership of their practice. Mentors play a significant part in encouraging practitioners to engage in reflective practice by supporting them and working alongside them as role models in the reflective process (Blenkin and Kelly 1997). Dewey (1933) in his review of learning used the term 'critical thinking' but preferred to call it 'reflective thinking', and it is this 'critical' or 'reflective' thinking that may be seen as conducive to high-level practitioner learning. The process of reflective thinking ensures that issues meaningful and relevant to the content of practice (everyday life) can be highlighted, confronted, reviewed and addressed, resulting in 'reflective action' and ultimately recognised as 'reflective practice'. It is generally considered (Dewey 1933; Kolb 1984; Gibb 1988; Ghaye and Ghaye 1998; Leeson 2004) that reflective practice is rooted in a willingness to engage in self-appraisal and development with the learner/practitioner engaging in the discovery of self as a learner within any context and with emphasis placed upon the role of experiences, reflection, action and new experiences. Schön (1983) further explored reflection and suggested that 'reflection-in-action' is reflection occurring during action and 'reflection-on-action' is reflection after action, the purpose of both being to improve future action and thus practice.

Reflective practice therefore implies that practitioners:

- are actively concerned about the aims and consequences of the work they are doing;
- can monitor, evaluate and revise their own practice continuously;
- have an ability to look carefully at practice in order to support the development of new skills and understanding;
- have an open-minded attitude;
- enhance professional learning and personal fulfilment through collaboration and dialogue between practitioners.

(Fowler and Robins 2006: 33)

Before we consider how we can support our practitioners in their reflective practice and subsequently personal and professional development it is worth considering if reflective action is dependent on learning how to reflect or if it is instinctive or intuitive. Referring again to Dewey (1933), it is at his suggestion that we know intuitively that we need to do things in order to learn from our experiences and to deal with our expectations.

More recently, Atkinson and Claxton (2000) have pursued the notion of 'ways of thinking', 'learning' and how this is influenced by intuition, and it could be argued that there are some people who can intuitively see potential for personal and professional development in any situation. They are able to assess a situation and its worth; reflect upon and change things to ensure personal progress and maintain a favourable atmosphere in which their learning continues to take place. These changes or choices made during the course of their practice are largely intuitive because they see the need for action as being immediate. But can these skills be taught?

As mentors, we should, first and foremost, challenge our own reflective skills and consider the power of intuition. Are we truly reflective in our own practice? Have we learned how to reflect and, if so, how do we do it? Do we reflect in and on action? Who supports us in this process? It is important to consider these questions from a very personal perspective before going on to consider how we encourage and teach those whom we are mentoring to reflect and to 'trust' their intuition (Atkinson and Claxton 2000).

Reflective practice is easily encouraged and facilitated by simply asking questions and the first step as a mentor might be to ask hard questions about yourself as a practitioner:

*   What is my role as a mentor?
*   What is my practice like?
*   Do I do a good job and if so how do I know?
*   How has my role developed since I began?
*   What are the effects of my practice on the practitioners I mentor?
*   How can I improve what I do?

Having considered ourselves as active reflective practitioners we will be well placed to support the practitioners we mentor. It is then our responsibility as mentors to use strategies which include the posing of questions in order that our practitioners can be encouraged to reflect and move forward personally and professionally.

Paulo Freire (1998) advocated that conversations should be examining, questioning and interpreting practice critically in an open arena supported by a significant other (mentor) who has the experience and expertise to pose questions in order that the practitioner can further reflect. Subsequently, Ghaye and Ghaye (1998: 11) urged practitioners to engage in critical reflective conversations not only with themselves but in collaboration with others, as 'reflection does not have to be a solitary activity' and they suggest even more determinedly that 'we can learn by talking to others about our practice, having it challenged, in a constructively critical manner'. These questions need to be systematic, and to have a consecutive order as 'successive portions of a reflective thought grow out of one another and support one another' (Dewey 1933: 4).

However, it is important to remember as a mentor encouraging practitioners to reflect that they may sometimes be uncomfortable when asked about their opinions since this is a new experience. Dadds (cited in Robins *et al.* 2003) points out that confronting and questioning practice, knowledge and understanding can sometimes cause significant discomfort for even the most experienced or qualified professionals. There is therefore a need for careful questioning, guidance and support in order to preserve self-esteem when we encourage reflection upon thoughts, understanding and practice. As a mentor we should be careful to provide encouragement and support by validating and confirming any emerging thinking with, at least initially, a minimum of evaluative feedback on the content of that thinking, as the practitioners resolve their own dilemmas. They often do not need answers, but rather opportunities to find their own and a mentor may facilitate this process by posing questions that will encourage reflective thought.

Brookfield (cited in Dryden *et al.* 2005) suggests four viewpoints from which to consider an 'event', but Peters (cited in Dryden *et al.* 2005: 4) structures reflective thoughts around a describing, analysing, theorising and acting (DATA) cycle. This again could be a useful structure when teaching practitioners to reflect. It gives a starting point and then guides them through a reflective process step by step.

D – describe the problem, task or incident that needs to be looked at and possibly changed;
A – analyse the description, looking at assumptions that were made at the time and also any that are being made about how to respond now;
T – theorise about a range of ways to respond to the problem, task or incident;
A – act using one or more of the theories above.

The above lines of questioning may appear quite basic but they are systematic, and the next point to consider is: Do they actually encourage the practitioner to think beyond the event in question? Do they actually challenge practitioners to consider where they may go or what they might do next? This is a vital step in the reflective process because it is important that reflections made on practice lead to effective changes being made. The DATA approach begins to do this in the theorising and acting stages.

A final set of questions that may be used when facilitating and teaching practitioners to reflect have slightly more detail to them. These will be preceded by a discussion about the actual 'event'.

- What new knowledge, ideas or skills have you gained from this session/ training/experience/discussion?
- How might this impact upon your own thinking, values and/or practice within your setting or role?
- How might it impact upon the children with whom you/I work in terms of their learning and/or behaviour?
- What impact might it have on other colleagues or even parents/carers?
- What changes may it lead you to make to your practice?
- Is there any further training that could be undertaken that might enhance this new knowledge, ideas or skills?

(Fowler and Robins 2006: 40)

It is through the asking of questions of significant learning experiences which provoke true reflection that it should be possible to gain a greater understanding of personal and professional actions and thus the opportunity to improve practice.

The pursuit of quality within the field of early childhood is high on the political and social programme and is embedded within *Every Child Matters* (DfES 2003, 2004). The subsequent *Children's Workforce Strategy* (DfES 2006: 5) sets the challenge of 'building a world class workforce for children, young people and families' and has a clear remit and intention to strengthen interagency and multi-disciplinary working. It may be said that a vision recognising the development of practitioner skills as a core element requires practical approaches which include practitioners who are 'reflective' and who are supported by 'reflective' mentors. There is emphasis throughout these policies suggesting that the 'quality' within early childhood settings is to be found in the interactions among settings, practitioners, the children and their families.

Reflective practice and quality issues are interdependent since unless practitioners engage in the process of reflection their practice is at risk of becoming ill-informed and potentially dangerous 'because that is the way it has always been done and no-one has questioned whether it is still appropriate', as suggested by Leeson (2004: 146).

Critical skills of reflection are crucial to all workers in the field of early childhood as the importance of insight and understanding will shape and form not only immediate practice but also potentially the lives of children in our care and their families. Our role as reflective mentors, supporting and teaching reflective practitioners, is vital to the ongoing maintenance and development of quality provision within our early childhood settings.

Notes

1   This chapter draws upon Robins (2006). For further information visit www.paul chapmanpublishing.co.uk (part of Sage). © Sage Publications 2006.
2   For the purposes of this chapter the term 'practitioner' is used to describe any person being supported by a mentor. The term 'senior practitioner' relates to a third person within a setting, usually in a more senior position, who needs to be mindful of the mentor/practitioner relationship and its outcomes.

References

Atkinson, T. and Claxton, G. (eds) (2000) *The Intuitive Practitioner: On the Value of Not Always Knowing What one is Doing*. Maidenhead: Open University Press.

Bandura, A. (1977) *Social Learning Theory*. Englewood Cliffs, NJ: Prentice-Hall.

Blenkin, G.M. and Kelly, A.V. (1997) *Principles into Practice in Early Childhood Education*. London: Paul Chapman.

Bronfenbrenner, U. (1979) *The Ecology of Human Development*. London: Harvard University Press.

Brookfield, S.D. (1995) *Developing Critical Thinkers – Challenging Adults to Explore Alternative Ways of Thinking and Acting*. Buckingham: Open University Press.

Bruner, J. (1996) *The Culture of Education*. Cambridge, MA: Harvard University Press.

Callan, S. (2006) What is mentoring? In A. Robins (ed.) *Mentoring in the Early Years*. London: Sage.

Callan, S. and Copp, E. (2006) The mentor as the one in the middle. In A. Robins (ed.) *Mentoring in the Early Years*. London: Sage.

Clutterbuck, D. (2000) Ten core mentor competencies. *Organisations and People*, 7(4): 29.

Clutterbuck, D. (2004) *Everyone Needs a Mentor: Fostering Talent in your Organization* (4th edn). London: Chartered Institute of Personnel and Development.

Department for Education and Skills (DfES) (2003) *Every Child Matters* (summary). London: DfES Publications.

DfES (2004) *Every Child Matters: Next Steps*. London: DfES Publications.

DfES (2006) *Children's Workforce Strategy; Building a World-class Workforce for Children, Young People and Families* (response to consultation). London: DfES Publications.

Dewey, J. (1933) *How we Think: A Reinstatement of the Relation of Reflective Thinking to the Educative Process*. Chicago, IL: Henry Regner Publishers.

Downie, C.M. and Basford, P. (eds) (2003) *Mentoring in Practice; A Reader*. London: University of Greenwich.

Dryden, L., Forbes, R., Mukherji, P. and Pound, L. (eds) (2005) *Essential Early Years*. London: Hodder Arnold.

Fowler, K. and Robins, A. (2006) Being reflective: encouraging and teaching reflective practice. In A. Robins (ed.) *Mentoring in the Early Years*. London: Sage.

Freire, P. (1998) *Pedagogy of Freedom: Ethics, Democracy, and Civic Courage*. Lanham, MD: Rowman & Littlefield.

Gardiner, C. (2003) Mentoring: towards a professional friendship. In C.M. Downie and P. Basford (eds) *Mentoring in Practice; A Reader*. London: University of Greenwich.

Ghaye, A. and Ghaye, K. (1998) *Teaching and Learning through Critical Reflective Practice*. London: David Fulton.

Gibbs, G. (1988) *Learning by Doing: A Guide to Teaching and Learning Methods*. Oxford: Oxford University Press.

Hamilton, R. (1993) *Mentoring*. London: The Industrial Society.

Knowles, M.S., Holston III, E.F. and Swanson, R.A. (1998) *The Adult Learner* (5th edn). Foley, TX: Golf Publishing.

Kolb, D.A. (1984) *Experiential Learning: Experience as the Source of Learning and Development*. Princeton, NJ: Prentice-Hall.

Leeson, C. (2004) In praise of reflective practice. In J. Willan, R. Parker-Rees and J. Savage (eds) *Early Childhood Studies*. Exeter: Learning Matters.

Moyles, J., Suschitzky, W. and Chapman, L. (1999) Mentoring in primary schools: ethos, structures and workloads. *Journal of In-service*, 25: 161–172.

Parsloe, E. and Wray, M. (2000) *Coaching and Mentoring: Practical Methods to Improve Learning*. London: Kogan Page.

Pegg, M. (2000) *The Art of Mentoring*. Gloucester: Management Books.

Robins, A., Ashbaker, B.Y., Enriquez, J. and Morgan, J. (2003) Professional practice for professionals and paraprofessionals. *International Journal of Learning*, 10. Available online at http://IJL.cgpublisher.com/products_index (accessed 10 May 2008).

Schön, D.A. (1983) *The Reflective Practitioner: How Professionals Think in Action*. New York: Basic Books.

Vygotsky, L.S. (1978) *Mind in Society*. Cambridge, MA; Harvard University Press.

Wilkin, M. (ed.) (1992) *Mentoring in Schools*. London: Kogan Page.

Willan, J., Parker-Rees. R. and Savage, J. (eds) (2004) *Early Childhood Studies*. Exeter: Learning Matters.

Zachary, L.J. (2000) *The Mentors Guide*. San Francisco, CA: Jossey-Bass.

Endpiece

Janet Moyles and Theodora Papatheodorou

These five chapters conclude our exploration of relational pedagogy in this collection. As can be seen, some writers are still clearly exploring the concept and working towards a greater understanding. This is how it should be, since relational pedagogy is still a new and evolving concept, as we saw in Chapter 1 and as other writers have emphasised in different chapters. The overlapping and integrated nature of the concept makes it difficult to write about in definitive terms but it seems to us, the editors, that our contributors have all captured the spirit of relational pedagogy. We feel certain that all the chapters will help you, our readers, to begin an exploration of your own understandings, interpretations and practices in order to familiarise yourselves with this important way of thinking, working and learning in early childhood education and care. If the book can do even some of this, then we have well and truly begun the processes of relational pedagogy.

Author index

Subject index